SELU

SELU

Seeking the Corn-Mother's Wisdom

Marilou Awiakta

Illustrations by Mary Adair

Fulcrum Publishing
Golden, Colorado

Other books by Marilou Awiakta

Abiding Appalachia: Where Mountain and Atom Meet

Rising Fawn and the Fire Mystery:
A Story of Heritage, Family and Courage, 1833

Library of Congress Cataloging-in-Publication Data
Awiakta, Marilou.
    Selu : seeking the Corn-Mother's wisdom / Marilou Awiakta ;
illustrations by Mary Adair.
        p.   cm.
    Includes bibliographical references (p.   ) and index.
    ISBN 1-55591-144-7
    1. Cherokee Indians—Religion and mythology. 2. Cherokee Indians–Philosophy. 3. Human ecology—Southern States—Religious aspects. 4. Environmental degradation—Southern States. 5. Southern States—Social conditions. I. Title.
E99.C5A95 1933   93-26645
299'.785—dc20   CIP

Printed in the United States of America
0 9 8 7 6 5 4 3 2 1

Fulcrum Publishing
350 Indiana Street, Suite 350
Golden, Colorado 80401-5093
(800) 992-2908

This doublewoven basket—
this book of seed-thoughts—
is for you
your family and loved ones
as it is for mine—
especially
Chelsea
born March 23, 1991
to daughter Drey and Dwayne,
Gregory
born October 6, 1991
to daughter Aleex and Jack,
and for our son Andrew
and for Paul.

CONTENTS

WEAVING II: SELU, SPIRIT OF SURVIVAL

FOREWORD

Wilma P. Mankiller
Principal Chief, Cherokee Nation of Oklahoma

In the old days the Cherokee people believed that the world existed in a precarious balance and that only right or correct actions kept it from tumbling. Wrong actions were believed to disturb the balance. For hundreds of years, since the Cherokees signed the first peace and friendship treaty with Britain, and later a land cession treaty with South Carolina, our world has been spun out of control, and we have been searching for that balance. In our current state we are so very distant from that time when our world had balance. But even though we do not ourselves fully understand why, we have returned to searching our own history and teachings for answers to today's problems. Perhaps, like Selu shaking the kernels from her body so that the people can live, we are shaking hundreds of years of acculturation and dehumanization from our minds—also so that our people may live. This book, *Selu,* gave me and gives the reader some practical advice on how to use ancient wisdom in contemporary life.

We human beings are sometimes so oriented toward scientific explanations for everything that we seldom are able to suspend that analytical state of mind and just believe that Selu can be our mother, that the stars can be our relatives, that the river can be a man, and that the sun can be a woman. We have never really understood that we are one small part of a very large family that includes the plant world, the animal world and our other living relations. How can we possibly keep our world from spinning out of balance if we don't have a fundamental understanding of our relationship to everything around us? We continually fail to see our own insignificance in the totality of things.

I am grateful for the fleeting moments when I experience the rare harmony and balance that our ancestors frequently referred to. Such was the case when I began reading this wonderful collection of history, stories, poetry and feelings—and contemplating, woven among them, Mary Adair's stellar drawings. I took a break from reading this book to look out my window. When my gaze settled on several stands of beautiful, proud Selu in my own small garden, I smiled and knew such a moment was at hand. Selu is always special to my family and me. Every year Charlie and I grow a garden, but no matter how many vegetables we plant, the success of our garden is measured by how Selu does. I can tell you she did well this year. Perhaps she knew her story was being read and appreciated in my home and soon would be shared with many others.

As you read through this extraordinary book, you will be helped onto a path that will enable you to gain a clear sense that there is a way we can stop destroying the very world that sustains us, and we can return to a time of balance and harmony. *Selu* is a book that will lead the way, but, above all, *Selu* is a book about hope.

ACKNOWLEDGMENTS

Creating community is the Corn-Mother's specialty, and she set a field of people working to bring this book to harvest. All the while, we talked, told stories, joked, sang—and wiped sweat from our brows. My thanksgivings to everyone for sharing their time and gifts.

Along the path to Selu and in the field as well, my husband Paul kept watch, provided sustenance for body and spirit (and often cooked meals) so I could bend to my work.

Through her drawings Mary Adair clearly has been integral to the book. Implicit in its custom-production is my editor, Carmel Huestis, indefatigable, and unstinting with advice and support. In the fall of 1991, when I sent her four pipe cleaners and two lengths of yarn to convey the manuscript's doublewoven construction, she wove her own basket—and has been weaving with me ever since.

For setting an example of the "good mind" and for encouraging me through the years, I'm grateful to my parents, Wilma and Bill, my sister Adele, Joseph Bruchac, Wilma Mankiller and Phyllis Tickle.

In the oral tradition, "knowings" is a more accurate term than "research," because insightful conversation deepens the connotation of the printed word. In the order in which they arrived from the Four Directions to help with *Selu*, I acknowledge the following people: *EAST*: Saul Slapikoff and Elizabeth Ammons of Tufts University; Gladys A. Widdiss, Chair Emeritus of the Wompanoag; Joan Lester, chief curator of the Boston Children's Museum; Rayna Green of the Smithsonian Institution; and Doris Seale; and Bill and Pat Garner. *NORTH*: Susan Dixon, managing editor of *Akwe:kon* (formerly the *Northeast Indian Quarterly*); Margaret Raymond, director of the Minnesota Indian Women's Resource Center; Ginny Carney of the University of Alaska; and Marie Dawson, a Celt from the Old Country, who now lives in New York City. *WEST*: Leslie Silko; Sharon Patacsil of United Indians of All Tribes Foundation, Seattle; Bruce Johansen of the University of Nebraska shared the galleys of *Exemplar of Liberty*, which he and Donald A. Grinde wrote, and introduced me to the work of Sally Roesch Wagner. *SOUTH*: Sam McCollum shared his fifty years' experience of raising corn; Ellen Rolfes, inspirer; Joan Greene, archivist, Museum of the

Cherokee Indian (N.C.), tracked Attakullakulla and Outacite (Ostenaco). Via various media in Memphis, Lisa Procter and Audrey May brought in Barbara McClintock. For insight into the continuing saga of Tellico, I'm grateful to Reba McGinnis, Judy Card, Dwayne Herron, Jack Hopkins, Nick Fielder, archeologist for the state of Tennessee, Memphis State University archeologist David Dye, and the staff of TVA's *River Pulse*, an environmental advisory magazine. The Cherokee Director of the Sequoyah Birth Place Museum, Carroll Hamilton, told me the story of the Cherokee experience with TVA since 1980.

People who use technology creatively worked with great patience on the book. Patty Maher wove the layout design. Jackie King, Carolyn Moody and Pat Cloar transcribed the manuscript to computer discs. And Nita Cochron, Cherokee scout extraordinary, used the telephone to guide me to a place I'd despaired of finding.

Traditional stories always have been preserved and held in trust by families. For the stories of *Selu*, I am grateful to Mary Chiltoskey and her niece, Regina Galloway, and to Jack F. Kilpatrick, Jr., who gave me permission to quote from *Friends of Thunder*, written by his parents Jack F. and Anna G. Kilpatrick, and long out of print. I hope interest in reprinting it will be generated. The Chiltoskey-Galloway book, *Aunt Mary, Tell Us a Story*, is new and readily available.

All of us who have worked on *Selu* give thanksgivings to the indigenous people of the Americas, who have preserved the whole corn—grain and spirit—from time immemorial, and to Ginitsi Selu herself, who has taught us an eternal truth, "One alone can't bring in a harvest."

Selu Is Always Singing

Every month
somewhere in the world
a crop of corn
comes ripe.
Every day
somewhere in the world
Selu sings
of survival.

Wilma Mankiller says,
"We must expand our concept
of home and family
to include our environment
and our people.
We must trust
our own thinking.
Trust where we're going.
And get the job done."
The Principal Chief,
Cherokee Nation of Oklahoma,
says this.

Somewhere in the world
Selu is always singing ...

INTRODUCTION

"Write a straightforward introduction," my editor says. "Tell your readers what the book is about, how it's organized and what they can gain from reading it."

I smile. "Up in Appalachia where I'm from, we never do that when a story's afoot. And this one about Selu is long and winding."

Being from a storytelling culture herself, she laughs. But she holds firm. "Most of your readers are rushing through the high-tech world. They're used to literal language. They want the facts—fast!

"Like a TV commercial?"

"Or better yet, like a fax."

"My mind to theirs, right? Concise, quick, personal. ... Fax is a good idea—akin to poetry, in fact. I'll do it."

FAX

To: The Reader
                 Fax No.: Wherever you are

From: Awiakta
                 Fax No.: East Tennessee mountains

NOTE: If there is a question or problem concerning the information transmitted, please read *Selu: Seeking the Corn-Mother's Wisdom.*

REMARKS

Subject: Corn, Mother of Us All
                  Ginitsi Selu (Cherokee name)

Content: Her survival wisdoms (time tested) and other seed-thoughts.

Organization: Doublewoven basket (Cherokee-style) Essays/stories/poems interweave in a pattern. Outer side of basket is a path to Selu. Inner side is Selu herself. We walk the path together, gather thoughts, then contemplate Selu's wisdoms as presented by Native Americans who have preserved them. We consider applications of wisdoms to life, government and the general good.

Reason for Making Our Journey:
        So we won't die.
        Neither will Mother Earth.

10/7/93   4:00   pages: 1   usage time: 00'27

WEAVING I
A Path to Selu

SECTION I

TRAILHEAD
Where Path and Stories Begin

The spirit always finds a pathway. ... If you
find a deer trail and follow that trail,
it's going to lead you to medicines and
waterholes and a shelter.
　　　　　　　　—Wallace Black Elk
　　　　　　　　The Sacred Ways of a Lakota

To take shape
a journey must have
fixed bearings,
as a basket has ribs
and a book its themes.
　　　　　　　　—Awiakta

Take your bearings at the trailhead
or you'll wind up lost.
　　　　　　　　—Appalachian Mountain Maxim

HEADING EAST BY WAY OF
FOUR DIRECTIONS

Wounds ✦ Mother Earth ✦ Healing ✦ Selu

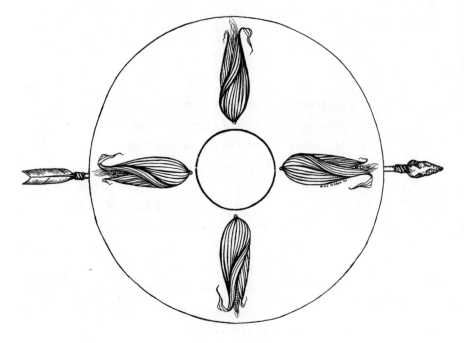

Dying Back

On the mountain
the standing people are dying back—
hemlock, spruce and pine
turn brown in the head.
The hardwood shrivels in new leaf.
Unnatural death
from acid greed
that takes the form of rain
and fog and cloud.

In the valley
the walking people are blank-eyed.
Elders mouth vacant thought.
Youth grow spindly, wan
from sap too drugged to rise.
Pushers drain it off—
sap is gold to them.
The walking people are dying back
as all species do
that kill their own seed.

When Earth Becomes an "It"

When the people call Earth "Mother,"
they take with love
and with love give back
so that all may live.

When the people call Earth "it,"
they use her
consume her strength.
Then the people die.

Already the sun is hot
out of season.
Our Mother's breast
is going dry.
She is taking all green
into her heart
and will not turn back
until we call her
by her name.

Out of Ashes Peace Will Rise

Our courage
is our memory.

Out of ashes
peace will rise,
if the people
are resolute.
If we are not
resolute,
we will vanish.
And out of ashes
peace will rise.

In the Four Directions ...
Out of ashes peace will rise.
Out of ashes peace will rise.
Out of ashes peace will rise.
Out of ashes peace will rise.

Our courage
is our memory.

I Offer You a Gift

Still of the night ...
   moon on the wane
   sun deep in sleep.
Cricket, bird and wind lay low
as rhythms of earth and sky
   suspend
   prepare to turn.

Awake in the dark
   you know
   I know
We may not make it.
Mother Earth may not make it.
   We teeter
on the turning point.

Against the downward pull,
against the falter
of your heart and mine,
I offer you a gift
a seed to greet the sunrise—
   Ginitsi Selu
Corn, Mother of Us All.
   Her story.

COMPASS FOR OUR JOURNEY

SELU, A Rare Portrait

"SELU ... *Say-loo* ... *Selu* ... *Say-loooo* ..."

Her name echoes through the centuries. But who is Selu? Knowing just her name is not enough.

She will speak for herself in the following traditional Cherokee story. Like Siquanid', who tells it, from my childhood I have found this story interesting.

For thousands of years, indigenous peoples of the Americas have formally recognized corn as a teacher of wisdom, the spirit inseparable from the grain. Through corn's natural ways of growing and being, the spirit sings of strength, respect, balance, harmony. Of adaptability, cooperation, unity in diversity. Songs of survival.

As a link to the spirit, many tribes long ago composed an Origin of Corn story, which they tell to this day. They designed the story to create a synapse in the mind, a lens in the eye, a drum in the ear, a rhythm in the heart. Listeners take the story in, think it through and, when the need arises, apply its wisdoms to life. Although the stories vary in content from tribe to tribe, they have a spiritual base in common, which began when the People first cultivated maize from a wild grass. They perceived corn as a gift from the All-Mystery, the Creator, the Provider. In telling Selu's story to a general audience recently, a Cherokee medicine man established its spiritual base immediately. "In the beginning, the Creator made our Mother Earth. Then came Selu, Grandmother Corn."

Used in this ritual sense, "Grandmother" connotes "Mother of Us All," a spirit being who is eternally wise. And if the medicine man had been speaking his native tongue instead of English, the indivisibility of grain and spirit would have been apparent, for both are spelled s-e-l-u. Saying one evokes the other. In the Smoky Mountains of my homeland, the Cherokee pronounce the word "say-loo." In Oklahoma they pronounce it another way but with the same meaning.

Especially during the past decade, I've been seeking deeper under-standing of Selu's wisdoms and ways of applying them to contemporary life,

9

including my own. I invite you to share my path of thought to the place it has led me in the early 1990s—the cusp of the millennium, a time of upheaval and change for us all. Our compass for the journey is Selu's traditional story *and its cultural context*. To be accurate and useful, a Native American story, like a compass needle, must have its direction points.

The following version of Selu's story, thought to be very old, is rare in other ways. During the mid-twentieth century, Siquanid', an elder who lived in the lonely hills east of Tenkiller Lake in Oklahoma, told it to Jack and Anna Kilpatrick, distinguished Cherokee scholars, who spoke, read and wrote their native language. Included in their book *Friends of Thunder*, this story, unlike many published versions that appear to be retellings from the English, was translated directly from the verbal text. Told in the unaffected, friendly manner in which the older Cherokee talk, it provides a word-portrait of Selu. To make a story relevant to listeners, details are sometimes altered. For example, Siquanid' substitutes guns for bows and arrows. Because Native American cultures relate wisdom to age, it is significant that Selu is a "very old woman."

THE ORIGIN OF CORN

At one time there was a very old woman who had two grandsons. These two grandsons were always hunting. They hunted deer and wild turkeys. They always had plenty to eat.

Later on, after many hunting trips, when they got ready to go hunting early in the morning, they were cleaning their guns. When their grandmother noticed that they were ready to go, she thought to herself, "They are getting ready to go hunting," so she went to them where they were cleaning their guns, outside the fenced-in yard.

When the grandmother came to them, they were busily cleaning their guns. She said to them, "I see that you are getting ready to go hunting," and they replied, "Yes. We are going to hunt deer today."

"Well, when you come back, I'll have the most delicious of dinners ready. I'm going to cook all of the old meat, and I'm going to put into it something they call corn and we're going to drink the broth from it," she said to the young men.

"All right," said the young men.

When they got to the forest, they wondered about the word *corn* that she had used. They didn't know what that was, and they wondered where she got it.

"I wonder where corn comes from?" they asked each other. "When we get home, we'll find out," they said. They killed a deer, shouldered it and went home.

When they got home, they saw the large pot bubbling. They noticed that with the meat, corn in small ground-up pieces was boiling in there. (If anyone had ever seen it before, he would have known what it was; but then these boys had never seen it before.)

They asked their grandmother, "What is that that you have in the pot?"

"It is called grits."

They didn't ask her where she got it.

When they ate their dinner, the young men had the most delicious meal that they had ever had. After dinner they told their grandmother what a superb meal she had cooked. The grandmother was pleased.

"Well, tomorrow at noon we will have some more delicious food."

The next day they went hunting again, but they already had some dried turkeys. So the grandmother cooked these dried turkeys and cooked grits with them.

When they returned home that evening with their bag of turkeys, dinner was announced. With this meat were these grits, and the young men said, "This is the best meal that we have ever had." They thanked their grandmother again and told her that her food was delicious.

The grandmother was very pleased and said, "I'm so happy that you said what you did."

Next day they again went to the forest. While they were in the forest, one of them kept thinking about the corn. "This thing she calls corn ... she said that today about noon she is going to start cooking again," said one to the other; and the other said, "Yes, that's what she said."

"I'll go hide around somewhere and see where she gets it if you want me to," said one.

"All right," said the other. "You had better go before she begins cooking."

So one of them went. This thing called corn was troubling this young man; so he hid behind the smokehouse and watched for his grandmother.

Later on the grandmother came carrying a large pan and went into the smokehouse. The young man peeped through a small hole. When the grandmother got into the smokehouse, she put the pan under where she was standing. Then she struck both of her sides, and when she hit her sides grits fell from every part of her body. They fell until the pan became full. When she came out of the smokehouse, she carried this pan of grits, dumped them into the pot, and began cooking them.

That's what the young man learned, and he went back to his brother and told him about it. When he arrived where his brother was, his brother asked him what he had learned.

He said to his brother, "This delicious food of Grandmother's that we have been eating comes from her body. She shakes it off from all over her body. She puts a pan under her. She strikes her sides, and it falls off her body and falls into the pan until it is full, and that is what we have been eating," he told his brother.

His brother said, "We really eat an unsavory thing, don't we!" So they decided that they would not eat any more of it when they got home.

When they arrived home, their grandmother had dinner ready. Again she had the same kind of food. They both didn't each much.

"What's wrong? You're not eating very much. Don't you like me?" said their grandmother.

The young men said, "No. We're just too tired from walking so much in our hunting."

"But I think that you don't like me," she said. "Or maybe you learned something somewhere, and that's the reason that you don't want to eat," they were told.

At that moment the grandmother became ill. She knew that they had found out [her secret]. The grandmother took to bed, and she began to talk to them about what they should do.

"Now that I'm in bed, I'm going to die." (She told them all about what was going to happen in the future.) "When you bury me, you must put a large fence around me and bury me just right out there. Something will grow from right in the middle of my grave. This thing will grow up to be tall. It will flower at the top, and in the lower part will come out beautiful tassels, and inside of them will be kernels. It will bear two or three ears of corn with corn silk on them.

"You must leave the ears alone and take care of the plant. Put a fence around it. They [the ears] will dry; they will be very white; the shuck will be brown and crisp; and the silk will be dark brown. That is when you gather it.

"This thing they call corn is I. This corn will have its origin in me.

"You must take the kernels off the cob and plant them. Store them away until spring. When spring comes, make spaced-out holes in the ground and put about two of the kernels in each hole. By doing this you will increase your supply—and it is surpassingly good food—and when it sprouts, it will go through the various stages of growth that you will have seen in this one of mine.

"Then it will bear corn that you can use, either to boil (boiled corn is very good to eat all summer long, while it is green) or in winter you can use it to make meal.

"I will be the Corn-Mother," said the old woman (a long time ago, they said).

That's the injunction that the young men were taught to carry out. They thought about this deeply as they were burying her after she died. After they buried her, they made the fence; and all that summer [the corn plant] grew and bore corn just as she told them it would do, and when the corn became dry, they gathered it and took the kernels off the cobs.

Then again next spring they planted it. Then the two young men said, "It would be better if we each had a wife."

One of the young men said, "Let's just one of us get a wife. You get a wife, and I'll be a bachelor and live with you."

The other said, "All right," and left to search for a wife.

The young man said to the one who left to get a wife, "Just walk some distance over there, blow into your hands, and there will be a girl run to you."

So he arrived away off into the forest near a house, I believe. In that house was an old couple with a large number of young women. These young women were all outside playing. Some of these young women were frolicking about, and others were laughing and making a lot of noise.

The young man came quite near, blew into his hands, and whistled. One of the young women who was playing stopped and said, "I'm going to stop playing because someone is whistling for me," and left the group.

She ran directly to the young man. The young man said to her, "We'll marry, if it's all right with you."

She said, "All right." So they went to his home.

The young man told her that in the spring they would plant corn, and each year they would plant more and more of it. So when spring came, they used their hoes to make holes so that they could plant corn. They hoed and hoed and had a very large field of corn, and that was the beginning of there being so much corn. And they remembered what the old woman had said to them, "I will be the Corn-Mother," she had said. "Don't ever forget where I am buried," she had told them when she talked to them.

From this beginning there became so much corn that everyone in the world had some. They say that corn had its beginning from a human being, that the plant called corn started from a woman, and that when this man took a wife, they had such a huge field that they had much corn and much food to eat.

That's what I know, and that's the end of it: that's all.[1]

Making the Compass-Story "User Friendly"

Undoubtedly with a twinkle in his eye, Siquanid' tells the story in perfect harmony with its design to entertain, instruct and inspire. Subtle as sunlight playing through forest leaves, humor backlights the depth of the Corn-Mother and her teachings—especially the law of respect—and makes them familial, accessible. Unavoidable. Run as fast as you can to any corner of the universe and the Law will be there waiting for you.

Even as a child I understood this lesson because the elders kept the story's direction points firmly in place. Throughout our mountain county, my grandfather was known to "have a way with corn," meaning he grew it exceptionally well. Early one morning I was helping him pick green corn for lunch. My grandmother had told us when to go, because she was doing the cooking. To keep its best flavor, she said, the corn had to be pulled before the sun warmed it—and cooked the same day. Making a good meal is hard work, so when she'd said "Go," we hopped to it. Since I was too short to reach the ears, I held the basket. A question had been on my mind and I broached it through the familiar story.

"Papa, was Grandmother Selu mad at the boys for spying on her?"

"She wasn't mad or mean-spirited. She just told them how it is. Way back in the beginning of time, the Creator put the Law in Mother Earth and all she gives us. If you take from her, you have to give back respect and thankfulness. If you don't do that, why then she quits giving. So when the boys were disrespectful, Selu had to leave. That's the Law."

Circling the conversation closer to the mark, I said, "But the boys didn't mean to hurt her. They just wanted to know ..."

From Papa's smile, I knew he had caught my drift. We'd just reached the bare spot in the corn row where several weeks earlier he'd caught me digging up germinating seeds to see if they were growing. He'd explained why the seed had to die, by showing me the tiny taproots broken off and the hair-fine ones that were also damaged. "You can't spy on a corn seed—or any other seed—when it's doing its private work," he'd said, calling up Selu's whole story with that one word "spy." "And Selu gave her grandsons another chance. She told them how to show their respect by taking care of her. Then she changed to her other self and came back as a corn plant to see if they would do it. When they did, there was plenty of corn for everybody. They were smart boys. They didn't have to be told but once." His glance said, "A word to the wise is sufficient."

And that was my unspoken question as Papa and I gathered the corn together. Had he noticed that I'd learned my lesson? As we moved on down the row, Papa said, "Yessir, this corn looks real good. There'll be plenty for everybody." Knowing he was answering the question I was thinking as well as the one I was asking made me feel good, like the rich earth on my bare feet and the scent of hot sun on the plump, milky-sweet ears I laid in the basket. In natural ways like this, the elders plant a story such as Selu's in young minds, where one day—maybe years later—it will bear fruit.

When I tell Selu's story to a general audience, some people are disturbed because Siquanid' says the grandsons used guns. How can the story be authentically old if modern weapons are in it?

This inquiry is usually earnest and respectfully asked. I've gradually realized that it signifies a basic cultural difference. American society (and Western society as a whole) is so oriented toward science, technology and legality that a discrepancy in a fact calls the validity of what is being said into question. If the facts are wrong, how can the statement be true? But the arts are not about facts. They are about creating images and mental connections.

I'm always glad when the subject of guns comes up because it underlines the necessity of keeping the story's cultural context—its direction points—in place. Revealing spiritual truth, not facts, is the purpose of Selu's story, which the storyteller keeps alive and current by adapting details such as guns to the times. Long ago the grandsons may have been sharpening arrowheads or restringing bows. Locations are varied also. Sometimes Selu goes into a smokehouse, other times into a hut. In one oftentold version of the story, Selu lives with her husband, Kanati the Lucky Hunter, and the boys are their sons— one by blood, one by adoption. What cannot be changed are the spiritual base and the spine of the story, which include Selu's identity, the grandsons' (or sons') disrespect, the consequences of it, and Selu's teaching of how they can restore harmony for their own good and the good of the people. Used as it was originally designed, the story is a timeless and reliable compass to right relationships with Mother Earth, with the human family and with oneself.

Take away its cultural context, cut out its spiritual heart—as many people do who are unaware or unmindful of Native storytelling tradition—and instead of a compass, you have an archaic legend of "How Corn Came to the World." A literary play-pretty in which an old woman, quaintly calling herself the Corn-Mother, teaches her grandsons a lesson in respect. A thoughtful person might draw some interpersonal wisdoms from the story, such as "respect your elders" or "share good things with others" or, perhaps, "you must take care of seeds to make them grow." Important lessons certainly, but it wouldn't take years to grasp them. The surface mind can do it. And a legend carries no spiritual imperative to change one's behavior. It simply suggests a lesson one might take to heart.

With extraordinary precision, the Cherokee medicine man sets the story to its fixed point, the constant to which all other points relate and from which all life and wisdom flow: *"In the beginning the Creator ... "* Through this source all that exists is connected in one family. Traditionally, the philosophic magnetic direction is East, the direction of triumph and the deep red light that immediately precedes the rising of the sun, which the Cherokee say is "impregnated with miraculous creative power." East is the heading for hope and determination and life.

The story of *Ginitsi Selu*, Corn, Mother of Us All, faces East. What does the story mean?

"Think it through," the elders advise, but they mean a special kind of thinking. And this is a crucial cultural difference. In Western culture, thought is a function of the mind; feeling a function of the heart. Rational thought is generally considered superior to feeling (emotion), which may deceive. The soul is a third entity.

In *Walk in Your Soul*, Jack and Anna Kilpatrick emphasize that the word they translate as "soul" could just as fittingly be rendered "mind" or "heart." All derive from the verb stem *da:n(v)dh* ("to think purposefully"). The soul is conceived to be in the heart. To "walk in your soul" is to think purposefully from the center of your whole being.[2] It is this kind of thinking, not intellect, that perceives wisdom. Through the centuries, sages of many cultures have taught a similar principle, and, in their search for balance and wisdom, people of many races have communed with nature. For indigenous people, this communion has also been a study, for nature contains the Original Instructions, the laws.

To think from the center of one's being has always been easier in the solitude of mountain, plain, desert or sea. To do it on the freeway is a different matter. Or in the subway, airport, train station or shopping mall. At the office telephones ring, computers click, the fax machine rolls relentlessly. These machines are in many of our homes also, along with the inexorable voice of television, which at regular news intervals spins us "around the world in thirty minutes." Although technology undeniably helps us, it also drives us, creates a feeling of being whirled faster and faster until we fear we'll be flung off into space.

How remote Selu seems in this world. How inaccessible her singing.

And yet, corn is almost everywhere in America—in our fields, in our food. Through its byproducts, it is even in many machines. And where corn is, the Corn-Mother is also. "This thing they call corn is I," she said. Through her story, which creates a spiritual dimension of mind, eye, ear and heart, we can perceive the Corn-Mother and her wisdoms. She teaches by precept and example. One wisdom immediately apparent is strength. *Ginitsi Selu* faces life as it is.

To seek her we start where we are—in the midst of the high-tech age. There are many paths to Selu. We pick up the trailhead of one in a machine that has become almost as familiar as a wristwatch: the fax.

Fax/Facts

You may want the facts fast: "Can you explain the wisdoms now? Will they work for me? And who is Selu *exactly*?"

Your questions point in the right direction. They also tell me that we must be very clear about this path. It's my "thinking through"—one person's view—of Selu's story along with some practical applications of her wisdoms as, with the help of Native American traditions, I understand them so far. Since they've worked for Native people for thousands of years, it's likely they still work. As to who Selu is *exactly* ... our compass-story gives specific direction. When the Corn-Mother's grandsons spied on her, when they disrespectfully looked the Mystery in the face, they broke their relationship with her. We won't delve into Selu's secret or into tribal ceremonies or counsel that elders have given me in confidence. Only what Selu and Native people offer to the public will be considered. We'll stay on the path. But we need to stop here at the trailhead and take our bearings, or we'll wind up lost.

"Can't you just fax the bearings?" Your joke makes us both laugh. Here we are, living in a society so speed-driven that most of us hardly have time to think where we're going, and I'm inviting you to veer off onto a long, quiet path that obviously spirals into another country. Not only that, I'm asking you first to stop, be still and take bearings, the general ones first: Where we are. Where we're going. How we get there. Encounters along the way.

Before the twinkle fades from your eyes, I offer you something so small that my thumb and forefinger almost cover it. It's a communication that's faster than fax, more personal than poetry and more ancient than words. When you hold out your hand, I lay a deep red corn seed in your palm.

Seven thousand years of concentrated energy emanate from the seed. Instantly you know that it's alive, coded with ways of growing. Without human cooperation, without planting and care, the seed will keep its life to itself. This is the essence of corn's nature, wherever it grows in the world, and most people are familiar with it.

But your understanding is deeper because Selu's story (or a similar one, if you are Native American) is already at work in your mind. I know this from the expression in your eyes. From the way you listen when I say, "I offer you a gift." From the openness of the palm you extend to me. We'll be good traveling companions.

All these communications transpire in the split second when the red kernel and the tip of my finger touch your skin. Energy to energy, life to life create a spark. And we make a quantum leap out of linear time and into a warm, wet place in Mexico where indigenous people are having a similar experience as, for the first time, they touch a certain wild grass. They perceive a presence sacred in matter and spirit, who they say is a gift from the All-Mystery, the Creator, the Provider. Over time, they contemplate the grain and work in harmony with the spirit manifested in its natural ways. They also ponder the meaning of the gift for their own lives. Under their reverent, patient care, the wild seed gradually relinquishes its protective husk and entrusts its reproductive life to human hands, a process that the People interpret according to their sacred law and covenant with Mother Earth: Respectful care brings abundance. Lack of care brings nothing. If you take, you must give back—return the gift.

The People keep the covenant. From the seed they develop infinite varieties of what is now called the "supreme achievement in plant domestication of all time": *Indian maize*, corn. Its capacity to adapt to climate, soil and altitude is extraordinary. So is its balance. The plant is strong, in both stalk and curving leaf. From the union of its male and female parts—the tassel and the nubbin of silks—comes the nutritious ear. Every other part of the plant can be used for the People's needs as well: stalk, shucks, cob and roots. According to the region where they grow, the plants and their ears vary greatly in size and the kernels in color. But the essence of corn remains the same.

From the spirit—the nature of corn—the People learn survival wisdoms, common-sense ways of living in harmony with their environment and with each other. To reverence the spirit and convey the wisdoms, each tribe, according to its custom, creates ceremonies, rituals, songs, art and stories. Each story is itself a seed, where the spirit of corn, as well as her basic teachings, is concentrated. Planted in a child's mind, the story matures along with the child, nourishing her or him to grow in wisdom and in stature. Story and life interweave. Like the grain, the stories vary from tribe to tribe, but the spirit is the same.

The People also give corn's spirit proper names. Round names that encompass all expressions of their reverent relationship. Some of the names are "Our Mother," "She Who Sustains," "Our Life." Although I know the spirit by the Cherokee name of Selu, I usually refer to her as the "Corn-Mother" or "Grandmother Corn." There are two reasons. One is that knowledge of her wisdoms is shared among indigenous peoples. It is not exclusive to one tribe or individual. The other reason is that especially in a property-oriented society like America, where great debates arise even over whose idea is whose, it is crucial to remember the magnetic direction of our compass-story, which clearly points to the source of corn and the wisdom contained therein. "In the beginning, the Creator made our Mother Earth. Then came Selu, Grandmother Corn. ..."

In the faraway times of which we are speaking, the People acknowledged this source. And they came to know corn in two or more of these senses: mother, enabler, transformer, healer.[3] From time immemorial, wherever the People have migrated, in the Four Directions, they have taken Grandmother Corn with them, passing the whole corn—the grain and its story, its sacred meaning—from generation to generation.

Today in America corn is a national food. People of all races eat it daily in some form—fresh kernel, meal, syrup or oil. At an early age, schoolchildren learn that corn was "a gift from the Indians" and that early settlers would have starved without it. But the recipients of the gift have always written the official history of America. In the minds of most of their descendants—and therefore, in the national mind—corn remains a grain only, an "it" appropriated for their use. What about the Indians themselves as people? And who do they say is the donor of the gift? What about Grandmother Corn and the law of giving back?

General respect for Native Americans as well as for their skill and thought that developed this plant and other "gifts" is just beginning. Does this shift in consciousness indicate a willingness to accept the traditional teaching—still very much alive among Native people—that corn and all that lives are imbued with spirit and that a reciprocal relationship is crucial to survival? Will the concept of dominance over nature, so entrenched in Western thought, also shift enough to make this change possible? Will the shift occur in time?

Perhaps. Science has proven that the earth is one great ecosystem. That everything on the earth and in the sky above is interconnected. Principally through television, the National Storyteller, even very young children are aware of damage to the environment. When I speak with first graders, for example, about Mother Earth, the Web of Life and how we are all one family, they take this concept for what it is—the literal truth. They tell me about endangered species, oil spills, the destruction of the Amazon forest, air pollution. "There won't be anything left when we grow up," they say. And they want to do something about it.

As the decade of the 1990s begins, times are hard in America. People are thinking about survival. A Memphis cab driver put it fax-style: "The country's going broke and the planet's dying out from under us. Prices and taxes are going up. People are losing their jobs. The homeless are everywhere. Crime is so bad that you don't feel safe—even locked up in your own house. And it's gonna get worse because a few people are getting richer and the rest of us are getting poorer. We're getting to be like Europe when the Pilgrims came over. If America's not careful, we're gonna eat ourselves alive."

The last sentence strikes home. Image is the quickest and most resonant way in speech or print to convey a concept. Combined with facts, it conveys the whole idea. "We're gonna eat ourselves alive!" When they are deeply moved, many people reach for an image, usually without realizing they are speaking poetry in its broadest sense. (Test this by listening to your own words for a day. Poetry may be as familiar to you as fax is.)

It is true that America is a high-tech, speed-driven, "Gimme-the-fax/facts-and-get-on-with-it" society. Few can escape this dynamic. But it's also true that most of us, down deep, yearn for relationship, connection and meaning. Facts alone are not enough—for communication or for survival. *Balance is the key*. And used creatively, technology can help us achieve it. Fax, for example, is akin to poetry. It is concise, quick, and requires a recipient who takes time to understand the message.

Poetry resembles the corn seed in that its energy is concentrated and evokes a reality beyond the surface. Again, understanding takes time. The seed, however, is reality itself ... a living poem ... a message instantly conveyed. But what does it mean? The human mind has spent seven thousand years in contemplation and has not yet plumbed the mystery.

In each traditional Native story, the people who originated it concentrated their understanding of the mystery. The story is alive. It creates that path in the human mind and heart that conveys wisdom from the whole corn—the grain and its spirit—and this constitutes an even more profound achievement than the domestication of the plant. And it is just as practical for survival. As the storyteller explains in Leslie Silko's novel *Ceremony*, traditional stories "are all we have left to fight off illness and death. ... There is life here for the people. ... In the belly of this story the rituals and the ceremony are still growing." Like the corn seed, the story is reality itself. There is no way to fax it. And understanding takes time, as experience has gradually taught me.

SELU AND KANATI

Genesis of Human Balance

In all versions of the compass-story, respect between genders is an implicit wisdom. Casting the relationship in familial terms—grandmother and grandsons or mother and sons—keeps the focus off "the battle of the sexes" and *on* the basic issue: Humanity has two genders. Sexual preference is a separate issue. To preserve the balance, the genders must cooperate and get along, for themselves, for the sake of the community and the environment. Perhaps one reason versions of this story are still often told is that they so well express the Cherokee philosophy of harmony, which begins in the tangible world with Mother Earth. Selu and Kanati model this harmony between genders.

There is another story that is more specific to the relationship between man and woman. Selu's husband, Kanati the hunter, is the mythic father of humankind and the bringer of hunting and woodlore to the people. There are many stories in which he is central. To those who know them, the mere mention of Kanati's name calls up a powerful and important presence who is associated with the deer. Kanati and Selu are sometimes called First Man and First Woman. There is a traditional story about their meeting.

My version of it derives from one told by the renowned storyteller Mary Chiltoskey, of the Eastern Band of Cherokees in North Carolina. (Her version appears on pages 296–98 and is called "The Legend of the First Woman.") Like the compass-story, this one about Selu's birth and marriage runs through my mind all the time—a clear melody that takes on different accompaniment, according to the times I'm living through, which are now very much out of balance. The present adversarial relationship between genders is indicative of our societal and ecologic dilemma.

Especially orally, storytellers may vary language and add amplifications adapted to a specific audience and specific circumstances, but they cannot change the story's basic elements. My poetic version is designed with the themes of this book in mind and for general audiences. There is also one phrase that carries special intensity in the South (and perhaps elsewhere): "Sick and tired." It means that you've been pushed to the limit of endurance. Something's got to give. And you'll consult the highest power to see that it does. I think the animals in the story had reached that point.

The Birth of Selu

Selu came into the world singing. From the top of a cornstalk she came—strong, ripe, tender. A grown woman.

Kanati, the First Man, heard the song. At first he didn't know where it was coming from, but he was glad to hear it. It sounded like company.

Kanati was lonely. Bored. As a hunter, mostly of deer, he'd always had plenty to do. That was the problem—he did too much. He killed too many of the animals, more than he needed. It seemed all he could think about was hunting—and sleeping in the sun.

The animals got sick and tired of his ways. *Sick and tired.* They met in council and decided to ask the Creator's help. "Kanati is killing too many of us," they said. "If he keeps on going like he is, there soon won't be any of us left." The Creator pondered the situation, then sought out Kanati, who was sleeping in the sun, and caused a corn plant to grow up beside him, near his heart.

The stalk was tall and straight, the leaves curved and gleaming green. From the top of the stalk rose a beautiful brown, black-haired woman, the First Woman. From the top of the cornstalk she came—strong, ripe, tender. And singing ...

Kanati woke up, looked around. Then he saw Selu ...

Kanati had been lonely for such a long time that he might have been rude and in a rush. But he remembered the original courtesy—the sweetness of his own heart—that the Creator had given him. Respectfully, he asked Selu to come down and held up his hand to help her.

She smiled, but signaled him to wait ...

Politely, Kanati waited while she reached behind her for an ear of corn, for Selu knew you must always take your heritage with you, wherever you go.

Then she gave Kanati her hand and stepped down. They went home together.

Selu took the corn and went into the kitchen. Soon the kettle was bubbling and Kanati smelled the most delicious aroma he'd ever known—the sweet heart of the corn. Maybe it reminded him that the pollen from the tassel has a similar aroma, equally sweet.

Kanati felt in harmony with all that lives.

> *Strength and tenderness.*
> *Tenderness and strength.*
> *Balance*
> *in the human dimension ...*

for the individual, regardless of gender. And for the community, where traditionally the Cherokee, like many other Native peoples, have applied the principle of gender balance to all levels of their society, from family to ceremonies to government. Woman and man represent cardinal balances in nature. Among these balances are:

- the balance of forces—continuance in the midst of change;
- the balance of food—vegetables and meat;
- the balance of relationships—taking and giving back with respect.

Regardless of the era in which this ancient story of Selu is told, one of the unchanging elements is that a basic imbalance, a lack of respect, between genders disturbs the balance in the environment, just as imbalance in an individual invades the web of his or her life and affects all relationships. Or as a basket's rib that is out of kilter will throw the whole weaving awry.

One of the most sustaining elements common to all of the Selu stories is healing. Even a break in the cardinal balance may be restored to wholeness and harmony. Broken strands in the web of life may be repaired, as a basket out of kilter may be returned to balance if one unweaves it back to the original error, corrects it and reweaves from there. Hope strengthens the will to survive. Determination and work make survival possible.

As we set out to seek the Corn-Mother's wisdoms, our compass-story will keep us on the path. It will help us hear Selu singing of strength, respect, balance and harmony. Of adaptability, cooperation, unity in diversity. And through the teachings of Native speakers and tradition, we may realize, if we think purposefully, that *Ginitsi Selu* has been in our midst for longer than we ever supposed.

FOLLOWING THE DEER TRAIL

Although Selu's story was implanted in my childhood, I only recently became aware that it has grown and matured with me. Looking back I see that for more than a decade Selu has increasingly influenced my life and work, singing and weaving through them.

I should have realized all along what was happening. During the latter part of the 1970s, I'd had (and am still having) a similar experience with the spirit of another Cherokee traditional story. He is *Awi Usdi*, Little Deer—Selu's counterpart, a teacher of the sacred law of respect to hunters and other people as well. It's important for you to know him because in Native ceremony, art and thought, as in nature, the deer and the corn are usually companions. They signify balance and harmony in nature, as well as in human gender—male and female. Understanding Little Deer is important also because, by a long and circuitous route, he led me through the 1980s to Selu.

As Wallace Black Elk says, "The spirit always finds a pathway." Before retracing mine, you'll want a landmark map that gives an idea of what to expect along the way and at our destination. The path weaves and spirals through the years of the past decade in the same way a trail moves through the mountains (or reeds through the ribs of a basket). The terrain of my life itself shaped the path (and the form of this book). Whether for deer or human, a mountain trail rarely runs straight-on for long. You've probably already sensed its circular, weaving motion: over ... under ... over ... under, round and round, each time going a little higher.

Our heading is East—toward the Corn-Mother and her wisdoms—by way of Four Directions: Wounds, Mother Earth, Healing, Selu. In some places the going is steep and rough. In others, it smooths out and overlooks vistas of harmony and peace. We move in the natural continuum of past, present and future—time flowing back on itself, as Albert Einstein theorized and Native tradition has always held to be true. And as many other people have experienced, especially when moving through the vast expanses of nature. Our destination is a spiraling meditation on the wisdoms of *Ginitsi Selu*—Corn, Mother of Us All. In this era, when we "teeter on the turning point" and struggle for balance, what can we learn from her? Contemporary Native speakers give traditional paradigms for perceiving and applying her wisdoms, which are appropriate for the individual and society alike. Our journey must be made with respect. Part of that respect is patient and careful preparation; we should not and must not *plunge* into the presence of *Ginitsi Selu*. (Also, "plunging" in the mountains can get you killed—or snakebit.)

National balance begins with the individual. That's why this book of thoughts is our personal journey together as well as a contemplation of issues, events, places and people. An individual's life intertwines with the whole; it is a strand of the web. In each of us, as we weave our lives, there's a thread, a path, that goes back to the beginning. My balance as a person and as a poet and writer began in the summer of 1977, when I first encountered Little Deer as a living spirit—and in a most scientific place. He centered my life and later showed me the path to Selu, experiences as real as if I'd laid my hand on his antlers.

Along with the maxim of "Take your bearings at the trailhead," mountaineering wisdom says, "Make sure your guide is trustworthy." I'll leave myself to your judgment, but via his story, Little Deer (and Selu as

well) has been afoot in my native mountains as long as the Cherokee themselves—about twenty-five hundred years. His step is sure and time-tested. To
this day, Little Deer is well known among the Cherokee in the Eastern Band of
North Carolina and in the Nation of Oklahoma. To give you a feeling for the
contemporary Cherokee's relationship to Little Deer, we listen to conversations
between Anna G. Kilpatrick and two leaders, Asudi and Dôi in *Friends of
Thunder*. Asudi shows how naturally one may come upon *Ahw'usti* (this is the
precise Cherokee translation of his name; the more familiar spelling of "Awi
Usdi" is phonetic). Dôi touches on Little Deer's tutelary role in the confirmation
of Ahw'usti's being a *lar* (cherished guardian spirit) who lived in the house:[4]

A.K.: What about Ahw'usti that they tell about?

Asudi: He's still living. Up there on the hill, straight through here,
there is a salt spring. In Asuwosg' Precinct, a long time ago, I was
walking by there, hunting horses. There was a little trail that went down
the hill (nowadays there is a big highway on that hill up there), and
farther up on the flat the road divided. Beyond that, in the valley near
Ayohli Amayi, hunting horses early in the morning, I was walking there
in the valley when I saw them walking, and I stopped in amazement.

They were [a foot] high and had horns. The first one was just this
high, and he had horns. They were beautiful, and they were going in that
direction. There were no houses there. It was in the forest, and I
wondered where they were going. Several in number, they were all
walking. He [Ahw'usti] was going first, just this high, and he had horns.
His horns were just as my hands are shaped—five. *Five points*, they call
them five points. That's the way it was. Just this high, and so beautiful!
And there was a second one, third one, fourth one. The fifth one was a
huge one, and he also had horns with five points.

They stopped awhile, and they watched me. I was so afraid of the
large ones! They were turning back, looking at me. They were pawing
with their feet, and I was truly afraid then! They were showing their
anger then. First they would go right and then left and go: "Ti! Ti! Ti!
Ti!" They kept looking at me and pawing, and I just stood still.

They started again and disappeared away off, and I wondered
where they went. I heard my horses over there, and I went there as
quickly as I could. I caught me a horse and took the others home.

There was a man named Tseg' Ahl'tadef', and when I arrived
there, he asked me, "What was it that you learned today?"

"I saw an amazing thing down there," I told him.

"What was it?"

"A deer. He was just this high, and he had horns like this, and he was walking in front. ...

"It was Ahw'usti," he said.

A.K.: Did you ever hear of Ahw'usti?

Dôi: I have ...

A.K.: I wonder what he was like. ["The old people"] claim that they fed him.

Dôi: Yes, they did.

A.K.: Was he like a man, like a dog, or like a deer?

Dôi: He was a deer, very small deer.

A.K.: He lived in the house, didn't he?

Dôi: Yes, he was a small creature [indicating a foot and one-half or so].

A.K.: He was small, a small creature, wasn't he? They used to tell about [spirit animals] a long time ago, didn't they?

Dôi: Yes, they did ...

A.K.: And this Ahw'usti—did you say that they "used" him for [ritual] "medicine"?

Dôi: The old people who lived long ago used to "use" him. And they loved him.

A.K.: That's true.

Dôi: Yes ... They knew a lot, those people who lived long ago.

The essence of Little Deer's story is this: Long, long ago the hunters were killing too many animals (imbalance is apparently an immemorial problem for Homo sapiens). Meeting in council, the animals discussed ways of resolving their dilemma. Awi Usdi, the chief of the deer, came up with the solution.

"I see what we must do," he said. "We cannot stop the humans from hunting animals. That is the way it was meant to be. However, the humans are not doing things in the right way. If they do not respect us and hunt us only when there is real need, they may kill us all. I shall go now and tell the hunters what they must do. Whenever they wish to kill a deer, they must prepare in a ceremonial way. They must ask me for permission to kill one of us. Then, after they kill a deer, they must show respect to its spirit and ask for pardon. If the hunters do not do this, then I shall track them down. With my magic I will make their limbs crippled. Then they will no longer be able to walk or shoot a bow and arrow." Then Awi Usdi, Little Deer, did as he said.[5]

This is the essence of the story as it is told in the Eastern Band (as recorded in Michael J. Caduto and Joseph Bruchac's *Keepers of the Earth*) and in the Nation of Oklahoma. Its essence does not change. The sacred law is eternal and immutable. You must take and give back with respect.

In the pre-industrial society of the Cherokee, the primary physical consequences of breaking the law were clear: Overkilling the deer would cause depletion of the herds and hunger for the people. But how could such a story apply to life in the mid-1970s?

The synapse in my mind that could have made the connection was inactive. I'd grown up during the 1940s on a government reservation—for atoms, not Indians. It was the atomic frontier, Oak Ridge, Tennessee, a city that was part of the secret Manhattan Project. Seventy-five thousand people from many regions of America had converged there for a purpose unknown to most: to split the atom. With the exception of native mountain people and a few others, Oak Ridge was a science-oriented, literal-minded society. Anyone who spoke in images usually was labeled "backward," or most damaging from a scientific point of view, "romantic."

In the Oak Ridge schools and later at the University of Tennessee, I received an excellent Western education, with a double major in English and French and a minor in European and American history. I had three dreams: to write, to go to France and to have a life-partner/family. Declining a scholarship to the Sorbonne, I chose to marry Paul, who promised he would support my two other dreams. Seven years later, when we were twenty-eight years old and had two toddler daughters, he joined the U.S. Air Force, and we moved to a reconnaissance base in Laon, France. Laon is situated on a northern route used by invading armies eighty-seven times since the days of Julius Caesar. Vestiges of Caesar's camp are still visible. For two and a half years I worked as a translator and social liasion officer for the Air Force during the NATO withdrawal.

I learned that Machiavelli is alive and well and living wherever power and politics mix, which is to say, *everywhere*. In general, the French viewed Americans as romantics who've not yet lost their illusions. They said, "When Americans come to Europe, they fall among the Old Foxes." Gallic shrugs evoked flurries of bloody chicken feathers.

"But your Benjamin Franklin was a different type entirely," they said, as if he'd just left Paris. "He was shrewd. Very shrewd. A philosopher in a coonskin hat! *Formidable!*"

I felt at home. The French spoke in images. They were realists. And their concept of time was familiar, too: the past informing the present, influencing the future. They burnished the raw edges of life with their sense of ceremony, style, art and ironic humor. Appalachian mountain people think this way, the Cherokee, the Europeans (primarily Celts) and the Africans, who came much later. The ways of the fox are well known among us, as well as the ways of the formidable raccoon. Shrewd Franklin. The French took one look at his hat and saw a worthy adversary. In the same century, many French in the American South came to know the Cherokee leader and master diplomat, Attakullakulla. They embraced him as a chief among Old Foxes. His wily diplomacy, especially in negotiating treaties, is still legendary. From the Tellico area in East Tennessee, he was often at Chota, the Cherokee capital on the Little Tennessee River, which was formerly called the Cherokee River. Tellico is about fifty miles as the crow flies from my childhood home. East Tennessee was part of the Cherokee Nation for many centuries.

Living in France made me think deeply about who I was, about the value of my heritage, and about the necessity of working out harmonies with peoples from different cultures. By the time I returned to America, I knew that I was a Cherokee/Appalachian poet. I was determined to sing my song. ...

But it turned out to be excruciatingly difficult. Backlash to civil rights was closing doors to many ethnic groups. The women's movement had not yet changed the general concept of "woman's place." Technology was getting bigger, language more literal and technically oriented. Pollution of the environment was a growing concern. This outer turmoil exacerbated my inner one as I tried to make a harmony from my three heritages: Cherokee, Appalachian and scientific. The atom, after all, had been the companion of my childhood and youth. It was part of me, too. And high technology is a culture, with its own worldview, value system and language. I was immeshed in a tangled skein. Like a wire vine, it was shutting me up and shutting me down. Neither I nor my work had a center.

I had no idea that Little Deer's story was lying dormant in my mind, waiting for the right climatic conditions to germinate. One afternoon in 1977,

I went to the Museum of Science and Energy in Oak Ridge. For a long time I stood in front of a giant model of an atom—an enormous, translucent blue ball with tiny lights whirling inside, representing the cloud of electrons. Stars whirling … whirling … whirling … drew me into an altered state of consciousness.

Suddenly I saw Little Deer leaping in the heart of the atom.

In that instant, as if irradiated, his story sprouted, shot up and bore fruit. The synapse in my mind electrified. With my whole being I made a quantum leap and connected Little Deer to the web of my life—at the center. The vision was clear.

But what did it mean? That night, I drew what I'd seen: a white stag leaping at the heart of three orbits. To signify the electrons, I put a tiny star in each orbit. And I wrote these lines:

> From the heart of the mountain he comes
> with his head held high in the wind.
> Like the spirit of light he comes
> the small white chief of the deer.

I understood that he embodied the sacred law of taking and giving back with respect, the Sacred Circle of Life. I was certain that Little Deer and his story would reveal ways to make harmony in my own life and in the world around me. But deepening my understanding took time and work.

Slowly I began to combine facts and images into poems and prose that fused past, present and future. With Little Deer as the unifying theme, I wrote about the Cherokee, the Celts, the atom; about the earth, about men, women and children; about the interconnection of all that lives and the need for reverence for all. The resulting book, *Abiding Appalachia: Where Mountain and Atom Meet*, was published in 1978 by St. Luke's Press (now by Iris Press). *Abiding* raised the question: Do humans have enough reverence for life to cope with the atom? Is the spirit of Awi Usdi still with us? Shortly after publication came the nuclear accident at Three Mile Island, and several years later, the one at Chernobyl.

Abiding is the "eye" of my mature life and work. The vision of Little Deer changed all my relationships—with my husband, with my children, with other people and with the turmoils of contemporary life that confront us all. Primarily, it changed my relationship with myself. I understood who I was and the meaning of my middle name which I had never used in print: *Awiakta*, a derivation of the Cherokee word for "eye of the deer." To bring my inside in harmony with my outside and also to mark the mature season of my life, I would, in time—and after consulting with my family—choose to be known by this name. From this center, my work expanded.

I'm speaking literally when I say that Little Deer was my guide along the path to Selu during the next decade. But while he came like a lightning bolt, Selu arrived as what the Navajo call a "she-rain"—gentle, steady, long-term and deeply permeating. And the cycles of deer and corn overlapped, as seasons do. As I came to the end of my path and to Selu herself, I realized that Little Deer truly had led me to "medicines and waterholes and a shelter."

Selu holds my writings of a decade in balance, as the hometone of the dulcimer holds the notes of a melody. As we go along the path, you will hear her voice weave in and out, gradually growing stronger. With Selu's compass-story in mind, you will sense her presence more easily than I did the first time I traveled this way. Now, we must take some immovable points of reference and understand how they relate to the whole. Otherwise, we still may "wind up lost."

FIXED BEARINGS

The Doublewoven Basket

How can a book have the form of a basket? The same way a bowl can be shaped like a shell, a net like a web. Or as a flute takes up the song of a bird. The forms transpose through a basic affinity.

A round, doublewoven basket in the Oklahoma Cherokee style is this book's natural form, arising from the thoughts themselves. As I worked with the poems, essays and stories, I saw they shared a common base—the sacred law of taking and giving back with respect, of maintaining balance. From there they wove around four themes, gradually assuming a double-sided pattern—one outer, one inner—distinct, yet interconnected in a whole. The outer side became my path to Selu, the inner one was the Corn-Mother herself. The basket image conveys the principle of composition quickly. Reading will be easy if you keep the weaving mode in mind: Over … under … over … under. A round basket never runs "straight-on."

The clearest way to understand how this book, and our journey through it, is organized is to look at a *single* woven basket's basic design in its simplest form. First, two splits or reeds are centered, like the cardinal points of a compass. Then two more splits of equal size and length are added. These are the ribs of the basket:

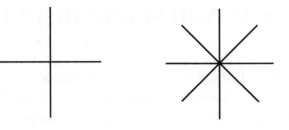

Weaving begins at the center. The base is tightly woven to hold the ribs in balance. The weaving may become slightly more relaxed as the basket takes shape ... over ... under ... over ... under ... until it is finished. From the simplest basket to the most complex of the doublewoven ones, this principle is the same: *The ribs must be centered and held in balance.* In a sense, they are the fixed bearings that guide the rhythm of the weaving.

Similarly, in the very beginning of this book, the themes are presented as poems, one poem for each of the Four Directions: Wounds, Mother Earth, Healing, Selu. With these themes fixed in your mind, you will see how my thoughts weave over and under them, first tightly at the base (the trailhead), then slightly more relaxed as the work progresses up the outer side. This is "Weaving I: A Path to Selu."

In the *doublewoven* basket style, buckbrush vines, called "runners," are used instead of reeds. At a certain point, the ribs are turned down inside and weaving begins again, back toward the base.[6] In a similar manner, about halfway through the book, my thoughts and themes become "Weaving II: Selu, Spirit of Survival." The two sides are distinct, yet interconnected, and they reconverge in the basic law of respect and balance.

The ribs of Wounds, Mother Earth, Healing and Selu hold the book, as well as each section's individual pieces, in shape. The four parts, whose titles are derived from the poems of the Four Directions at the beginning, are "Killing Our Own Seed," "When the People Call Earth 'Mother,'" "Our Courage Is Our Memory," and "Selu, Spirit of Survival." Essays, poems and stories are grouped according to theme, as in most varieties of corn kernels of the same color range onto one ear—yellow, white, red, black (deepest indigo shading to blue). Of course, since corn has "jumping genes," a few red kernels may pop up on another ear, but that's considered lucky hereabouts.

SISTERS AND SEED-THOUGHTS

The numbers four and seven appear often in my writing, as well as in Mary Adair's art, because they are traditionally sacred to the Cherokee and are used in ceremony, ritual, art, social organization and government. Four has direct relation to the cardinal points of direction and balance. One significance of seven is as the mystical number of renewal and return. The terms "Seven Clans" and "Seven Clan Districts" are commonly employed in Cherokee magic as figures of speech to signify the whole of the Cherokee people. They are sometimes used as a symbol for the entire world,[7] which is important to know in contemplating Mary's final drawing, "The Future Unfolding."

You might wonder, "Did you and Mary get together and work this harmony of art and text out in an elaborate plan?"

We didn't. And that's the magical part of our collaboration. We've met physically for only a few minutes: once at the Cherokee National holiday in 1986 and again at the National Women's Symposium in Tahlequah, Oklahoma, in 1989. But at the Reunion of the Cherokee Councils at Red Clay in 1984, I'd bought a print of Mary's painting *Nanyehi (Nancy Ward) Ancient Mother of Many*. I was powerfully drawn to it, and the print has been on the shelf by my round writing table ever since—at eye level. Mary is a descendant of Nancy Ward.

When I began working on the Selu manuscript in the fall of 1990, I called Mary in Oklahoma and asked if she'd like to do some drawings for it. Our conversation was brief. I said, "I'm working on a book called *Selu: Seeking the Corn-Mother's Wisdom*. It's about Selu at work in the contemporary world." I read her the poem "I Offer You a Gift," as well as a one-page introduction to the Selu section.

"I think I could do that," she said. Soon I received the title picture and all of the others except those for "Trailhead" and "Killing Our Own Seed." Without reading a word of the text, she had drawn the perfect pictures! In fact, her pictures helped me organize the book. I said, "Mary, how can this be?"

She chuckled. "Well, I know the story."

The power of culture, of roots, is a mysterious phenomenon. Mary's ancestors also lived in the southern Appalachians. Our families' paths may have crossed then also. Mary's strong, beautiful work is a great gift. It keeps constantly before me not only the value of the Cherokee heritage, but the value of others' heritages as well. All people in America—and especially the children—should be able to sing their songs, be proud of their roots and be received in a society that values their heritages. Red, black, yellow, white—in a circle, as Grandmother Corn exemplifies in her calico variety, which is commonly called Indian corn. America seems to be moving slowly in the direction of a truer democracy. I believe in that movement with my whole heart. And that is why in the fax at the beginning I called the path to Selu "our journey." Inasfar as technology (print and paper) can make interaction possible, I want this to be a book in which you and I are companions, especially as we gather what I call seed-thoughts about Selu's survival wisdoms.

The concept of seed-thoughts comes from one of my mother Wilma's maxims for life: "The seeds of one decade are the harvest of the next." This seems to hold true for most things, such as health, education, work, history, art, politics, issues, love or hate, relationships, marriage, family and most literally with children, who are "planted" in one decade and mature in the next. Mother says, "The reason the maxim holds true is that cycles are Mother Nature's way, and she *will* take her course, so you're well advised to work with her. 'The seeds of one decade are the harvest of the next' is an old saying and that's why it's old—the principle never changes. Even high-tech can't change Mother Nature."

This is Selu talking, the Eternal Wise Mother, Wisdom. And Wisdom speaks in all cultures. Whatever your ethnic roots, there is probably someone in your family or among your writers and poets who has passed along a similar maxim, a seed-thought for survival, which will bear fruit in its time, an investment for the future. (The term "seed money," so often used in America today, derives from this natural principle of deferred returns.)

In 1990, as I stood in a great singing cornfield and looked down my path winding through the past decade, I saw that the maxim holds true, for both my life and my work. It also holds true for issues. Not only are racism, sexism and disdain for Mother Earth coming to harvest in the 1990s, they also seem to be reseeding themselves. Thoughts and energy to counter them are also coming to harvest and, hopefully, will reseed in an even stronger strain, so that the twenty-first century will begin a new era of peace and justice. I dream this not because I am a romantic, but because I come from survivor peoples who revere the sacred law.

Although this book contains my seed-thoughts about survival and the Corn-Mother, as you gather them up, please add your own. Contemplate the value of your heritage, remember the stories that are meaningful to you, underline, write responses in the margin, tuck between the pages clippings and notes of other survival wisdoms you've found. Make this *our* book.

By the trailhead, Mary Adair has set a Cherokee gather-basket, a singlewoven basket of split-oak, sturdy enough to hold seven ears of corn—and more! At the very end of the book, she has placed a smaller, doublewoven basket of the kind the Cherokee use to hold seeds. It is made of buckbrush vines, sturdy in sinew and beauty. It images the real basket that has sat on my desk during the writing of this book. I've studied its construction and held it often, drawing strength from it. Because of the spirit and love that must go into the weaving, a basket made by hand is, like the corn seed, reality itself ... a living poem ... a message instantly conveyed. For this reason it is said that, ideally, a basket should never be sold but always offered as a gift. And thus this one has passed, hand to hand, from the woman who made it to the cherished woman friend who gave it to me for my fiftieth birthday, and then to Mary via a photo and to you via paper and ink—creative technology bringing you a gift from the daughters of Selu and in her honor.

At the end of our journey, when we've gathered all the ears, we'll ease off beyond the confines of print and paper to a place that exists only in our minds. We'll sit down with the ears—shuck 'em, shell 'em. Then you can sort out the seed-thoughts you want to keep and put them in the basket. All the while, we'll chat, laugh and sing, as people have done from time immemorial in the presence of the Corn-Mother. Most of all, we will give back respect and gratitude for the gift of her birth so long ago—and for the indigenous people who received her into their care and shared her great bounty with others.

We also will give respect and thanks for the deer, the Corn-Mother's eternal companion and counterpart in the balance, and for those who have preserved his wisdom in ceremony and story. The deer, like Selu, is part of the history of democracy in this land now called America. He will be with us on our path and of course, in the meditation on Selu herself.

A deep red corn seed lies in the palm of your hand. In the split second the shell first touched your skin, the tip of my finger touched you also. Energy to energy, life to life, an invitation to a journey ...

I call your attention to a small sign by our path that distills a philosophy of all my mountain ancestors.

Trail Warning

Beauty is no threat to the wary
who treat the mountain in its way,
the copperhead in its way,
and the deer in its way,
knowing that nature is the human heart
made tangible.

I plunged past this sign without heeding its warning the first time I came this way. I also forgot what my parents have always advised, "If you meet a copperhead—snake or person—give 'em a wide berth. If you have to go in close, take a hoe."

SECTION II

Killing Our Own Seed

M.Adair '92©

ARROW OF WARNING AND HOPE

The Cherokee vs. Tellico Dam Controversy

It seems like I already heard these
stories before ... the only thing is,
the names sound different.
—Old Grandma in *Ceremony*
by Leslie Marmon Silko

In truth, our cause is your own. It is the cause of liberty and of justice. It is based upon your own principles, which we have learned from yourselves, for we have gloried to count your Washington and your Jefferson our great teachers. ... We have practiced their precepts with success. And the result is manifest. ... We have learned your religion also. We have read your sacred books. Hundreds of our people have embraced their doctrines, practiced the virtues they teach, cherished the hopes they awaken. ... We speak to the representatives of a Christian country: the friends of justice; the patrons of the oppressed. And our hopes revive, and our prospects brighten, as we indulge the thought. On your sentence our fate is suspended. ... On your kindness, on your humanity, on your compassion, on your benevolence, we rest our hopes.
—Cherokee Memorial to the United States
Congress, December 29, 1835[8]

Little Deer and the Snail Darter

A phone call in the spring of 1978 set me on the path to Selu. The caller was Carroll McGinnis, a physician in East Tennessee, a Celtic man, who is a reverent hunter. He loves the land and believes implicitly in the truth of Little Deer. (I was living then, as I am now, at the other end of the state, in Memphis.) Our families have been friends for years; his wife, Reba, and I are "milk sisters," that is, we nursed our first babies together. Carroll was even more cryptic and wry than usual.

"Awiakta, get up here and do something about this damn Tellico Dam. They're going to ruin the Little Tennessee River and drown Chota."

"I thought the controversy was about the snail darter."

"So does the rest of the country," he said. "But I'm sitting up here right on top of the dam and I'm telling you if something isn't done quick, they're going to close the gates and wipe out the heartland of Cherokee history. The Cherokee have protested the dam for fifteen years!"

I was stunned. Angry. How could such a momentous issue go unnoticed by the national media? And even the Memphis media? And what could I do? Obviously I had to do something. This was family business, homeland business.

"All I can do is write," I said. "I'm not well known. I don't have any clout. Who will publish it? And even if somebody did, what good is it to sling a poem at a dam? Even King David himself couldn't ..."

"Do it," he said. And then less brusquely, "Little Deer will get you if you don't."

For more than a year, I wrote letters to the editors of newspapers across the state, urging attention to the Cherokee component of the issue and suggesting that investigative reporters be dispatched to cover it. I queried national magazines about doing articles myself. The usual reply was, "What does a dam in Tennessee have to do with the rest of the country?"

Finally, in September 1979, an underground newspaper in Memphis, *The Dixie Flyer*, agreed to publish an article and scheduled it for mid-November. As fast as possible, I gathered up facts and images; Tellico was a story I'd heard before by a different name.

At European contact in 1540, the Cherokee Nation covered parts of what are now eight southern states, approximately following the Appalachian mountains from southeast Virginia to north Georgia and from eastern North Carolina to middle Tennessee. Through treaties and attrition, the nation was gradually reduced in size. In 1838, the federal government forced seventeen thousand Cherokee on a fifteen-hundred-mile march to Oklahoma. About a fourth of them died. The Cherokee called it "the place where they cried," or the Trail of Tears. In North Carolina, a small group had eluded the federal troops. They fled to the high mountains, where they held out. Later, they became the nucleus of what is now the Eastern Band of Cherokees.

In researching my article, I talked with many Cherokee of the Eastern Band. To them, as to me, the Trail of Tears was not only a vivid memory, it was an old pattern they saw repeating in the Tellico Dam controversy. Their eyes were deep with pain, anger and sorrow. As one young man said, "Tellico is the Removal all over again. First our ancestors. Then our history. Then us."

To recognize the pattern as well as to understand what it means to the Cherokee, you must not only know the facts, you must feel their meaning. The following prose-poem is based on James Mooney's "Historical Sketch of the Cherokee" (19th Annual Report, the Bureau of American Ethnology, 1900).

The Removal

A cradle still warm ... a bubbling pot with no lid. ... So swiftly did Government troops sweep down that the Cherokee hardly found time for a fast look at home. Removal. "The cruelest work I've ever known," one soldier said, "the cruelest. ..."

It began in 1838, in June. And so many perished from the heat that the General waited 'til fall to move all the rest along the Trail of Tears. When next year's spring had come, 17,000 had gone to alien ground and 4,000 had sunk along the way.

Tsali's family marched the Trail and when his frail wife trudged too slow, soldiers struck her with their guns. And Tsali rose up. With his brother

*and his sons, he rose up to avenge the blows, attacking the guards and killing
one. And then they fled—back to the high, lonesome mountains—and hid
near Utsala's band, who had sworn to stay in the native land or die. Then
the General conceived a plan and told his aide, "I'll send Utsala word that
if he hunts Tsali down and brings him in to me, the rebel band may be allowed
to stay. William Thomas is the man to go. The Cherokee call him 'Little Will.'
He's their lifelong friend and still has their trust. Bring me Colonel Thomas. ..."*

*In silence Utsala heard the words of Thomas. In silence took them to
his heart that brimmed with bitter thoughts—of his wife and little son who
had died for lack of food. Of thousands who already walked the Trail of
Tears. Of his gaunt band and the years that lay before them. In the deep
silence of his heart Utsala knew—better to sacrifice the few than let the many
die. With an inward prayer for pardon, he nodded his assent.*

*Then Thomas went to Tsali. Refusing guards, he went alone and sought
the old man and his sons. Standing between them and their guns, he spoke
all he knew. With silence drawn round him like a cloak, Tsali heard Thomas
out. Then he said, "I will come in. I don't want my own people to hunt me
down."*

*And so they came—Tsali, his brother, and all his sons save one, who
was spared because of youth. And it was the General's plan that they should
die by the hand of their own kind, so that all the Cherokee might see their
helplessness before the law. A squad of prisoners aimed the guns. And Tsali
raised his tired eyes and saw they asked for pardon as they fired. The sound
faded from the air. ... But not the hope. Thomas held it to his heart. In
Washington he took the part of the Cherokee, claiming the promise in their
name. A remnant did remain and is here still. For Little Will kept his word.
And while he lived and was of sound mind, the Cherokee could find dignity
and peace.*

Most Tennesseans grow up knowing this story; they feel it in their
bones. For them, the title of my newspaper article and the lead poem were
a fax of the whole situation.

TELLICO: END OF THE TRAIL

The Covenant

The firing squad takes aim
and I, Tsali, fix my eye
on the mountain
on the promise—
a remnant shall remain
the Cherokee shall take again
their old and noble paths.
For this I go ...
my brother and my sons also.
Our blood shall seal
the exiles' pass
and make fast our mountain home.
And the Trail of Tears
shall be made dry
as by a mighty wind.

Will the Trail of Tears be made dry as by a mighty wind? Or will the gates of Tellico Dam slam shut and rising waters drown the historic and spiritual heartland of the Cherokee nation? That heartland includes the sites of Chota, holy city and ancient capital of the nation; Tuskegee, birthplace of Sequoyah, inventor of the Cherokee syllabary; Tenase, for which Tennessee was named; and many other towns, as well as the sacred burial mounds. None of the sites is more than 20 percent excavated. All will be lost—if the waters rise.

Fortunately, a vigilant remnant of the people does remain. Fifteen years ago Cherokee leaders perceived the threat. In October 1979, I discussed their feelings and protest strategy with Dr. Duane King, director of the Museum of the Cherokee Indian in Cherokee, North Carolina. Dr. King has been active for many years in tribal affairs. He said that in 1965, when the Tellico Project was in the planning stages, Cherokee leaders protested strongly. Tennessee Valley Authority (TVA) officials replied, "Why did you wait so long?" (A question they repeated when the Cherokee brought suit to halt the dam in 1979.)

In 1966, Congress passed the Historical Preservation Act. The Cherokee were encouraged. They thought it included *their* history. The Endangered Species Act also engendered hope. But the Cherokee didn't let up on their work through democratic channels. During the early 1970s the chief of the tribe and the chairman of the council called on Governor Winfield Dunn and asked him to speak on their behalf to TVA. He did. With earnest support.

TVA was not cooperative. However, officials appeared willing to listen, at least during the following years of litigation from landowners as well as environmentalists, who fortunately discovered the snail darter—a three-inch fish sufficiently piquant and obscure to capture the imagination of press and public.

As for the Cherokee cause, the major media seemed uninterested. Although the Cherokee talked openly with reporters, no one really picked up on it. The Cherokee were just one more voice shouting against the dam, just another endangered species—obscure but definitely not "piquant."

It is the old question: If a tree falls in the forest and there's no one to hear it, does it make a sound? If an issue is raised and the major media don't "hear" it, is it an issue at all? Certainly, the sound of it will never reach the public. January 1979 brought hope. A cabinet-level committee ruled the Tellico Dam project economically unjustified and refused to exempt it from the provisions of the Endangered Species Act. If saving the snail darter helped their historic sites, thought the Cherokee, so be it.

But a blow was being prepared on the House floor. On June 18, the crucial initial stage was so cleverly executed that it required only forty-two seconds to complete. Most of the few congressmen present were Appropriations Committee members who had come to take up routine committee appropriations in the energy and water development bill.

Knowing that the House has a firm rule that forbids using an appropriations bill to change existing laws and that the word "Tellico" would spark immediate objection, John Duncan, representative from the Tellico area, quietly put his amendment on the agenda. Just as the clerk was about to read its substance, Duncan stopped him. By prearrangement, a minority member rose to say that the minority had reviewed the amendment and accepted it. Alabama Representative Tom Bevill said for the Democratic majority, "We have no objection." Before the clerk could continue, the chair called for a voice vote. Next morning members of Congress read in the *Congressional Record* what had *not* been said on the floor—that the House had adopted an amendment directing TVA to complete Tellico Dam and fill the reservoir, notwithstanding the Endangered Species Act and all other laws.

In the aftermath debate Paul McCloskey of California tried to reverse the action, pointing out "the danger of condemnation by the public if we adopt without reading an amendment of this degree of controversy." When the Senate took up the issue on September 10, Senator John Culver of Iowa attempted to emphasize the facts: that this project would generate just twenty-three megawatts in a TVA power grid already producing twenty-seven thousand megawatts; that, by TVA's own admission, the power was unneeded; that the dam would cost annually seven hundred thousand dollars more than it would provide in benefits; and, finally, that until there had been more years of successful transplant experiments, the snail darter might still be an endangered species.

With one minute to go in the debate, Tellico opponents had a slight majority. But Tennessee's Senator Howard Baker, a strong proponent of the dam, went up and down the aisles and persuaded six senators to change their votes. *Audubon* magazine (November issue) reported the entire proceedings in great detail, including the final result: Dam advocates won forty-eight to forty-four. The deed was done.

What of Cherokee rights? What of the "old and noble paths" that would disappear forever? What of the Trail that would end in a Lake of Tears? The government was silent.

So why didn't the Cherokee sue the government sooner? Dr. King explained, "The Cherokee wanted to exhaust all other possibilities first, because to bring suit against the federal government would be an admission to themselves and to the general public that their rights are being denied. They could not believe Congress would reverse its own laws."

Then the blow fell.

On September 25, 1979, President Carter signed the Duncan Amendment exempting Tellico Dam from every other federal law that would prevent its completion.

It was an old pattern: "Agree to this treaty and we'll never ask for any more land. Trust the law." In short, the government used the letter of the law to defeat its spirit. Jointly, the Cherokee of the Eastern Band and of the Nation of Oklahoma filed suit on October 12. They charged that completion of the Tellico project, which would destroy sacred burial grounds, "denies Indians their religious freedom guaranteed under the First Amendment."

They fixed their eyes on the Constitution, on the promise. ...

For the first time, major media took notice (although with the implicit attitude of "Why did they wait so long?"). The news was reported accurately but with a marked lack of crusading passion. As one reporter said, "People just don't turn on to burial mounds like they did to the snail darter." To be fair, several newsmen have been interested in the Cherokee issue, but their editors haven't. It would be intriguing to know why.

Evidently some people do "turn on to burial mounds," for several thousand Cherokee and supporters turned up at the protest rally at Chota in mid-October. Sixteen sticks of dynamite were found near the campsite. (Interestingly, the sheriff made the announcement during the press conference.) Roads leading to the rally were then blocked for "public safety," and fifteen hundred to two thousand protesters were turned back. Previous to that, an estimated one hundred fifty pounds of nails had been scattered along the roads and directional signs had been reversed. Who was responsible for the nails and the dynamite? Nobody knew. That is, no one had been arrested.

Along with their Constitutional suit, the Cherokee asked for an injunction to stop TVA from closing the dam gates until the courts ruled on the suit. The Federal District Court, the Sixth Circuit Court of Appeals and the Supreme Court denied the injunction. Ruling on the suit was postponed. "What that means is this," said Bob Blankenship, a tribal leader, "TVA can close those gates whether it violates our rights or not. Once the water starts rising, our case is moot. Our lawyers are in Cincinnati and Washington right now trying to get it all straight. We thought everybody was entitled to their day in court. That's what the Constitution says. We don't understand. It looks like the small people don't have a chance.

"Another thing, TVA has moved all the non-Indian graves. But the bones of our people—part of them are in the basement of the University of Tennessee, and the rest are going under water."

Removal. The cruelest work. ...

Thoughts turn to what might have been—if, at this point, it was decided to leave Tellico a "dry" dam, used for flood control only.

In 1972, state archeologist Mack Prichard made a formal proposal for the Tellico area (Prichard is now environmental coordinator for the Tennessee Department of Conservation). He envisioned Tenase State Park, "which could include reconstructed Cherokee houses on our state's namesake site; a rebuilt council-house at Chota, their ancient capital; and memorials to great leaders like Oconostota, Little Carpenter (Attakullakulla) and Old Hop. ... It would certainly honor the birthplace of Sequoyah, the Tennessee-born genius, who invented the Cherokee syllabary.

"A sensitive archaeologist would be employed to excavate the Toquo Mound and certain other features pertinent of the Cherokees' antecedents in that pastoral valley.

"Further, Cherokees would be employed as Indian guides to conduct visitors on float trips down the crystal waters of the Little Tennessee River. They would stop at the old towns 'come alive' again, and among the many islands to bargain for handicrafts that Indians-in-Residence would make. They might fish in one of the most productive trout streams in the eastern

U.S. Floating quietly down through history on thirty-three miles of that scenic corridor would be an unforgettable experience. As for the land that has been taken for the Tellico Dam project—it would be returned to the farmers and to the Indians who were forced to cede their homeland in 1819."

That was the vision. It was published in the *Tennessee Valley Historical Review,* fall 1972, and in *The Tennessee Conservationist* in February 1973. Mack Prichard also pointed out that as early as 1890, the Smithsonian Institution had alerted the public to the fact that the Little Tennessee Valley was the "richest archaeological section in the Appalachians." Proof of these riches has been emerging since 1967. Acting under federal law (the Reservoir Salvage Act of 1960, the National Historic Preservation Act of 1966 and two other preservation and protection acts passed during the course of the project), teams of archeologists from the University of Tennessee conducted surveys and excavations in the Tellico area. Funded principally by the National Park Service and TVA, this work was done to help guide land use so that cultural heritage could be preserved. What the archeologists found was a mother lode—twelve thousand years of Native American history. And the federal government gave them time to save only a fraction of it.[9] Apparently, four federal laws are not enough to protect this treasure. And even the U.S. Constitution cannot protect the Cherokee.

Why have We-the-People waited so long to listen?

Or perhaps a more basic question is: "In the fight against injustice, can anyone ever start early enough?" How much more of our resources can we afford to lose in the name of industry and energy? There has to be a limit. For there comes a point where material progress is no longer a virtue. "Our claim," said tribal council chairman Dan McCoy, "deals with human rights and dignity."

But the talk is over. The gates of Tellico are poised to slam shut. Will we lament the Trail of Tears and shrug as the federal government drowns the historic heartland—and the hope—of the Cherokee? Or will we realize, with the Cherokee, that the Trail has come full circle. That we will walk it together. That the waters are rising for us all.

❖ ❖ ❖

At the eleventh hour ...

At the eleventh hour, just before the sluice gates of the dam were to be closed, some of the news media picked up on the cause of what the *New York Times* called "the forgotten folk battling against Tellico" (November 11, 1979). These folk were the Cherokee and the 340 families, most of them small farmers, whose land TVA had claimed under rights of eminent domain: 16,000 acres for the reservoir (lake) and 22,000 acres for adjoining property. Some of the people favored the dam project. Many were forced to sell and move. Three refused to do either and held out to the last—Nellie McCall, Thomas Burel Moser, and Jean Ritchie. Like many others in the area, they were skeptical that TVA wanted the adjoining property to "regulate and control its industrial and recreational development as an economic draw in a job-poor area." They believed that TVA would turn the land over to developers for profit (which it later did with half of the acreage).

Mrs. McCall, aged eighty-four and recently widowed, was waiting in her home for federal marshals to evict her when she spoke to reporter Wendell Rawls, Jr. He described her as having "fire in her eyes and a voice as firm as her grip." She asked him, "How would you like it if somebody was trying to steal your land? When you'd worked all your life for your home and then an agency of the United States government, of all things, comes along and takes it away from you. ... The lake would take about an acre and a half and I offered them that for nothing, but they said everybody had to go. It's a land grab."

Benjamen Snider, owner of a large grocery store in the area, said that 340 families moving away from the valley had brought losses to local business, eroded the county tax structure and weakened the school system. "The endangered species wasn't the snail darter," he said. "It is the small businessmen, the people who live here, and nobody cared about us." He described Nellie McCall's deceased husband, Asa, as a "gut-busting farmer" who did his work for fifty years, then watched the "land men come."

Mrs. McCall said that her husband, as well as two of her farming brothers and a sister, had died in the last five years from being "grieved to death" over the loss of their farms to the dam project. She summed up her view of the government and its agency. "You can't trust somebody that'll steal your land and then tell you it's for your own good."

Another elder, Goliath George, age seventy-eight, who speaks only Cherokee, told in an affidavit about an elder he'd listened to as a boy—a medicine man, a spiritual leader. He "would talk to my people from atop a hickory stump, notched so he could climb up on top and look out over the valley. He talked about what would happen in four or maybe five generations. He said the valley would be covered with water—our forefathers would be on the bottom of the valley looking up through a wall of glass. Tears rolled down his cheeks when he said that one day the people would once again be put to the test of holding on to that which is sacred or giving up forever another part of their lives."[10]

For almost half a century, these elders had watched the story of Tellico Dam unfolding—from the proposal of it in 1940, to the formal announcement in 1961, and the beginning of construction in 1967. They knew this story and others before it. They could discern patterns, strategies, implications. They spoke their minds. Maybe that's why American society pushes older people aside, calls them "elderly," insists they're "over the hill," treats them like "little old ladies and little old men in tennis shoes" when they speak up. Maybe there are those who fear what the elders might tell the people.

On November 13, when federal marshals arrived to evict the last three holdouts at Tellico, a CBS television crew was there to film the removal. The film aired that night on the "CBS Evening News," with a narrator describing the scene. Thomas Burel Moser's house was bulldozed into a giant hole that had been dug for it. Moser told the nation, "It's a hell of a country, ain't it?" Jean Ritchie said that what TVA had done was "stealin'." When Nellie McCall was asked where she would go now, tears welled in her eyes and she could not answer. Back in New York, Walter Cronkite, the elder statesman of national news reporters, was so moved that he had trouble getting into the next story. So did many viewers. More powerfully than thousands of printed facts, the film imaged the implications of Tellico.[11]

My mind went back to July and the day that Paul, our children and I had floated the narrow river with our long-time friends, Carroll and Reba and their children. Two mountain families saying farewell to the valley. But the river hadn't let us dwell on sorrow. Lifting our spirits with scents of fresh water and evergreen, the steady, gentle current glided our three canoes by old forests, past open fields that revealed the smoke-blue mountains cradling the valley, and back into the sun and shadow of overhanging trees. When the canoes were close enough, we exchanged words or smiles. Mostly, we signaled with our hands and pointed out special beauties to one another ... a leaping fish ... rock cliffs ... a pair of hawks circling against blue sky ... a doe bending to drink at the water's edge ... on and on in peace and well-being ... until we beached the canoes and walked across the overgrown field to the closed and abandoned dig at Chota. A barbed wire fence and a rusty "No Trespassing" sign made it clear that, barring a miracle, the end of the trail was near. By rights of blood—the code of the hills—we climbed the fence and scattered quietly and respectfully over the site. Standing in solitude, each of us had said goodbye to this part of our homeland. ... On November 29, 1979, the sluice gates of the dam were closed and the waters of the Little Tennessee River began to rise.

It was the end. I called the Cherokee Museum in North Carolina to talk with a young woman who had helped me with research. Her voice was as downhearted as mine.

"We just can't believe it," she said. "We're walking around like we're dead."

"It looks like 'We-the-People' don't have a chance," I said. "What's happened to the Constitution?"

"Maybe it's drowning, too."

That was the most devastating thought of all. I felt America heading West, the direction of death and destruction: the Darkening Land. Why had the Cherokee trusted democracy again? Why did so many other Native people continue to trust it? Why did I, in spite of all logic against it, still in my deepest heart want to trust the Constitution? I saw no path to the answers. The waters of Tellico were rising. Years of protest from many sectors of society had failed. I gave in to despair.

Many other people did not. I'll tell you the story of one of them, a story that was said to have happened in December 1979. [12]

THE LAST DAY OF ROLAND THE CHEROKEE

In the still of a December night, Roland walked resolutely toward the deserted archeological dig at Chota. Ignoring the "No Trespassing" sign, he grabbed the barbed wire fence, felt the sharp memory of the day in court: The eye of the judge had been cool. Disdain flowed in the folds of his robe. Roland looked at him and knew—

The arrow is set to the bow.

The aim is drawn ...

The judge sped the verdict to the mark. "The gates of Tellico Dam will close. The waters will rise." His attitude was clear: This so-called sacred ground is nothing to us. The Cherokee are nothing to us.

The verdict echoed years of words, concrete words that lay heavy in Roland's heart: "Those Cherokee can't stop our dam for a mound of bones. Besides, it's heathen to dump the dead in a heap. If they'd done it the Christian way—one by one—we'd move 'em, just like we've moved our own. And that so-called sacred city, that Chota, it's nothing now but a fenced-in field down by the river. Those Indians left more'n a hundred years ago. We're gonna close those dam gates and let 'er flood."

Roland tightened his grip on the wire, for the words carried an old sound. "The Cherokee are nothing to us ... nothing to us ... nothing." Long before the Trail of Tears, his ancestors in the valley had heard the sound, and wise elders had said:

The arrow is set to the bow.

The aim is drawn ...

Blood dripped from Roland's palm, but he took no heed. Behind him the damned-up river was beginning to overflow its banks. Holding two of the barbed fence strands down with one foot, Roland pushed the other two upward with a thick coil of white rope held in his unhurt hand and climbed through. He walked across the field, through dry leaves and high, withered weeds to the site of the council house, whose traces he'd helped archeologists lay clear. A granite boulder marked the pit of sacred fire, a fire the Old Ones said still burned deep within the earth.

Here Roland stopped. Taking a bundle from his jacket pocket, he carefully unwrapped a long-stemmed pipe and a small pouch of sacred tobacco and began a special long prayer ceremony for the Cherokee people. The prayers were completed by daybreak. Then Roland stripped away his boots, his denim jeans and jacket and piled them like a cairn of stones among the weeds. Bared to the winter cold, as warriors had gone of old, he circled the boulder with rope, then sat cross-legged on the ground. Drawing the rope around his waist, he tied it in seven knots ... tight ... tighter ... until he felt the brace of granite against his back.

In silence Roland listened to the sigh of rising waters and watched the light in the eastern sky deepen from rose to powerful crimson. Fixing his eyes on the crest of the mountain, he aimed his spirit to the mark.

> You profane the sacred bones.
> You pour concrete on the living.
> I, Roland the Cherokee,
> call this ground sacred.
> I set myself an arrow to the bow.

On a distant hill, as he'd promised Roland he would do, an old kinsman sat in the notch of a tall oak stump and kept the watch until the young man's spirit arced into the sky. Then the old man climbed down from the stump and took the message to the people: "Begin again."

After the flood ...

After the flood, public reaction varied. Of the local people who loved the beautiful valley, few could bear to look on its death. Nationally, some people "switched channels," moved on to the next story—and the holiday season. Others, many others—especially those who had followed the Tellico controversy closely—were stunned. A debate that had begun with the initial proposal for building the dam almost forty years before had ended suddenly, cut off by a congressional maneuver that showed staggering contempt for democracy, for the people: the Baker-Duncan Amendment.

Reactions of anger and outrage gathered momentum, from the press and from public individuals. The *Christian Science Monitor* called Tellico "a boondoggle if there ever was one." Letters of protest poured in to President Carter and members of Congress. Increasingly, Tellico was perceived as a warning arrow about America's direction—national imbalances in government, human rights, conservation of the environment, heritage preservation and the mass communications that shape public opinion.

It was the latter imbalance that the *Houston Chronicle* asked me to address in its "Outlook" section (March 24, 1980). Excerpts from my article follow.

THE PRESS: WATCHDOG WITH A BLIND EYE

Most Americans still believe the Tellico Dam controversy centered on the snail darter. For years, that's where the press focused its attention. Last November, when the TVA closed the gates of the dam in East Tennessee and began filling the reservoir, the typical public reaction was, "It's about time. When it's a choice between 'progress' and a three-inch fish, the fish has to go."

The Cherokee reacted differently. What their leaders had protested vigorously since 1965—when the dam was in the planning stage—came to pass. Rising waters drowned the spiritual and historic heartland of the Cherokee nation. ... But the Cherokee are determined to survive. They continued to press for a ruling on their suit that their constitutional rights had been violated.

After a long period of indifference, the national press is taking notice of the Cherokee cause. But the public asks the press, "Why didn't you tell us sooner?"

And conscientious members of the press ask each other, "Why didn't we know about the Cherokee cause before now?"

A nationally syndicated political cartoonist says, "I feel betrayed. I myself drew a cartoon satirizing the dam vs. the snail darter. Until recently, I never heard anything about the Cherokee issue. I depend on my sources— the wire services and other articles from reporters covering Tellico. Somewhere down the line our information system is breaking down. How can the press be the 'watchdog of the people' if we are blind in one eye?"

The people are asking the same question. And we want to know: Who focuses "the good eye" of the press? Who decides which issue is worthy of attention? What criteria do they use in making the judgment? And, with Tellico specifically, how did it happen that for fifteen years the major media did not emphasize Cherokee protests?

A large metropolitan daily allowed me to review its files on Tellico. It contained clippings from magazines, the *Congressional Record* and newspapers that ranged from New York to Florida, Los Angeles to Connecticut. Most articles focused on the snail darter vs. the dam. It is also fair to say that in-depth coverage was given to the economic unfeasibility of the dam; the waste of valuable farmland; the "pork barrel" arrangements involved; the political sleight of hand used to exempt the dam from laws that would prevent its completion; and, of course, the environmental impact. *U.S. News and World Report* (September 17, 1979) briefly mentioned Cherokee protests and quoted the response of the mayor of Tellico Plains, a small town near the dam site, "Indians moved off 200 years ago," he said. "Live Americans—be they black, white or red—are more important than the remains of dead Indians."

But the Cherokee are "live Americans." Their ancestors didn't just "move off" the land. And "the remains of dead Indians" include the rich and highly developed culture they left behind, a culture that is part of the heritage of all Americans, "be they black, white or red." Archeologists have established that that indigenous habitation of the Tellico area goes back twelve thousand years. The valley contains a national treasure of knowledge. How could the watchdog of the people fail for so long to pick up on an issue of such magnitude?

Ironically, it may be because the Cherokee trusted the democratic process. They did not riot in the streets, kidnap officials or blow up buildings. Instead, beginning in 1965, they presented carefully reasoned arguments to whomever would listen: TVA officials, governors of Tennessee, environmental groups. They also appealed directly to the press. But the major media said Cherokee protests were not an issue and reported them briefly if at all. ...

If the watchdog of the people can be blind for so long to a domestic issue such as this, how can we be sure what really is happening abroad, in places like Afghanistan and Iran? ... The antagonism many Americans feel for the press springs not from resentment that we are told the truth, but from fear that we are told only half the truth.

As the cartoonist said, "Somewhere down the line our information system is breaking down." Something must be done about the "blind eye." And only the press itself can do it. Only conscientious, dedicated professionals can regulate a profession that is so intricate and powerful. And we, the people, must forego our own penchant for the sensational and the piquant. We must settle down to the sober, vital task of being well-informed, active citizens. Otherwise, the words of J. C. Wachacha, a young Cherokee from the Qualla Reservation, may foreshadow the fate of us all:

> Chota has gone under water now and as I watched, some time back, the waters going up, a part of me went also. But gone will never be the memories of the summer I spent working with an archaeologist some years ago. Just to have been on the very soil where my ancestors walked means a lot. Often after work, I would go back to the Chota site and wander around and sit by the river and visualize the village and its people and somehow, which I can't explain, I could feel the very presence of these people. I think, with just the tiniest smidgen more of faith, I could have stepped back into time and lingered with my people. But all I have left now are a few artifacts.

"A few artifacts" ...

A few artifacts—is that all we'd one day have left of Mother Earth, of our nation, of "We-the-People"? My heart almost dragged the ground as I trudged through the next two years, looking for an upward path.

During this time TVA announced (and shortly afterward implemented) a proposal to turn over half of the 22,000 acres adjoining the lake to developers. As lakefront real estate, the land was already estimated to be worth twice what TVA had paid for it.

Jean Ritchie said, "What TVA, Howard Baker and the Congress took away from us with eminent domain, they are going to give away. They took our land under false pretenses. They said they wanted to control the development. At Tellico, our government stabbed a certain sector of its people in the back. This newest proposal by the Tennessee Valley Authority is just more of the same." Calling the entire Tellico controversy "a sad chapter in American history," Mrs. Ritchie said, "This just makes me madder and madder. I'll go to my grave bitter about this."[13]

The other "forgotten folk," the Cherokee, fared no better. In mid-April, 1980—when the Tellico reservoir had long been filled—the Sixth U.S. Circuit Court of Appeals in Cincinnati, Ohio, rejected the Cherokee appeal to protect their ancient burial grounds by preventing TVA from filling the lake behind the dam.

When they realized that the ruling would be delayed, the Cherokee had filed a motion with the same court, asking for a temporary injunction to halt the flooding until the remains of their ancestors, which had been removed during archaeological excavations, could be reburied. The Cherokee claimed racial and cultural discrimination and contended that remains of whites had been reburied, while remains of Native people were boxed and stacked in a basement at the University of Tennessee in Knoxvillle. They did not object to flooding the area after the remains were reburied, because "if this is done and the valley is then flooded, the Cherokee people can know that these remains will not be disturbed or desecrated again by the federal government." The motion was denied. The Cherokees' last hope was that TVA Chairman David Freeman would abide by his promise to honor a request they had made in 1974 (to a previous chairman of TVA) to have the remains reburied above the new lake's high water mark.[14]

In its 1980 ruling, the court used the letter of the law to contradict its spirit, in much the same way the courts had done in the early 1800s, when they adjudicated land disputes with the Cherokee prior to the Removal. In a 2–1 decision, the court said the evidence was overwhelming that the flooding of the area would damage tribal folklore and tradition, but that it would not threaten religious observances. Judge Pierce Lively, who wrote the majority decision, said, "Though cultural history and tradition are vitally important to any group of people, these are not interests protected by the Free Exercise Clause of the First Amendment."

Although Lively called the decision "a difficult and sensitive determination," he said there was insufficient justification for the claim of indispensability of the Little Tennessee Valley to Cherokee religious observances. The court also said the bill signed by President Carter on September 25, 1979, authorized completion of the dam and "no clearer congressional command is imaginable."

In his dissent, Judge Gilbert Merritt wrote that the case should be sent to the U.S. District Court in Tennessee to permit the Indians to offer proof on the centrality of the burial grounds. A most sensible opinion, for if the Cherokee appeal were to be judged on the basis of religious freedom, the nature of the religion in question would have to be defined. Native Americans had just been granted religious freedom under the Constitution in 1978. It would seem that their definition of religion had been established as valid by the Supreme Court. In any case, the deed was done; the reservoir had been filled for four months. The rejection of this last appeal ended the Cherokees' fifteen-year struggle to save their ancestral homeland.[15]

Tellico had become a Lake of Tears. Tears from "the folk," from conservationists, historians, archeologists, scholars, lawmakers. Tears from farm families, poets, writers, artists, musicians. Tears from everyone who loved the beautiful valley of the Little Tennessee and had tried in vain to save it. And tears welling up from the bottom of the lake, from the eyes of the Cherokee ancestors. We are all part of the web. What affects one strand affects us all. In time, even the fish of Tellico Lake would have cause to weep.

In the fall of 1981, my heart was still dragging along. If I could have seen into the future I would have been partly reassured, partly warned to vigilance. That future is now the past, which feeds the continuous story of Tellico. Some losses were permanent, including scars on the hearts of the people. But the cumulative power of public pressure ameliorated others. The seven-state bureaucracy of TVA, like a giant ocean liner, slowly altered its course of the previous two decades. From enforcing the principle that the end (industrial progress) justifies the means, it changed to identifying its goals decisively and publicly. Instead of being negligent of the environment, the agency became its bellwether, keeping the public informed through various media about the condition of the lakes and rivers in its service area. And a nuclear project was scrapped, with a loss of sunk costs many times greater than what it would have cost to drop the Tellico project. The power of the agency scaled down to a size more compatible with the land and its people.[16]

Some of the valley's rich heritage was preserved. Fort Loudon, an eighteenth-century British fort, was moved to an artificial bluff and developed into a tasteful museum. Many of the Cherokee artifacts taken from the excavations were put on display and interpreted there, as well as in the nearby Sequoyah Birth Place Museum. TVA had helped the Cherokee establish the museum on a tract of land the agency gave them, as it had promised to do. In June 1986, in the vicinity of the museum, Cherokee from the Eastern Band conducted a small, private reinterment ceremony. The bones of 191 ancestors were returned to their rest in the valley that had been their home. (Carroll Hamilton, Cherokee director of the museum, says TVA has maintained conscientious support of the museum and the Cherokee for many years.) Scholars began to write about Tellico. Its metaphorical significance became increasingly clear.

The snail darter was found to exist elsewhere in America.

Few industries came to the valley, but in the mid-1980s, a nine-mile luxury residential area was begun around the lake, with prime lakeside lots of about one-third acre selling for up to sixty thousand dollars. Plans included golf courses and a four-million-dollar yacht club. Developed by Cooper Communities of Bentonville, Arkansas, Tellico Village was projected ultimately to have eight thousand to ten thousand residents. Weston Tucker, a senior vice president overseeing the development, said in 1988 that most of the lots were sold and the snail darter had made them easier to sell. "You don't have to wonder if anybody knows what you're talking about when you say Tellico Village." Such is the power of image to last in the public mind—all facts to the contrary.[17]

In the 1992 edition of TVA's *River Pulse*, the graphic of Tellico Lake and its tributaries had the shape of a twisted and disintegrating arrow, coded red—for warning. Fish are contaminated. Oxygen levels in the deeper water above the dam are low because during the summer this layer of water is stagnant, which causes problems for animals living in the bottom mud. Cold and low in minerals, water flowing into Tellico from Chilhowie Lake is affecting the diversity and abundance of aquatic life. Common sense says that when fish and plants are having trouble with the water, people should beware of it, too.

The "forgotten folk" of the battle against the dam have survived, as mountain people always have, by beginning again. They have relocated, regrouped, gone on with life. But many of them today look at Tellico Lake and wonder if it will continue as it was conceived—in tears. They cannot see into the future, as I could not, in that fall fourteen years ago. ...

In those days all I saw were wounds and hopelessness. Anger froze my mind, made it impossible for me to write. Although my parents had lived through the Great Depression in Appalachia and were wise about survival, I listened with only one ear to what they said. "Do what you can. Give the Constitution time to work. It's like the land. Mother Earth may go down for a while, but she always comes back. Even when things look worst, down underneath, she's on her way. When you've done all you can, stand and wait. Have faith." In short, "Head East."

I was too focused on the negative of Tellico to do that. And I didn't realize until a decade later that my parents had dropped a microscopic seed in a crevice of my mind, a clue to the mystery of why Native people—and perhaps many other people as well—persist in believing in the Constitution. And why "this thing they call corn (selu)" is part of the whole.

But in the fall of 1981, I was discouraged, dispirited and had resolved to quit writing. Images and facts alike were spit against the wind. Useless. Trying to lift my heart, my friend Sonia sent me a photocopy of Alice Walker's essay, "In Search of Our Mothers' Gardens." (Blessings on the creative use of technology!) I was so moved by the essay that I overcame my shyness in writing to a famous person. Her thoughts were such a meaningful gift that I had to give back my appreciation. Never expecting a reply, I wrote Alice Walker on my notepaper with the logo of Little Deer on it. By return mail came a response: "When you come to San Francisco, come to see me."

In the fullness of time, I did go. We sat in her apartment, talking and drinking tea. She had just returned from Diablo Canyon and a protest about the nuclear reactor proposed for that site. It pleasured me to hear that she had read one of my essays, too, and to see the logo of Little Deer pinned on the wall above her typewriter. But the deepest pleasure was our conversation, which went on for hours. Alice also nudged me in a new direction. "Tell me what you think about the atom." Beginning with my experience with Little Deer, including his traditional story, I went on with thoughts I'd had about connecting him with the atom and about doing the same with the traditional spirit and history of Cherokee women, connecting them with what I called "the atom's mother heart."

"Write all that down, write it just like you're talking to me."

Although her enthusiasm urged me on, I shied off. "But where would I send it? Who would want to read an article like that?"

"Send it to me," Alice said. "I'll help find a place for it."

For a long while, I quietly mulled over the unexpected wonder of her response, hesitating before the leap she suggested I make and thinking ... of a title. "How does 'Baring the Atom's Mother Heart' sound to you?"

"Perfect."

As we sat sipping tea and honey, sharing thoughts, outside the open window a wind soughed the boughs of a nearby pine ... a song in harmony with Alice's voice.

Alice has three heritages—African, Cherokee, European. When I told her the long story of Tellico, she said (as you have perhaps been thinking as you read it), "It seems like I've heard this story before ... the only thing is, the names are different."

We talked about family and heritage, about race and the future, about the atom, about tears and "trudging along" and questing for an upward path. Tellico began to take on the image I would forever carry with me—an arrow of warning and hope, arcing toward the sunrise. Through Alice's voice but coming from beyond it, I faintly heard singing, strong and lively, even at a distance. I didn't know who was singing, but I set out in the direction of the sound, heading East. This time I remembered to take a hoe.

Star Vision

As I sat against the pine one night
beneath a star-filled sky,
my Cherokee stepped in my mind
and suddenly in every tree,
in every hill and stone,
in my hand lying prone upon
the grass, I could see
each atom's tiny star—
minute millions so far-flung
so bright they swept me up
with earth and sky
in one vast expanse of light.

The moment passed. The pine
was dark, the hill, the stone,
and my hand was bone and flesh
once more, lying on the grass.

BARING THE ATOM'S
MOTHER HEART

"What is the atom, Mother? Will it hurt us?"

I was nine years old. It was December 1945. Four months earlier, in the heat of an August morning—Hiroshima. Destruction. Death. Power beyond belief, released from something invisible. Without knowing its name, I'd already felt the atom's power in another form. Since 1943, my father had commuted eighteen miles from our apartment in Knoxville to the plant in Oak Ridge—the atomic frontier where the atom had been split, where it still was splitting. He left before dawn and came home long after dark. "What do you do, Daddy?"—"I can't tell you, Marilou. It's part of something for the war. I don't know what they're making out there or how my job fits into it."

"What's inside the maze?"

"Something important ... and strange. I see long, heavy trucks coming in. What they're bringing just seems to disappear. Somebody must know what happens to it, but nobody ever talks about it. One thing for sure—the government doesn't spend millions of dollars for nothing. It's something big. I can't imagine what."

I couldn't either. But I could feel its energy like a great hum.

Then, suddenly, it had an image: the mushroom cloud. It had a name: the atom. And our family was then living in Oak Ridge. My father had given me the facts. I also needed an interpreter.

"What is the atom, Mother? Will it hurt us?"

"It can be used to hurt everybody, Marilou. It killed thousands of people in Hiroshima and Nagasaki. But the atom itself ... ? It's invisible, the smallest bit of matter. And it's in everything. Your hand, my dress, the milk you're drinking—all of it is made with millions and millions of atoms and they're all moving. But what the atom means ... ? I don't think anyone knows yet. We have to have reverence for its nature and learn to live in harmony with it. Remember the burning man."

"I remember." When I was six years old, his screams had brought my mother and me running to our front porch. Mother was eight months

66

pregnant. What we saw made her hold me tight against her side. Across the street, in the small parking lot of the dry cleaner's, a man in flames ran, waving his arms. Another man chased him, carrying a garden hose turned on full force, and shouting, "Stop, stop!" The burning man stumbled and sank to his knees, shrieking, clawing the air, trying to climb out of his pain. When water hit his arms, flesh fell off in fiery chunks. As the flames went out, his cries ceased. He collapsed slowly into a charred and steaming heap.

Silence. Burned flesh. Water trickling into the gutter ...

The memory flowed between Mother and me, and she said, as she had said that day, "Never tempt nature, Marilou. It's the nature of fire to burn. And of cleaning fluid to flame near heat. The man had been warned over and over not to work with the fluid, then stoke the furnace. But he kept doing it. Nothing happened. He thought he was in control. Then one day a spark ... The atom is like the fire."

"So it *will* hurt us."

"That depends on us, Marilou."

I understood. Mother already had taught me that beyond surface differences, everything is in physical and spiritual connection—God, nature, humanity. All are one, a circle. It seemed natural for the atom to be part of this connection. At school, when I was introduced to Einstein's theory of relativity—that energy and matter are one—I accepted the concept easily.

Peacetime brought relaxation of some restrictions in Oak Ridge. I learned that my father was an accountant. The "long, heavy trucks" brought uranium ore to the graphite reactor, which was still guarded by a maze of fences. The reactor reduced the ore to a small amount of radioactive material. Safety required care and caution. Scientists called the reactor "The lady" and, in moments of high emotion, referred to her as "our beloved reactor."

"What does she look like, Daddy?"

"They tell me she has a seven-foot shield of concrete around a graphite core, where the atom is split." I asked the color of graphite. "Black," he said. And I imagined a great, black queen, standing behind her shield, holding the splitting atom in the shelter of her arms.

I also saw the immense nurturing potential of the atom. There was intensive research into fuels, fertilizers, mechanical and interpretative tools.

Crops and animals were studied for the effects of radiation. Terminal cancer patients came from everywhere to the research hospital. I especially remember one newspaper picture of a man with incredibly thin hands reaching for the "atomic cocktail" (a container of radioactive isotopes). His face was lighted with hope.

At school we had disaster drills in case of nuclear attack (or in case someone got careless around the reactor). Scientists explained the effects of an explosion—from "death light" to fallout. They also emphasized the peaceful potential of the atom and the importance of personal commitment in using it. Essentially, their message was the same as my mother's. "If we treat the atom with reverence, all will be well."

But all is not well now with the atom. The arms race, the entry of Big Business into the nuclear industry, and accidents like Three Mile Island cause alarm. Along with me, women protest, organize anti-nuclear groups, speak out. But we must also take time to ponder woman's affinities with the atom and to consider that our responsibilities for its use are more profound than we may have imagined.

We should begin with the atom itself, which is approximately two trillion times smaller than the point of a pin. We will focus on the nature and movement of the atom, not on the intricacies of nuclear physics. To understand the atom, we must flow with its pattern, which is circular.

During the nineteenth and twentieth centuries, scientists theorized about the atom, isolated it, discovered the nucleus, with its neutrons, protons, electrons. The atom appeared to resemble a Chinese nesting ball— a particle within a particle. Scientists believed the descending order would lead to the ultimate particle—the final, tiny bead. Man would penetrate the secret of matter and dominate it. All life could then be controlled, like a machine.

Around the turn of the century, however, a few scientists began to observe the atom asserting its nature, which was more flexible and unpredictable than had been thought. To explain it required a new logic, and, in 1905, Einstein published his theory of relativity. To describe the atom also required new use of language in science because our senses cannot experience the nuclear world except by analogy. The great Danish physicist, Niels Bohr, said, "When it comes to atoms, language can be used only as in poetry.

The poet, too, is not nearly so concerned with describing facts as with creating images and mental connections."

As research progressed, the word *mystery* began to appear in scientific writing, along with theories that matter might not end in a particle after all. Perhaps the universe resembled a great thought more than a great machine. The linear path was bending ... and in the mid-1970s the path ended in an infinitesimal circle: the quark. A particle so small that even with the help of huge machines, humans can see only its trace, as we see the vapor trail of an airplane in the stratosphere. A particle ten to one hundred million times smaller than the atom. Within the quark, scientists now perceive matter refining beyond space-time into a kind of mathematical operation, as nebulous and real as an unspoken thought. It is a mystery that no conceivable research is likely to dispel, the life force in process—nurturing, enabling, enduring, fierce.

I call it the atom's mother heart.

Nuclear energy is the nurturing energy of the universe. Except for stellar explosions, this energy works not by fission (splitting) but by fusion—attraction and melding. With the relational process, the atom creates and transforms life. Women are part of this life force. One of our natural and chosen purposes is to create and sustain life—biological, mental and spiritual.

Women nurture and enable. Our "process" is to perceive relationships among elements, draw their energies to the center and fuse them into a whole. Thought is our essence; it is intrinsic for us, not an aberration of our nature, as Western tradition often asserts.

Another commonality with the atom's mother heart is ferocity. When the atom is split—when her whole is disturbed—a chain reaction begins that will end in an explosion unless the reaction is contained, usually by a nuclear reactor. To be productive and safe, the atom must be restored to its harmonic, natural pattern. It has to be treated with respect. Similarly, to split woman from her thought, sexuality and spirit is unnatural. Explosions are inevitable unless wholeness is restored.

In theory, nature has been linked to woman for centuries—from the cosmic principle of the Great Mother-Goddess to the familiar metaphors of Mother Nature and Mother Earth. But to connect the life force with *living* woman is something only some ancient or so-called "primitive" cultures have been wise enough to do. The linear, Western, masculine mode of thought has been too intent on conquering nature to learn from her a basic truth: *To separate the gender that bears life from the power to sustain it is as destructive as to tempt nature herself.*

This obvious truth is ignored because to accept it would acknowledge woman's power, upset the concept of woman as sentimental—passive, all-giving, all-suffering—and disturb public and private patterns. But the atom's mother heart makes it impossible to ignore this truth any longer. She is the interpreter of new images and mental connections not only for humanity, but most particularly for women, who have profound responsibilities in solving the nuclear dilemma. We can do much to restore harmony. But time is running out. ...

Shortly after Hiroshima Albert Einstein said, "The unleashed power of the atom has changed everything save our modes of thought, and thus we drift toward unparalleled catastrophe." Now, deployment of nuclear missiles is increasing. A going phrase in Washington is, "When the war starts ... " Many nuclear power plants are being built and operated with money, not safety, as the bottom line. In spite of repeated warnings from scientists and protests from the public, the linear-thinking people continue to ignore the nature of the atom. They act irreverently. They think they're in control. One day a spark. ...

I look beyond the spectres of the burning man and the mushroom cloud to a time two hundred years ago, when destruction was bearing down on the Cherokee nation. My foremothers took their places in the circles of power along with the men. Outnumbered and outgunned, the nation could not be saved. But the Cherokee and their culture survived—and women played a strong part in that survival.

Although the American culture is making only slow progress toward empowering women, there is much we can do to restore productive harmony with the atom. Protest and litigation are important in stopping nuclear abuse, but total polarization between pro- and anti-nuclear people is simplistic and dangerous. It is not true that all who believe in nuclear energy are bent on destruction. Neither is it true that all who oppose it are "kooks" or "against progress." Such linear, polar thinking generates so much anger on both sides that there is no consensual climate where reasonable solutions can be found. The center cannot hold. And the beast of catastrophe slouches toward us. We need a network of the committed to ward it off. Women at large can use our traditional intercessory skills to create this network through organizations, through education and through weaving together conscientious protagonists in industry, science and government. Women who are professionals in these fields should share equally in policy making.

Our energies may fuse with energies of others in ways we cannot foresee. I think of two groups of protesters who came to Diablo Canyon, California, in the fall of 1981. Women and men protested the activation of a nuclear power plant so near an earthquake fault. The first group numbered nearly three thousand. The protest was effective, but it says much about the dominant, holistic mode of American thought that an article about the second group was buried in the middle of a San Francisco newspaper.

After the three thousand had left Diablo Canyon to wind and silence, a band of about eighty Chumash Indians came to the site of the power plant. They raised a wood-sculptured totem and sat in a circle around it for a day-long prayer vigil. Jonathan Swift Turtle, a Mewok medicine man, said that the Indians did not oppose nuclear technology but objected to the plant's being built atop a sacred Chumash burial site as well as near an earthquake fault. He said he hoped the vigil would bring about "a moment of harmony between the pro- and anti-nuclear factions."

The Chumash understand that to split the atom from the sacred is a deadly fission that will ultimately destroy nature and humanity. I join this circle of belief with an emblem I created for my life and work—the sacred white deer of the Cherokee leaping in the heart of the atom. My ancestors believed that if a hunter took the life of a deer without asking its spirit for pardon, the immortal Little Deer would track the hunter to his home and cripple him. The reverent hunter evoked the white deer's blessing and guidance.

For me, Little Deer is a symbol of reverence. Of hope. Of belief that if we humans relent our anger and create a listening space, we may attain harmony with the atom in time. If we do not, our world will become a charred and steaming heap. Burned flesh. Silence ...

There will be no sign of hope except deep in the invisible, where the atom's mother heart—slowly and patiently—bears new life.

Where Mountain and Atom Meet

Ancient haze lies on the mountain
smoke-blue, strange and still
a presence that eludes the mind and
moves through a deeper kind of knowing.
It is nature's breath and more—
an aura from the great I Am
that gathers to its own
spirits that have gone before.

Deep below the valley waters
eerie and hid from view
the atom splits without a sound
its only trace a fine blue glow
rising from the fissioned whole
and at its core
power that commands the will
quiet that strikes the soul,
"Be still and know ... I Am."

GRANDMOTHER ISHTOUA
TEACHES WISDOMS OF THE CORN

Published in 1983, *Rising Fawn and the Fire Mystery: A Story of Heritage, Family and Courage, 1833* is a book for people of all ages. It interweaves the stories of two Choctaw families who lived near Friar's Point, Mississippi, when the Indian Removals began. The plot is based on events in the life of Irving Knight's great-grandmother, the Rising Fawn of history, and background is taken from the account of Tushpa, who was about fourteen years old at the time of the Removal. Recorded by his son, James Culberson, this account is known to scholars as the rare Tushpa Manuscript. Tushpa is the great-grandfather of Beverly Bringle, who illustrated *Rising Fawn*. In the text, only material approved by elders of both families was used.

From October 1983 I have included the following from *Rising Fawn* in every public reading and offered a corn seed as a gift to each person in the audience. I've always carried the seeds in deerskin pouches—one large, one small—made by Dan Hanrahan, an Irish American, who cut and sewed them in the traditional way. When he gave them to me in 1983, he said, "These pouches are my contribution to the hope. They're gifts for you and the people, especially the children." Dan was a Vietnam veteran. He died in 1988 from an illness apparently caused by exposure to Agent Orange during the war. His gifts and his spirit travel on.

GRANDMOTHER ISHTOUA'S LESSON

"Grandmother, will we have to leave our home?"

"Your father comes home from the council tonight, Rising Fawn. He will tell us."

Gathered around the hearth of their cabin, the family waited. Rising Fawn, who was seven years old, nestled on her grandmother's lap. Her mother and brother sat nearby. At last, the father arrived with the council's decision: "Any of us who stay in Mississippi are a marked people. Already soldiers have burned our cabins to force us out. We must go to Indian Territory.

We must leave our home. ... The government will not send the boats and wagons they promised, so we will have to build rafts and canoes to cross the Big River (the Mississippi). After that we will walk. The distance is 400 miles." Staggered and grieved for a time, family members gradually recovered their balance and began preparations for the journey—and for survival.

As the Cold Moon waxed larger, many of the Twin Lakes Clan came to the cabin—grandmothers, grandfathers, aunts and uncles. They spoke of sorrow and fear, of how to help each other. Most of all, they came to touch the wisdom of the Grandmother, who was the eldest. Her name was Ishtoua, the deliverer.

Watching the family gather strength, Rising Fawn grew hopeful. But she went even more quietly than usual about her chores. Her mother smiled and said, "You are a child of your name—silent and quick. And those calm deer eyes miss nothing—you and your grandmother are alike in that. You two should choose the seed corn."

On one end of the worn plank table she heaped shucked ears. Some were deep orange. Others had gold kernels mingled with russet and soft black. "The chiefs and elders have given everyone a task for this journey and for making a home in the new land. We are to take choice seed corn for the fields. Your father and brother have brought deerskins for pouches. The fur will shed water and keep the seeds dry."

"And we must have seed enough for a large field," said the Grandmother. "The corn is like our people; it draws strength from its clan. A single stalk will bear nothing." How well the Grandmother knew the ways of corn. As she twisted an ear in her hands, kernels pattered onto the table so fast that Rising Fawn was kept busy scooping them into a willow basket. When it was full, she poured the kernels onto the table. They began to cull those too dark and hard to sprout.

From a pile of skins beside the fireplace, the mother took one, laid it on the floor and knelt to measure it. Rising Fawn peered over the edge of the table. "I want to carry seeds too. Will you make me a pouch?"

"I will make one small, like you, and put it on a thong so you can wear it around your neck. You must not lose it. It is a sacred task to carry seeds for the people, for if the seeds are lost, the people will go hungry."

Rising Fawn was pleased, and her curiosity quickened about the new land. "In the West, Grandmother, will there be a new sky? Will there be a Cup of Stars in the sky like we have here to tell us when to plant the corn?"

Her question made the Grandmother chuckle. "Of course, little one. Only land changes. The sky will be the same. When the Cup of Stars turns upside down like a dipper spilling water, we will know that Mother Earth is ready to receive the seed. The Great Spirit has made all things in harmony and the wisdom of the Great Spirit is within each thing."

She pressed a round, russet kernel onto Rising Fawn's palm. "Its heart is like a tiny flame of sacred fire. But feel how tough the shell is. You can throw the seed on the floor, put it in a pouch, carry it in your hand, but it will sprout only in warm earth. If it sprouts too soon, it will die. It protects itself until it is safe—that is its wisdom. The seed lives deep in the spirit until the time to come forth."

Closing Rising Fawn's hand around the kernel, she held the small fist in her root-like fingers. "The journey to the West will be hard. You will have to endure much. Be like the seed. Protect yourself. Live deep in your spirit until the time to come forth."

Rising Fawn turned this thought in her mind; then she asked, "How will I know when the time has come?"

"Listen to the wisdom within, where the Great Spirit speaks to you."

"Grandmother, when you pray before the fire, are you listening?"

"The fire is brother to the sun, the life giver. It helps me listen for the Great Spirit. When I pray I am listening ... with my spirit-eyes and my spirit-ears."

Rising Fawn looked at the fire. "I see flames. I hear them snap and roar. That is all."

"You are using your body-eyes and body-ears," said the Grandmother. With her finger she tapped Rising Fawn's chest. "You must listen with your spirit-eyes and spirit-ears."

"Can you teach me how to listen?"

The Grandmother shook her head. "All I can teach you is to be still. You must ponder the fire mystery for yourself."

That night Rising Fawn tried hard to be still and pray with the Grandmother. She kept her eyes on the fire, but her mind circled the room.

It touched the heavy deerskin pouches piled by the door ... the loft where her brother was sleeping ... the corner bed where her parents slept ... the gourds filled with sugar and meal ... the spinning wheel, her father's gun ... baskets of berries, beans and squash ... firelight dancing on her beaded moccasins ... the snakeskin design glistening on her red dress ... the small pouch, plump with seeds, around her neck ... the Grandmother's eyes.

The eyes of the Grandmother were smiling, a smile that seemed to say, "To ponder a mystery takes patience. You are young. There is time."

Long after the Grandmother had gone to her bed in the loft, Rising Fawn lay on the blanket and gazed into the fire. She was warm and drifting to sleep when she felt a darkness gather about her, a faint tremor in the boards beneath her. Her first dazed thought was "Earthquake!" Then she realized horses were galloping close to the cabin. A shout brought her wide awake, a white man's shout ...

"Burn it down! Gimme that torch. I'll throw it!"

Above the sound of hooves, another taut, urgent shout. "At least wake the family first, for god's sake!"

For answer, there was a thud against the cabin wall.

"Soldiers!" cried the father. He leapt from bed and climbed the loft ladder, "Wake up! Wake up!" Suddenly everyone else was moving— grabbing blankets, clothes, and as many pouches as they could carry. Rising Fawn stood by the hearth, holding her blanket around her. Through the cracks between the logs of the walls, smoke seeped into the room and she heard the warning of the flames.

Her mother thrust a heavy pouch into her hands. "Quick! Unbolt the door!"

She slid back the bolt, darted among the skittish horses. Startled, one horse reared above her. An arm jerked her out of the way, her dress sleeve tore ... the large pouch dropped. Hooves crashed down on it, seed corn scattered across the muddy snow. At the same time, she felt herself being drawn onto a saddle and held tightly against a rough coat that smelled of smoke and damp wool. She struggled and cried out, but the grim-faced soldier muttered, "At least I'll save one." Beneath the pounding feet of the horse, the earth seemed once more to shake and crack. The crescent moon swung back and forth in the sky. Rising Fawn felt herself falling into a darkness that became a dream. Her arms grew heavy, her eyelids heavier. She woke once in a half-daze. After a time, the pounding hooves gave way to a powerful rocking and sound of churning water. She dreamed the Big River flowed cold around her. A cottonwood tree torn from its bank somewhere upriver swung heavily at her. She fought the wet branches—her fingers tore at the bark. She seemed caught in an endless cycle—rocking, rocking. She pulled her blanket around her and pressed the deerskin pouch against her cheek. She tasted the salt of her tears.

In the sky, the Grandmother's hand tilted the Cup of Stars toward the earth. A voice like the embrace of wind in the pines whispered, "Be like the seed ... live deep in your own spirit ... "

All motion stopped. Rising Fawn opened her eyes. She was in a box! Air and sunlight filtered through a crack in the lid, and she saw long scratches in the wood where she had tried to get out. Her fingers were raw and sore.

She heard a knocking. ...

A white man's voice shouted, "Christmas gift!"

A bolt sliding back. A door opening.

"Michael!" a woman cried, " ... come quick, James."

Another man's voice, this time heartier and older. "Welcome home, Michael. You're early. We didn't expect you in Memphis 'til Christmas Eve. Here, let me help you with that box." Rising Fawn felt a lifting, a carrying, a setting down. "I see you've marked it 'Clothes,' Michael. Mighty heavy for just clothes. ... "

"It isn't clothes," said the soldier. "It's something much more valuable. Something you and Amanda have wanted for a very long time ... "

Light thumps of rope untying. Then the lid slowly sliding off.

In the bright light, the white faces blurred above her and Rising Fawn saw clearly only a grizzled beard, a yellow mustache and a coil of yellow braided hair. She clutched her deerskin pouch and felt tough kernels press against her palm. *Be like the seed ... Be like the seed.*

The woman bent closer. "It's a child, James ... an Indian child!"

"Well, now ... " The man with the grizzled beard laid his calloused hand on Rising Fawn's. Then he lifted her in his arms and went to sit in a chair beside the hearth.

Rising Fawn glanced furtively about the room—wood chimney, log walls, plank table, square bed in the corner. The cabin could be her own home—except that the people were white, and strangers. Like a young doe trying to escape notice, she became very still. For a few moments the strangers were also. Rising Fawn heard their soft breathing, the steady whisper of the fire ... the flutter and cluck of chickens nesting under the floor.

From the box the woman brought the blanket and tucked it around the child. Kneeling beside the chair, she smoothed Rising Fawn's hair and touched her cheek. "She has beautiful eyes ... so brown you can't see the bottom." She looked at the torn dress, the fingers raw with scratches. "How did you come by this child, Michael?"

"Last night some men in my company got drunk and set on meanness. They knew about a Choctaw cabin in the woods near Friar's Point. They got it in their heads to burn it down. I tried to stop them. When I couldn't, I rode along to try to warn the family. I couldn't do that either. Things like this— and worse—happen all the time, Amanda. This removal is cruel work. I'm sick of it. When I saw that little girl run out of the burning cabin, something in me snapped. I grabbed her up and cut out ... caught a steamboat at Friar's Point."

"What about her family?"

"Dead, maybe. If not, the cold will get them ... or they'll die on the long walk west. I just said to myself, 'At least I'll save one.' And I did. Then I thought of you and James ... 'Course, some folks hereabouts might say bad of you for taking an Indian girl for your own ... If you don't want her, I guess I could. ... "

Rising Fawn looked up at the man holding her. His eyes were warm and brown. "Hmf," he said. "Somebody's always saying bad about something. If you're quality folks—or poor like us—nobody cares much what you do. Besides, after all these years clerking at Winchester's store, I've traded with an abundance of Chickasaws and Choctaws. I figure in the main, they're peaceable people—and honest. We'll love this little one and raise her for our own, won't we, Amanda? Now you can use that trundle bed you've been saving all this time."

The woman went to her brother and took both his hands. "The child will be a blessing to us. But you've brought trouble on yourself—you've deserted the army, haven't you?"

Her brother nodded. "I have. So I'm headed west. A man can disappear out there and get a new start."

"When will you go?"

"Right away. The army is probably already on my trail, but they'll be asking about a soldier with an Indian child. Nobody saw me with her, because of the box. Your place may be where they'll look for me next. On the way from the Landing, I stopped by Anderson's Hotel. Found some folks passing through on their way to Texas. I'm going with them on the next ferry."

The woman put her arms around him. "You're the only one of my family left, Michael. I can't bear to think of you so far away ... especially at Christmas ... among strangers."

"Don't fret about me, Amanda. Think of that little girl. You and James are all she has now."

Rising Fawn felt the three of them looking at her, but she fixed her eyes on the fire. The room, the faces, the things she had heard swirled in her mind and flowed away, except for the words, *What about her family? Dead, maybe.* In the curling flames she saw the currents of the Big River, and she knew, for her father had taught her, that in water all trails are lost. There was no way back to her family. No way for them to follow her, if any were alive to try.

Rising Fawn did not cry or speak ... her silence became a tough shell as she withdrew deep in her spirit ... to be like the seed and wait for the time to come forth ... to listen for the Great Spirit ...

From then on, only the fire was real to her. She thought of the white couple as simply "the Man" and "the Woman." With her body-ears and body-eyes she understood what they said, and she did as they asked, for they were Elders. But she never talked to them.

She turned her spirit to the fire. In the mornings she watched the Woman unbank the embers and stir them to life, then she helped the Man carry out ashes. When he brought in logs, she walked beside him, her arms heaped with branches and strips of bark, which she later fed, one by one, to the flames.

During the day, there were many chores to do—making butter and cottage cheese, spinning, weaving, plain sewing, beans to shell, meat to cook—but as she worked with the Woman, Rising Fawn listened to the fire sing and crackle and sigh. She smelled the burning wood as it changed to warmth and light. At night, she sat on her blanket before the sandstone hearth, following the mysterious shift and leap of the flames. If she were very still, the spirit of the Grandmother came to sit beside her. But when Rising Fawn asked, "Are you well? Is my family well?" the Grandmother would not reply. The Great Spirit, too, was silent. And Rising Fawn knew she had not yet learned to be still enough.

"The child is *here* ... but she isn't *with* us," the woman told her husband. "I wonder if she'll ever be our own."

"She's likely grieving for her own people, Amanda. We'd best leave her be. We've got to be patient and gentle her slow." They began by forbidding her to follow the Choctaw custom of bathing every day. "It'll weaken you to do that," they said. "Once every week or two is enough. The smell of their bodies and of her own was much too ripe. But Rising Fawn paid it no mind.

She was proud of her black hair, worn loose and shining in the way of the grandmothers. But while the Woman plaited it in two long braids, Rising Fawn stood without flinching. She paid them no mind.

The Man bought her a pair of high-topped shoes that laced up the front. The stiff leather hurt her ankles and the soles were so thick that when she went to the woodpile or to the spring, Rising Fawn couldn't feel the softness of Mother Earth beneath her feet, like she did in moccasins. She wore the shoes, but she paid them no mind.

"One last thing," said the Woman, "and you will almost look like one of us." She grasped the deerskin pouch to take it off.

Rising Fawn took her hand and gently pulled it away.

Stepping back, the Woman looked at her a long time, then shook her head sadly. Rising Fawn moved away and lay down on her blanket before the fire.

Later, when she thought Rising Fawn was asleep, the Woman said in a low voice, "The child understands what we say, James. I'm sure she could speak, if she would. There's a knowing in her eyes—and something else. Sometimes they seem like the eyes of an old woman, wise and distant. I think she has a pagan soul."

"Amanda, maybe it's just the difference you're seeing. You're used to white children."

"No. No. From the day she came I've been watching her. She prays to the fire, worships it. I know that pouch is a heathen thing. Tomorrow we must take her to church. It will do her soul good."

Rising Fawn was not asleep. She murmured to herself in Choctaw, "It is hard to be like the seed … "

Mutual respect grew slowly between adults and child. Finally, through the mystery of ceremonial fire—in their culture and in hers—Rising Fawn realized how to survive in this new world without abandoning her heritage and, like the seed safe in warm earth, she "came forth."

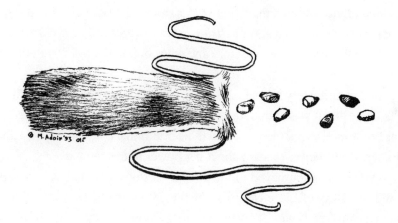

When I first set out …

When I first set out with *Rising Fawn* and the pouch of corn seeds, at the front of my mind was the gray December afternoon in 1982, when the idea for the book was born. Artist Beverly Bringle and I had stood on the Memphis Bluff, bowed against the cold. The Mississippi, heavy with snow and ice, was like a wide, white field moving slowly past us, carrying our thoughts back to the 1830s, when the Bluff was a crossroads of sorrow. The Chickasaw were forced into boats here and exiled to Indian Territory (now Oklahoma). From downriver came Rising Fawn—and later the Cherokee who took the southern route on the Trail of Tears. We looked across to Arkansas, where Tushpa had helped his family march overland. His father drowned while crossing the river, and his mother died on the trail. We stood for a long time, remembering …

In our thoughts also were Rising Fawn's adoptive parents and others like them, who, seldom noticed by history, quietly did what they could to alleviate suffering. Beverly and I resolved to create a story that would be like an Indian flute, an instrument that voices from the past could sing through to reach people of all ages. With *Rising Fawn* Beverly and I wanted to return the gift to those who lived the story and who continually offer to all the gift of hope.

What ultimately happened isn't relevant to this story of Selu. What is relevant is that it was at this stage of the path where Little Deer had led me that I first *recognized* the presence of his traditional companion, the Corn-Mother. And I began to learn about her power to convey wisdom.

Wherever I journeyed in the Four Directions, people listened to the traditional story of Little Deer and the law of respect he teaches. With my gift of a corn seed in hand, they listened to the words of Ishtoua as she passed wisdoms of the corn to Rising Fawn. "The corn is like our people. It draws strength from its clan. A single stalk will bear nothing." Always take your heritage with you. "And be like the seed. Protect your life. Live deep in your spirit until the time to come forth."

People also listened to the Cherokee story of Selu. When I held up an ear of calico corn, we would think together about this wisdom of the Corn-Mother. How the different colored kernels are ranged around the cob, no one more important than the other. How each kernel respects the space of those on either side, yet remains itself—red, black, white, yellow, or combinations of those colors. How the Corn-Mother, in her physical being, exemplifies unity in diversity, "from the many one"—democracy.

People understood, regardless of all the boxes that divide us: race, gender, age, religion, education, nationality, region. I thought a lot about the power that has been distilled into the traditional stories, about the capacity of people to "think purposely"—with mind/heart/soul. About what all of this might mean.

One night a Chinese-American elder gave me a clue. "The Corn-Mother's been talking to people for a long time. We've just forgotten how to listen. The story gives us ears." The truth of his words spurred me along in seeking the Corn-Mother's wisdom.

✧ ✧ ✧

As I continued my path, what I saw on the east side of it was hopeful. On the west side was the Darkening Land, devastation. Those who call Earth "It" were inflicting terrible wounds on "all of our relations"—the standing people, the walking people, the four-legged, the winged, the finned. My husband, Paul, and I retreated to the Great Smokies for a few days, the mother mountains that have always been green, regenerative, restorative. One afternoon we took a picnic to the highest peak, Clingman's Dome, one of our favorite places. We had in mind "a loaf of bread, a flask of wine, and thou beside me, singing in the wilderness." What we found is what you read in the poem "Dying Back." We went back to our motel. Some wounds are too terrible to look upon.

"Against the downward pull, against the falter of your heart or mine"—what would avail? The attitude of use and consume was rending the web of life at a brutal rate. And yet, to be healed, wounds must be examined. I saw many of them, and each boded death for the whole.

Old Students of the New Physics

A bulldozer slashed the breast
of the Indian mound—
  back and forth
  back and forth
scraping ancient soil
bone/pottery/prayer
into a dump truck
until the land was flat
  except
for one hip bone.
It stood upright—
a periscope from Mother Earth—
and drew into its dark socket
  the wide open wound
  with its ragged edge of grass,
  trees standing nearby
  dropped in dust and shock,
  machines receding ...

A monarch butterfly
drifted over the site.
She lit on the bone,
slowly flexed her wings.
"When I move my wings
energies change around the world
  round and round and
  up ... up ... up
I can cause storm/hurricane/tornado
when I move my wings."

"I know," said the bone.
"Now men have moved me."

If the Hand That Rocks the Cradle Rules the World

If the hand that rocks
the cradle rules the world,
why does the mother pace
row on row of white crosses,
seeking the one that
stakes her son motionless
in his lidded box?

If the hand that rocks
the cradle rules the world,
why do mother and daughter
leave the courtroom
with their freed rapist,
bowing their heads
against his gleeful stare?

If the hand that rocks
the cradle rules the world,
why does the mother
nurse a famished baby,
pressing her shriveled nipple
into a tiny mouth
too weak to take hold?

If the world wants the hand
that rocks the cradle to rule,
why does it slam its Council door
on the mother's wrist,
watching as she strains
her other hand toward
a cradle that rocks slower
        slower
            slower ...

*"Hell yes, we broke march going over a bridge. We didn't want
to shake the damn thing down!"*

—a veteran of Patton's Army

Memo to NASA

I see your mocked-up plans:
   stripmine the moon;
   hang guns on the stars.
You tramp into space
with a steady two-beat—
   Con-quer ... Con-quer ...
   Con-quer ... Con-quer ...
Break march, brothers.
You shake the bridge
of the sky.

Cherokee Woman on the Moon

The grandfathers have said,
"Let no one know
the path you have walked."
Brother Moon,
I draw the flagstaff
from your breast.
With an eagle feather
I brush away
first the man's step,
then my own.

Mother Nature Sends a Pink Slip

To: Homo Sapiens
Re: Termination

My business is producing life.
The bottom line is
you are not cost-effective workers.
Over the millennia, I have repeatedly
clarified my management goals and objectives.
Your failure to comply is well documented.
It stems from your inability to be
a team player:
  • you interact badly with co-workers
  • contaminate the workplace
  • sabotage the machinery
  • hold up production
  • consume profits
In short, you are a disloyal species.

Within the last decade
I have given you three warnings:
  • made the workplace too hot for you
  • shaken up your home office
  • utilized plague to cut back personnel
Your failure to take appropriate action
has locked these warnings into
the Phase-Out Mode, which will result
in termination.   No appeal.

Can We Head Off the Pink Slip?

That was my question. Almost everywhere I looked, consequences of breaking the law of respect were in motion. Strands of the web of life I saw severed around me were connected to those extending into the larger world. Society seemed bent on continuing in the direction we were going. And the children were following behind us adults, holding up their baskets. Was this insane and bitter harvest all we'd have to offer them? How could children anywhere survive on such unwholesome food?

I remembered the summer day in my childhood, walking the corn row with my grandfather. I remembered Selu's story and the law of respect. What I had forgotten was that the Corn-Mother gave her grandsons specific instructions about how to heal the break and restore harmony. And I had never perceived the importance of her attitude while doing so. She had maintained a "good mind." No blame, no recriminations. Selu had simply stated the situation, then firmly turned her grandsons toward the East, toward the future, as my parents always had tried to turn me. Farther along my way, I would re-learn this wisdom from the people who have practiced it for centuries: the Cherokee of east and west. It would happen in a meadow across the mountain from Tellico, in the place where the Trail of Tears began in 1838: Red Clay. A Cherokee leader prepared me for this event. I met her around the next bend in my path. Born at Chota in 1738, she later lived near Red Clay. For over half a century her voice was powerful in the council. Her last official message to her people reflects a cardinal value the Cherokee hold to this day, "Do not part with any more of our lands—it would be like destroying your mothers."[18]

SECTION III

When the People Call Earth "Mother"

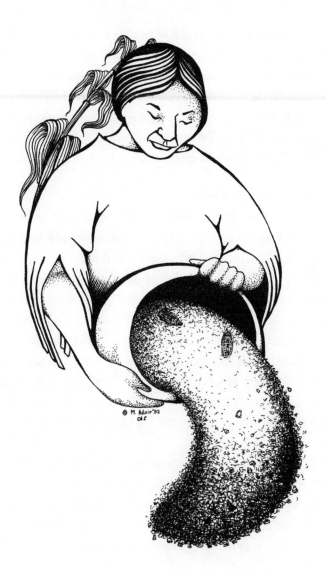

AMAZONS IN APPALACHIA

*The reader will not be a little surprised to find the story of the
Amazons not so great a fable as we imagined, many of the Cherokee
women being as famous in war, as powerful in the council.*
—Henry Timberlake, *Memoirs, 1765*

Are the spirits of these women accessible to us today? Yes! According to
Albert Einstein, there is a dimension beyond time and space where time stands
still—past, present and future are one. Native Americans have always known
this dimension as "the time immemorial," a spiritual place we enter to commune
intimately with all that is, a place abidingly real. Going there now, I return to my
native mountains in East Tennessee and walk with the strong Cherokee
grandmothers Timberlake met on his journey more than two centuries ago.

"Where are your women?"

The speaker is Attakullakulla, a Cherokee chief renowned for his
shrewd and effective diplomacy. He has come to negotiate a treaty with the
whites. Among his delegation are women "as famous in war, as powerful in
the council." Their presence also has ceremonial significance: it is meant to
show honor to the other delegation. But that delegation is composed of males
only; to them the absence of women is irrelevant, a trivial consideration.

To the Cherokee, however, reverence for women/Mother Earth/life/
spirit is interconnected. Irreverence for one is likely to mean irreverence for
all. Implicit in their chief's question, "Where are your women?" the
Cherokee hear, "Where is your balance? What is your intent?" They see that
balance is absent and are wary of the white men's motives. They intuit the
mentality of destruction.

I turn to my own time. I look at the Congress, the Joint Chiefs of Staff,
the Nuclear Regulatory Commission ... at the hierarchies of my church, my
university, my city, my children's school. "Where are your women?" I ask.

Wary and fearful, I call aside one of Attakullakulla's delegation. I
choose her for the gray streak of experience in her hair, for her staunch hips

and for the lively light in her eyes that indicates an alert, indomitable spirit. "Grandmother, I need your courage. Sing to me about your life."

Her voice has the clear, honing timbre of the mountains.

Song of the Grandmothers

I am Cherokee.
My people believe in the Spirit that unites all things.

I am woman. I am life force. My word has great value.
The man reveres me as he reveres Mother Earth and his own spirit.

The Beloved Woman is one of our principal chiefs.
Through her the Spirit often speaks to the people. In the Great
Council at the capital, she is a powerful voice.
Concerning the fate of hostages, her word is absolute.

Women share in all of life. We lead sacred dances. In
the Council we debate freely with men until an
agreement is reached. When the nation considers war,
we have a say, for we bear the warriors.

Sometimes I go into battle. I also plant and harvest.

I carry my own name and the name of my clan. If I
accept a mate, he and our children take the name of my
clan. If there is deep trouble between us, I am as free to
tell him to go as he is to leave. Our children and our
dwelling stay with me. As long as I am treated with
dignity, I am steadfast.

I love and work and sing.
I listen to the Spirit.
In all things I speak my mind.
I walk without fear.
I am Cherokee.

I feel the Grandmother's power. She sings of harmony, not dominance. And her song rises from a culture that repeats the wise balance of nature: the gender capable of bearing life is not separated from the power to sustain it. A simple principle. Yet in spite—or perhaps because—of our vast progress in science and technology, the American culture where I live has not grasped this principle. In my county alone there are twenty-six hundred men who refuse to pay child support, leaving their women and children with a hollow name, bereft of economic means and sometimes even of a safe dwelling. On the national level, the U.S. Constitution still does not include equal rights for women.

The Grandmother can see this dimension of time and space as well as I—its imbalance, its irreverence, its sparse presence of women in positions of influence. And she can hear the brave women who sing for harmony and for transforming power. "My own voice is small, Grandmother, and I'm afraid. You live in a culture that believes in your song. How can you understand what women of my time have to cope with?"

Grasping my chin gently, the Grandmother turns my face back toward the treaty council. "Listen to Attakullakulla's question again. When he says, 'Where are your women?' look into the eyes of the white delegation and you will see what I saw."

On the surface, hardness—the hardness of mind split from spirit, the eyes of conquerors. Beyond the surface, stretching future decades deep, are crumpled treaties. Rich farms laid waste. And, finally, the Cherokee, goaded by soldiers along a snowbound trail toward Oklahoma—a seemingly endless line of women, men and children, wrapped in coats and blankets, their backs bowed against the cold. In the only gesture of disdain left to them, they refuse to look their captors in the face.

Putting my arms around the Grandmother, I lay my head on her shoulder. Through touch we exchange sorrow, despair that anything really changes. I'm ashamed that I've shown so little courage. She is sympathetic. But from the pressure of her arms I also feel the stern, beautiful power that flows from all the Grandmothers, as it flows from our mountains themselves. It says, "Dry your tears. Get up. Do for yourself or do without. Work for the day to come. Be joyful."

"Joyful, Grandmother?" I draw away. "Sorrow, yes. Work, yes. We must work ... up to the end. But such a hardness is bearing down on my people. Already soldiers are gathering. Snow has begun to fall. This time we will walk the Trail of Fire. With the power of the atom, they can make the world's people walk it. How can you speak of joy?"

"Because, for those who die, death is death. A Trail of Tears for the Cherokee, a Trail of Fire for all—it is the same. But without joy, there is no hope. Without hope, the People have no chance to survive. Women know how to keep hope alive ... at least *some* women do."

The reproach stings and angers me ... because she is right. My joy, my hope *are* lost. I don't know how to find them again. Silently, my thoughts flow toward her. Hers flow back to me, strong, without anger.

"Come," she says.

"Where?"

"To Chota—the capital—to see the Beloved Woman."

I've heard of her—Nanyehi—"Whom many call a spirit person/immortal or 'the Path.'" Nanyehi, whom the whites call Nancy Ward and hold in great respect ... the Beloved Woman whose advice and counsel are revered through the Cherokee nation. She is said to have a "queenly and commanding presence," as well as remarkable beauty, with skin the color and texture of the wild rose.

Not ready ... I'm not ready for this. Following the Grandmother along the forest trail, I sometimes walk close, sometimes lag behind. Puny—that's what I am. Puny, puny, puny—the worst charge that can be leveled at any mountain woman, red, white or black. It carries pity, contempt, reproach. When we meet, the Beloved Woman will see straight into my spirit. I dread to feel the word in her look.

I know about her courage. She works ceaselessly for harmony with white settlers, interpreting the ways of each people to the other. From her uncle and mentor, Attakullakulla, she has learned diplomacy and the realities of power. She understands that the Cherokee ultimately will be outnumbered and that war will bring sure extinction. She counsels them to channel their energies from fighting into more effective government and better food production. To avoid bloodshed, she often risks censure and misunderstanding to warn either side of an impending attack, then urges resolution by arbitration. In the councils she speaks powerfully on two major themes: "Work for peace. Do not sell your land."

All the while, she knows the odds ...

As the Grandmother and I pass through my hometown of Oak Ridge, I look at the nest of nuclear reactors there and weigh the odds of survival—for all people. The odds are small. But not impossible. My own song for harmony and reverence with the atom is a small breath. But it may combine with others to make a warm and mighty wind, powerful enough to transform the hardness and cold into life. It is not impossible.

I walk closer to the Grandmother. In this timeless dimension, we could move more rapidly, but she paces my spirit, holding it to a thoughtful rhythm as we cross several ridges and go down into the Tellico Valley. We walk beside the quiet, swift waters of the Little Tennessee River. Chota is not far off.

What time and space will the Grandmother choose for me to meet the Beloved Woman? I imagine a collage of possibilities:

1755 ... Nanyehi fights beside her husband in a battle against the Creeks. When he is killed, she takes his rifle and leads the Cherokee to victory. Afterward, warriors sing of her deeds at Chota and the women and men of the Great Council award her the high office she will hold for more than half a century. She is seventeen, the mother of a son and a daughter.

1776 ... Having captured the white woman, Mrs. Lydia Bean, Cherokee warriors tie her to the stake. Just as they light the fire, Nanyehi arrives on the scene, crying, "No woman will be burned at the stake while I am Beloved Woman!" Her word is absolute. Mrs. Bean goes free. She teaches dairying to Nanyehi, who in turn teaches it to the Cherokee.

1781 ... At the Long Island Treaty Council, Nanyehi is the featured speaker. "Our cry is for peace; let it continue. ... This peace must last forever. Let your women's sons be ours; our sons be yours. Let your women hear our words." (Note: No white women are present.)

Colonel William Christian responds to her, "Mother, we have listened well to your talk. ... No man can hear it without being moved by it. ... Our women shall hear your words. ... We will not meddle with your people if they will be still and quiet at home and let us live in peace."[19]

Although the majority of Cherokee and whites hold the peace, violence and bloodshed continue among dissenting factions.

1785 ... The Hopewell Treaty Council convenes in South Carolina. Attending the council are four commissioners appointed by Congress, thirty-six chiefs and about a thousand Cherokee delegates. Again the Beloved Woman speaks eloquently. Knowing full well the pattern of strife that precedes this council, she bases her talk on positive developments. "I take you by the hand in real friendship. ... I look on you and the red people as my children. Your having determined on peace is most pleasant to me, for I have seen much trouble during the late war. ... We are now under the protection of Congress and shall have no more disturbance. The talk I have given you is from the young warriors I have raised in my town, as well as myself. They rejoice that we have peace, and hope the chain of friendship will nevermore be broken."[20]

Hope—that quality so necessary for survival. The Beloved Woman never loses hope. Perhaps I will learn the source of her strength by sharing her private moments: I may see her bend in joy over her newborn second daughter (fathered by the white trader Bryant Ward, to whom she is briefly married in the late 1750s) or hear her laugh among her grandchildren and the many orphans to whom she gives a home. Or I may stand beside her in 1817 as she composes her last message to her people. Too ill at age seventy-nine to attend the council, she sends the last message by her son. Twenty years before it begins, she sees the Trail of Tears loom ahead and her words have one theme: "My children, do not part with any more of our lands ... it would be like destroying your mothers."

The Grandmother's hand on my arm halts my imagings. We stand at the edge of a secluded clearing, rimmed with tall pines. In the center is a large log house, and around it women—many women—move through sun and shadow. Some walk in the clearing. Others cluster on the porch, talking quietly, or sit at the edge of the forest in meditation. Not far from us, a woman who is combing another's hair leans forward to whisper, and their laughter rises into the soughing pines.

A great weaving is going on here, a deep bonding ...

"This is the menstrual lodge," says the Grandmother. "When our power sign is with us we come here. It is a sacred time—a time for rest and meditation. No one is allowed to disturb our harmony. No warrior may even cross our path. In the menstrual lodge many things are known, many plans are made ... "

"And the Beloved Woman?"

"She is here."

"What year is this, Grandmother?"

"It is not a year; it is a *season*—you and the Beloved Woman are meeting when each of you is in her forty-seventh season." From the expression on my face the Grandmother knows I appreciate the wisdom of her choice: Four and seven are the sacred numbers of the Cherokee, four symbolizing the balance of the four directions. It is the season when no women should be or can afford to be puny. The Grandmother nods. Motioning me to wait, she goes toward the lodge, threading her way through the women with a smile of recognition here, the touch of outstretched fingers there.

With my hands behind my hips, I lean against the stout, wiry-haired trunk of a pine. Its resinous scent clears my mind. These women are not the Amazons of the Greek fable. While they are independent and self-defined, they do not hate men or use them only at random for procreation. They do not elevate their daughters, then kill, cripple or make servants of their sons. But did the Greek patriarchs tell the truth? If Attakullakulla had asked them, "Where are your women?" they would have answered with a shrug. I'm wary of the Greeks bearing fables. Although there is little proof that they described the Amazons accurately, ample evidence suggests that they encountered—and resented—strong women like my Grandmothers and characterized them as heinous in order to justify destroying them (a strategy modern patriarchs also use).

In any case, why should I bother with distant Greeks and their nebulous fables when I have the spirits of the Grandmothers, whose roots are struck deep in my native soil and whose strength is as tangible and tenacious as the amber-pitched pine at my back?

Like the husk of a seed, my Western education/conditioning splits, and my spirit sends up a green shoot. With it comes a long-buried memory: I am twelve years old. Mother has told me that soon I will be capable of bearing life. "Think of it, Marilou. It's a sacred power, a great responsibility." I think … and wait for the power sign. It comes. Mother announces to my father, "Our little girl is a woman now. …" He smiles, "Well … mighty fine." In the evening we have a dinner in my honor. Steam from corn on the cob, fried chicken, green beans and cornbread mingles in my mind with the private odor, warm and pungent, that Mother describes as "fresh" (the rural term for mammals in season). I feel wholesome, proud, in harmony with the natural order.

I am ready now to meet the Beloved Woman …

"What was it like," you ask, "to be in her presence?"

"Come. I will show you." It is midnight, June, the full moon. Behind a farmhouse near the Kentucky border, you and I walk barefoot through the coarse grass. Crickets and treefrogs are drowsy. Birds are quiet. And we are enveloped in a powerful, sweet odor that transforms the night. Too pungent to be honeysuckle. Too fecund for roses. It recalls a baby's breath just after nursing, along with the memory of something warm and private that lingers at the edge of the mind. …

Sniffing the air, we seek the source—and find it. The cornfield in bloom. Row on row of sturdy stalks, with their tassels held up to the moon. Silently, in slow rhythm, we make our way into the field. The faint rustle of growing plants flows around and through us; until we stop by a tall stalk, there seems no division between flesh and green. We rub the smooth, sinewy leaves on our cheeks and touch a nubile ear, where each grain of pollen that falls from the tassle will make a kernel, strong and turgid with milk. Linking arms around the stalk, we lift our faces to the drifting pollen and breathe the spirit of the Corn-Mother—the powerful, joyous, nurturing odor of one complete-in-herself.

"Where are your women?"

We are here.

RED CLAY: WHEN AWI USDI WALKED AMONG US

Reunion of the Cherokee Councils of East and West

"I feel what's happening at Red Clay, but I don't know how to take a picture of it." The veteran news photographer shakes his head, folds his hands on top of his camera.

I show him my blank notebook. "The energy field here is too strong. I've never felt anything like it. It's so peaceable."

We smile, wander on, he toward the West Knoll, with its crest of trees faintly tipped with leaves. I toward the amphitheater tucked in the lee of a wooded hill. Weeks of chilling rain have left earth and air so sensitive I can almost touch the sunlight, the pungence of loam and pine carried by brisk wind. I am in my native mountains again, where my blood feels at home.

It's April 7, 1984—the second and final day of the Eastern and Western Cherokee Council Reunion at Red Clay, now a state reserve nestled between steep ridges near Cleveland, Tennessee. This place is sacred ground, hallowed ground, a place that remembers. It was here in 1837 that the last council met, faced with the federal government's adamant demand that ancestral lands be relinquished; here in 1838 that federal troops began the Removal, the Trail of Tears that divided the people into what is now the Cherokee Nation of Oklahoma and the Eastern Band of Cherokee Indians, most of whom live on the Qualla Reservation in North Carolina. Other families and small communities are scattered along the Appalachian mountains from Virginia to north Georgia.

For the first time in 147 years, the chiefs and their councils have united to discuss mutual concerns about health, education, legislation, economics and cultural preservation. According to centuries-old tradition, the convening of the council is as much social and religious as it is political, and formal deliberations are being held outside, among the people—a crowd estimated, overall, at twenty thousand. Five to six thousand are of Cherokee heritage.

We've gathered in a remote mountain meadow, its fingers wedged among wooded knolls and its palm sparsely dotted, as it was in 1837, with a cabin and other tenements made of weathered logs. In the center, near a deep limestone spring, is the rectangular, opened-sided council house. The amphitheater is concealed behind a hill. At the entrance to the Historical Area, shaded by pines, the museum and offices are housed in a low, fawn-colored wood building with a long porch across the front. Ordinarily, to walk onto the council grounds is to pass into another time, into a quiet broken only by songs of birds or occasional conversations of other visitors.

None of the planners had expected twenty thousand people. As April 6 drew closer, however, attendance estimates rose swiftly. "We don't know what will happen," said Carol Allison, assistant to the principal chief of the Cherokee Nation of Oklahoma and one of the organizers of the event. "We've told everybody—the media, the public—that this reunion is to be dignified, a historic council meeting, not a 'drums and feathers' event. But what if the non-Indians come expecting that kind of thing anyway and are disappointed with the Indians for *not* having it? It's still winter in East Tennessee—what if people swamp the motels and others are left milling around in the cold? We can't let this reunion get out of hand."

"We" included the principal planners—the Cherokee of east and west, the officials and citizens of Cleveland, the supervisor of the Red Clay Historical Area and his staff and their assistants, as well as unknown numbers of other people preparing for the journey. One thought united us all: a reverent spirit *will* prevail at Red Clay. For months we beamed this thought toward the sacred ground. Energies fused, creating a powerful field that ultimately would draw human currents from the Four Directions.

On the eve of the reunion, people were pouring into the Cleveland area by plane, by car, by camper, by train. Everywhere the friendly exchange: "Where're you from?" "Florida!" "Connecticut!" "Minnesota!" "Hawaii!" and points between. At the Chalet Motel, where many Cherokee were staying, the mood was happy, expectant, quiet. Around us the mountains seem frozen, their trees bare-limbed against dark clouds. In just such weather the ancestors began the Trail of Tears. We were thinking of them and asking ourselves, *What will happen at Red Clay?*

Now I'm in the midst of it all. From the beginning the sun has been radiant, the wind benevolent, though steadily rising. At the amphitheater in the lee of the hill, however, all is quiet. On the grass stage, where the final council session is in progress, Chief Robert Youngdeer of the Eastern Band raises his arms toward woods and sky. "When we came to Red Clay the trees were closed and cold. See in one day how the leaves have unfurled. ..." His unspoken meaning is clear:

Remember
how our Mother Earth has renewed
herself
how the people have endured
how hope has unfurled
invincibly!
Red Clay!

Something is moving among us. I feel it in many images—an energy as invisible and real as the atom's. Governor Alexander calls it electricity. A reporter, an aura. As I walk the council grounds, I gather these images as healing medicines for bleak seasons I know will come again.

The most striking image is the ceaseless current of men, women and children, moving peaceably among the knolls, over the meadow. Here pooling quietly for a ceremony, there running in rivulets among the food and craft booths that edge the grounds, pausing in eddies of conversation, then moving on, a constant lively contented murmur.

"I've never seen anything like it," an Anglo man observes. "Nothing seems planned but everything gets done! People just *flow* around."

The Cherokee set the tone for the crowd. Though visually they often may be distinguished only by a deeper tint of skin or hair, a bit of beaded jewelry, an occasional ribbon shirt or dress, they are still, as an observer of the 1837 council described them, "the decorous Cherokee," and they behave in keeping with the dignity of the occasion. There can be no drinking, no rowdiness. By immutable tradition, where the council meets is sacred ground.

Red Clay Is Ground That Remembers

Maybe this is why so many people seem to listen inwardly to a different dimension. Even time images differently here. It is all of a piece, all in the present. I touch the railing of the open-sided council house. Once again it is the fresh of the morning, sunlit, chill with a light breeze. Paul, our son Andrew, age fifteen, and I huddle with about two hundred others waiting for the prayer ceremony that will open the reunion. Friends exchange news. Strangers chat like neighbors. The chiefs and councillors stand quietly discussing arrangements.

In response to a request for a photograph, a small wiry woman emerges from the councillors and stands apart. A blue kerchief is wrapped around her forehead and tied in back, in the traditional way. Her jacket and ankle-length skirt are dun colored. I recognize Maggie Wachacha, an eighty-eight-year-old member of the Eastern Band, scribe for the tribal council, and a "rememberer." I know of her through her grandson, who told me, "My grandmother heard her elders tell how they walked the Trail of Tears. When she speaks of it, we hear their voices. We feel their sorrow."

As she gazes unperturbed toward the steep ridge across the meadow, I study the seams of her face, the calm eyes, brown at the center, fading to hazy blue in the outer rims. Is she thinking of what an ancestor recounted, words recorded by George W. Featherstonhaugh, as the two men stood near the council house on that rainy August day in 1837?

> John Mason brought us greetings from President Van Buren. He said the president is guided by "justice" and is only concerned with our safety and well-being. He urged us to accept the treaty signed two years ago in New Echota [Georgia] and move west. He said this when he knows the signers were not authorized by the people. He told us, "In Oklahoma, the country will be yours—yours exclusively." We were not impressed.

Is Maggie Wachacha remembering this bitter sorrow? Or is she thinking of today, when the Cherokee diaspora has gathered from the Four Directions? As scribe of the Eastern Band, she knows the resolutions the reunion council will consider. Perhaps she is looking to the future, to the harvest that may come from seeds of unity.

Briefly her eyes meet mine, and I know. All are one to her: past, present, future, and the experiences they bring. I begin to understand the power that vibrates in this place.

Red Clay Is the Still Center of Time

As the Reverend Robert Bushyhead of Qualla begins prayers to the
Great Spirit in Cherokee, I think how at the council 147 years ago, similar
prayers "soothed the spirit" of Featherstonhaugh, an English naturalist
whose eyewitness account was used extensively in the modern reconstruction of the historic area. I hear his precise voice describe Red Clay:

> Rich, dry bottom of land ... the irregular street of huts, booths and stores
> hastily constructed for the subsistence of several thousand Indians ...
> the hilly ground upon which the council house was built ... the copious
> limestone spring ... and the most impressive feature—an unceasing
> current of Cherokee Indians, men, women, youth, and children, moving
> about in every direction, and in the greatest order, and all, except the
> younger ones, preserving a grave and thoughtful demeanor.

How much is the same and how much has changed. "If we hold fast in
the center," Maggie Wachacha's eyes tell me, "the good can be preserved
and the grievous made well."

The youth reflect the wisdom of Maggie Wachacha. They too feel
what's happening at Red Clay and respond energy to energy, a cloud of
electrons orbiting the nucleus. They are the future gathering strength. Two
merry teenage girls from Qualla sell red "Remember the Removal" T-shirts
at one of the folding table "booths."

"Proceeds go to a joint youth project with the Oklahoma Nation," they
explain. "This summer we're going to retrace the Trail of Tears so we'll
understand our heritage better."

I buy two shirts. "I'm from the Far Away Cherokee Association in
Memphis. We're going to host the group as you pass through. We'll be
looking for you."

Beyond the line of tables small children run in the meadow, dart in and
out of log tenements. In the barn loft they stick out their arms and wave
through interstices in the walls. Laughter and calls of "Wait for me" drift
over the grounds. A young couple is watching them. The woman's hands rest
on her abdomen, which is stretched almost to term. "We're from the Nation
in Oklahoma," the man says. And though I haven't asked, he adds, "My eyes

are blue and my skin is light because every other generation my family 'married out.' My wife is full-blood. We don't know what our baby will look like. But it's what's in the heart that counts. 'There's power in the blood. ...'"

"Wondrous working power." I finish the line of the old song, and the three of us smile. We are remembering that for more than a century the federal government subjected the Cherokee to a killing winter: divided the nation; forbade the teaching of language and culture; imposed the Dawes Act of 1890, which linked blood quantum to entitlement to land and federal services and which had the avowed purpose of fomenting "selfishness, which is at the bottom of civilization." Break up the land. Break up the tribal system. Break up the family. The strategy succeeded brilliantly in both geography and politics.

Blood, however, flowed east and west and also into remote coves and valleys in between, secluding itself in the genes of families (some of whom have married outside the tribe and back since 1540)—and biding its time. Memory of language and culture spiraled in the cells of children, where the "rememberers," including our Mother Earth, the greatest rememberer of all, have known how to call it forth. Although the quantum always has caused dissension, as it was intended, abetting the tendency of people to polarize into opposing groups, families have held fast. And now ...

Red Clay Is Blood Converging

Within its watery nest
a baby listens
to gathering kin
to its own blood singing
—and slowly unfurls
invincibly.

This baby, like all our others, reaches toward us unaware of color—either of skin or eye, or of hair that may be straight, curly or wooly. The baby remembers only its blood-song. If the child looks "politically incorrect," will we cut it in pieces? Or will we say, "It's what's in the heart that counts. Sing, child!"

Today, in the warm peace of Red Clay, I dare to hope that we can help our children sing a bridge over all that is closed and cold, that we can help them by singing the bridge ourselves—invincibly.

Thousands of people here carry the image of an invincible singer—Nancy Ward, the last Beloved Woman of the Cherokee. She is pictured on the reunion's commemorative poster, which is reproduced on the program book's cover. Her grave lies twelve miles from Red Clay, but the sacred ground remembers her vision—and so do we.

During her tenure as Beloved Woman (1755–1822), Nancy Ward worked steadily and against increasingly desperate odds for mutual understanding between Anglos and Indian people. It was a concept of peaceful coexistence that she maintained in her own family. She had two children with her first husband, who was a full-blood. After his death she was married briefly to a white man, Bryant Ward, and they had one daughter. According to the Cherokee matrilineal tradition, the children took the mother's name. There was no thought of "cutting them in pieces"—part this, part that. Both privately and politically, this system was a matrix to nourish peaceful coexistence.

However, the patrilineal system of the Anglo culture provided no such matrix, and by the 1820s, when Nancy Ward died, the vision of peaceful coexistence and the matrilineal egalitarian culture that would have nourished it seemed to have died with her. In reality, the system used nature's oldest survival tactic—it adapted, went underground, preserved its roots. Today, Nancy Ward's vision, which was shared by many other Cherokee leaders of her time, is greening again. At the first session of the reunion council, which is composed of both women and men as in the traditional times, Wilma Mankiller presides. She is deputy principal chief of the Cherokee Nation of Oklahoma, the first woman to hold high office since Nancy Ward.

Red Clay Is Unity Being Born

This unity is imaged by the principal chiefs—Robert Youngdeer of the East and Ross Swimmer of the West. Always accessible, they move easily among the people. But when they obviously are talking privately together, the crowd, including the national press, courteously avoids them. This unsolicited courtesy, in itself, is extraordinary. And I see it now, as the two men walk toward the West Knoll. They alternately listen, talk, sometimes serious, sometimes smiling. Weaving connections. Chief Youngdeer is medium height—sturdy, erect. His hair is white, his gaze often reserved and penetrating, though he is also noted for his compelling sense of humor. He is a master orator in the ceremonial tradition. Chief Swimmer is younger, tall and lithe, an attorney who moves astutely through the bureaucratic intricacies of Washington. His manner is urbane, firm, kindly. In both the Cherokee and dominant cultures, these men are highly respected for their knowledge, wisdom and governing skill.

Many things separate the eastern and western bands: twelve hundred miles, federal bureaucracy, lack of formal contact for nearly a century and a half. The Eastern Band numbers 8,882, is geographically enclosed, and has a low-income, tourist economy. The Cherokee Nation of Oklahoma owns several businesses, including a company that produces components for commercial and defense industries. Most of the Nation's 53,097 members are integrated into the dominant culture, although 30,000 of them live in the fourteen-county service area (not a reservation).

"But we have many points in common," says Chief Swimmer, "an ancestry, heritage, culture, and our outlook for the future. The future Red Clay brings is to renew tribal ties and family relationships that were ended in 1837. We will continue annual meetings, alternating locations east and west. (In June 1985, the council met in Tahlequah, Oklahoma.) We'll have opportunities to support each other on issues pertaining to one tribe and to strengthen our lobby effort in Washington on issues we have in common. Red Clay is not only historic but means a lot to contemporary Cherokees."

As the formal, major ceremony begins, Paul, Andrew, and I are part of the ceaseless current that has pooled quietly on the West Knoll. From our place midway, we can see the crest of trees, but can only hear the speakers as they step to the podium. As they speak, the images of Red Clay intensify— *ground that remembers ... the still center of time ... blood converging ... unity being born*—and they seem to be slowly resolving into one. I feel what's happening, feel the expectant vibration in the crowd as whispers pass, "They're coming. The runners are coming with the sacred fire."

Young women marshals in traditional ribbon dresses have cleared a path for them that leads up to a monument of crab orchard stone, which will shelter the flame. In 1838, when soldiers herded Cherokee families from Red Clay, someone secretly carried the sacred fire, tamped and hidden in moss. The fire signified the spirit of the Creator, of the sun, of the people—and the Cherokee have kept it burning for centuries. In 1951 an ember was brought back to North Carolina. Now the young men have run 130 miles in relay from the Qualla reservation in the mountains of North Carolina, bearing torches.

The crowd is silent as the men run slowly toward the crest of the knoll. There the torches are joined together and passed among the council members before coming back to the chiefs for the ceremonial lighting. The chiefs invoke the fire's ancient meanings, and Youngdeer extends its light to include the present when he says, "The flame stands for freedom, and friendship between the whites and the Indians. We hold neither hatred nor malice in our hearts. We remember the past but look to the future."

I stoop to touch the path, where the earth has used winter rain to bring forth grass—thick, buoyant, rippling verdant, and sweet in the wind. I sense the people thinking with one heart, evoking the seventeen thousand who walked the Trail of Tears, the four thousand who died along the way, the small band that held out in North Carolina. We move with them through years closed and cold, through the slow-warming cycle of justice that restored many rights. Now, in the seventh generation since the Removal, we have come to Red Clay, where new leaves unfurl and a fresh, green path shines in the sun.

We have survived.
We thank the Great Spirit.
We shall renew our strength and
mount up with wings.

A powerful presence sweeps silently through the crowd. It is more than an "energy field." More than "electricity" or an "aura." Many who know his traditional story say Awi Usdi walks among us. Little Deer, a spirit of reverence and justice.

The Coming of Little Deer

From the heart of the mountain he comes, with his head held high in the
wind. Like the spirit of light he comes—the small white chief of the deer.

When one of his own is slain
he instantly draws near
and finding clotted blood on the leaves
he bends low over the stain,
"Have you heard …
Has the hunter prayed words of pardon
for the life you gave for his own?"
If the answer be "No" then Little Deer
goes—invisible, fleet as the wind—
and tracks the blood to the hunter's home
where he swiftly pains and cripples his
bones so he never can hunt again.

From the heart of the mountain he comes, with his head held high in the
wind. Like the spirit of light he comes—the small white chief of the deer.

Once in a lifetime he may appear
to one whose spirit is deep
and a master's arrow may bring him down
so the hunter can take his horn
to keep as a charm for the chase—
a talisman reverently borne
for reverence alone sustains its power
and forestalls wrath and pain.
But the hunter must be swift of hand
for the arrow hardly strikes his throat
than Little Deer leaps for his ancient path
that slopes upward into the mist.

From the heart of the mountain he comes, with his head held high in the
wind. Like the spirit of light he goes—the small white chief of the deer.

Some say he can't be here. That our high-tech age is "too advanced" to believe such stories. But Awi Usdi was in these blue-hazed mountains twenty-five hundred years ago, when the Cherokee named his spirit. To him modern arrogance is a mere drifting leaf.

He has come to Red Clay because the heart's blood of the Cherokee was spilled here. This is hallowed ground.

He has come on the hunters' behalf, because their descendants have prayed the words of pardon through their deeds. It has taken time.

Today Governor Alexander announces the formation of the Tennessee Indian Commission, a historic first for our state and an expression of the concern for Native American Tennesseans that has been growing for decades. The history of the Red Clay Historical Area exemplifies this slow, steady growth. In 1929 Colonel James F. Corn of Cleveland saved Red Clay from becoming a factory site by buying the land and giving it to the state. In 1973, archeologists began excavation and reconstruction, funded by tax money, not donations, from all of Tennessee's citizens. Locally, the Red Clay Association supported the project. When the work was sufficiently done, Jennings Bunn, area supervisor, invited the Cherokee to return, with the hope that "the reunion of 1984 will in some small way help to heal this wound and reunite in oneness a great Nation. May the spirit of Awi Usdi watch over us all."

Because we have gathered here in reverence and love, Awi Usdi is watching over us, walking among us.

Swiftly, I gather his image: A peaceful power assuring all people that if justice and reverence prevail, in the fullness of time, sorrow may be eased, wounds may be healed. And within whatever morass we find ourselves, there is always a green path that leads us to the top of the hill, where the sacred fire burns for us all.

FIRMING MY STEP

Experiencing a whole nation turning toward the east is luminous—beyond prose or photographs or poetry. Fifteen thousand non-Indians had come to witness the event. Why?

Without my asking, a couple with four children in hand—ages three to ten—told me the reason many people came. After the council meeting I was walking down the hill beside them.

"We have a little farm up in Minnesota," the woman said. "We drove all the way here in our truck."

The man said, "We wanted our children to see this. If the Cherokee can survive, so can we."

Of course, at Red Clay there had also been people who were "just curious" and a charlatan or two (isn't there always?). One of them was a man in a long feather headdress and pilot's sunglasses claiming he was a "shaman who had healing hands." The Cherokee quietly shunned him, although one of the chiefs rebuked him indirectly by mentioning in a speech that the Cherokee did not wear feather headdresses. Although the only obvious security people were random park rangers, many others in ordinary clothes roamed through the crowd, including tribal police ("Beauty is no threat to the wary"). But a greater power was holding the twenty thousand people in check, and one expression of it came from those who live in the vicinity of Red Clay.

Before the reunion began, many of them had brought gifts for Cherokee families who had traveled long distances and were camped on the grounds. Firewood, jellies, fried chicken, cakes, charcoal. Welcome notes and names were attached to some gifts, others were left anonymously on the porch of Park Headquarters. At the beginning of the reunion, Chief Swimmer had instructed a staff member to make a list of all identifiable donors, so he could circle back letters of thanks on behalf of the Cherokee. When the reunion was over, as the chief was getting into his car to leave, a middle-aged man hurried up and thrust a painting into his hands. "I made this for you," he said. "The paint's not quite dry, but I wanted you to know how I feel about you and your people."

Harmony.
Continuance in the midst of change.
Peace.

The reunion at Red Clay convinced me that Homo sapiens have a chance to avert Mother Nature's "pink slip" and create a place where our children, the seeds of the people, can grow safe and strong. By unweaving contemporary life back to our original error, we might be able to restore the balance and heal the wounds. *"In the beginning, the Creator made our Mother Earth. ..."* If I could leave only one of my writings behind, it would be the poem "When Earth Becomes an 'It.'" We must call Earth "Mother" again, especially for the children. The baby who was "slowly unfurling" at Red Clay is now nine years old. Her English name is Alayna. Her Cherokee name is Jigeyu—"Beloved," after Nanyehi, the Beloved Woman. She, children like her, and those unborn are looking toward the future. They are expecting the sunrise.

From Red Clay on, my step on the path was firm. Gradually I realized where Little Deer was leading me.

REBIRTH OF A NATION

Interview with Wilma Mankiller

At age forty-two, Principal Chief Wilma Mankiller of the Cherokee Nation of Oklahoma is the first woman to head a major Indian tribe. It's no easy task: her jurisdiction includes eighty-six thousand of the ninety-five thousand Cherokees in the country. In charge of a budget of nearly $50 million, Mankiller has compared her job to running a small country and a medium-sized corporation at the same time. But anyone who doubts that she can handle it need only spend a few minutes in her presence.

Like the mountains of her native eastern Oklahoma, the chief is staunch and sturdy; nurturing, yet not to be trifled with; and deeply calm. Running beneath that tranquil surface is a reservoir of humor that helps her keep things in perspective. She chuckles as she quotes what the Cherokee say about her: "While other people get agitated and jump up and down, Wilma moseys on through and gets the job done."

Mankiller has defined the job on her own terms. Although her last name, passed down by her ancestors, could suggest that she's warlike and pushy, the opposite is true. The chief has an open-door policy and a philosophy of building programs from the grassroots up—helping people define their own needs and then developing systems to meet them. She always seems to have time for anyone who needs her.

Mankiller works almost around the clock, a cycle that includes making time for Charlie Soap, her husband of two years, two daughters, a grandson, and other family and friends. This is moseying, Mankiller-style, and last fall it not only got her elected to her second term as a chief but won her the Harvard Foundation Citation for Leadership and a *Ms.* magazine award as one of 1987's Outstanding Women of the Year.

One of eleven children, Mankiller was born on a farm in rural Stillwell, Oklahoma, to a Cherokee father and a Caucasian mother. When a drought in the late 1950s devastated the family's crop, a federal urbanization project for Native Americans relocated them to San Francisco.

While living in California, Mankiller studied at San Francisco State University, married a wealthy Ecuadorean businessman, raised their two daughters, and became increasingly involved in Indian issues. The marriage broke up after ten years, and in 1977 Mankiller returned with her children to the Nation and to her family's plot of land, Mankiller Flats. After receiving a degree in social sciences at a local college, she became a graduate assistant in architecture at the University of Arkansas. In the fall of 1979 she was seriously injured in a car accident. "That accident," says Mankiller, "changed my life. I always think of myself as the woman who lived before and the woman who lives afterward."

When Ross Swimmer resigned in 1985, Wilma Mankiller became Principal Chief. She was re-elected in 1987 and again in 1991. I interviewed her for *Southern Style* magazine in 1988.

What were you like before the accident?
I had a hard edge. I spent a lot of time being angry at injustices against people in general and the Cherokee in particular. During the '60s and early '70s, I had an us-and-them mentality.

What happened to give you that "hard edge"?
It was an ongoing process: growing up Indian in an urban environment, feeling my family members were victims of ill-advised federal policies, and realizing the government had not honored treaties or policies for health and education. My father had always been active in Indian issues. But the protest at Alcatraz in 1969 [against poor treatment of Indians] was the catalyst that made me an activist.

And in 1979 the accident occurred. What happened?
One morning I was driving from Stillwell to Tahlequah. At the top of a hill, a car coming from the opposite direction pulled out to pass and hit me head on. The driver of that car was my best friend, Sherry Morris. She was killed instantly.

The doctors told me later that I was so mutilated they didn't know at first if I was a man or a woman. One leg was crushed, one broken. My ribs were broken; my nose and other facial bones were, too. All I remember now is how I felt. I was dying, yet it was a beautiful and spiritual experience, warm and loving, soft. I no longer feared death. I saw how precious health and life are, how important it is to do something good with your life and to share. I realized how insignificant you are in the totality of things. It's a precious thing to be here and take part in the world.

How did the aftermath of the accident affect you?
I was incapacitated for almost a year. At home by myself I had time to examine my life in a new way—to reevaluate, refocus. But just when I thought I was finally getting well, my muscles began to weaken. I couldn't hold my toothbrush or my hairbrush, and I couldn't control my speech or my facial muscles. I had spells of not being able to breathe. Once I fell and rebroke the bones in my face. I was very frightened and didn't know what was happening to me.

Then I saw a muscular dystrophy program on television that described a case similar to mine. I called a muscular dystrophy center and was referred to specialists. The diagnosis was moderately severe myasthenia gravis.

"Creeping paralysis," the old-timers in Appalachia called it.
Exactly. Doctors removed my thymus gland and put me on an intensive medical treatment. I'd suddenly gone from being an active, positive person

to a person who was struggling to stay alive. I was very discouraged. Sometimes I just wanted to roll over and play dead.

You've said that tribal medicine men helped you recover from the accident. What did they do?
Medicine men are healers and spiritual counselors. They help restore harmony from the inside out. They taught me to approach life from a positive, loving perspective. Your chances of surviving are much better this way than with a negative outlook. I applied that concept to my work, too. What I really wanted to do was rebuild our tribe and our people.

Then I had the surgery. Afterward I was on a life-support system. Finally I got angry. I said, "Get me out of here and off this stuff. I'm not going to take this any more. I'm going to participate in getting well."

The doctors thought I'd have to stay on the support system for three weeks. Instead, I came off it in three days. Once I took charge of my life, my body gradually began to heal. Last year I finally was able to discontinue the medicine for myasthenia gravis.

So the real turning point for your health, as well as for your vision of your work, was a change in spirit?
Yes. Illness had slowed me down enough to make me think, listen and pay attention. The medicine men and the elders talked to me about how we should be as a people. They showed me the sacred wampum belts that teach the truths of Cherokee life: that we should have good minds, consider everything in the world—including nature—as brothers and sisters. We should not be judgmental, but accept all as family. They taught me not to be dragged down by the negative. That divides people.

I began to understand, to rethink. Out of all that, I grew determined to bring the people together as "we." In the old days, people talked about their problems and helped each other solve them. That was the genesis of my idea for the Department of Community Development. Instead of accepting the paternalistic approach that tells people what they need and gives it to them, we would define our own needs, develop resources, and do the work ourselves.

That reflects the principle of working from the inside out. Were there other ways that you changed inside?
Coming so close to death moved me beyond the ego to the calm. I can't imagine what could rattle me now. I also became a lot tougher and firmer, without becoming mean spirited. I don't worry so much about little things. I focus more on the good.

How has your experience influenced other people?
More than anything else, I give people hope. I'm a daughter of the Cherokee people, and they know that, a woman from a poor family who landed on her feet. Last year, when I was on the "Good Morning, America" television show, people back home said, "When you were talking, it was like *we* were talking."

Whatever the subject, your theme is unity: sharing, consensus, cooperation. Is that the historical role of Cherokee women?
Women were the center of the family and the tribe. They trained the chiefs and had their own council. The head of their council had a powerful voice in government. Women sometimes went to war alongside their husbands and sons. In the early 1800s, for the sake of survival, the tribe adopted a system similar to the federal government's, which had no place for women. But underneath, the people passed on the tradition of nurturing and assertiveness to both genders.

That's why it never occurred to me that anyone would be concerned about having a female chief. My husband was as confused by the furor as I was. Tribal people think holistically. Whether you're a man or a woman, you do what needs to be done. The nurturing skills I apply to my family apply to the tribe.

What advice do you have for women as a whole?
Many women internalize the stereotypes of "the woman's place," passivity and so on. We need to rethink where we are—there's a lot of unlearning to do—and extend our ideas of home and family to include our environment and our people. We need to trust our own thinking, trust where we're going.

Then "mosey on through"... ?
And get the job done.

Selu and Kanati: Marriage

The Chimney Tops are famous twin peaks in the Great Smoky Mountains National Park. One peak is softly rounded, one is sharp. Their beauty is their balance.

Two peaks
alone ... apart ...
yet join at the heart
where trees rise green
from rain-soaked loam
and laurel's tangled skeins
bear fragile blooms
and wind, a honing, ceaseless
sigh, blends with mirth
of streams defying heights
to wend their way unquenched.
Two peaks
they stand against the sky
spanned by a jagged arm of rock
locked in an embrace
elements cannot destroy
or time erase.

CHEROKEE EDEN

An Alternative to the Apple

Myth is a powerful medicine. For centuries, the proverbial "Eden apple" has rolled through Western culture—the arts, politics, theology, society—and pointed its accusing, wounding stem at woman: "You are to blame for sin and destruction. You deserve to be punished." I refuse the apple. Instead, I reach for the strawberry—the powerful, healing medicine of Cherokee Eden. This myth has endured perhaps twenty-five hundred years, as long as the Cherokee themselves. Here I have adapted it from James Mooney's *Myths and Sacred Formulas of the Cherokee.*

ORIGIN OF STRAWBERRIES

The first man and woman lived in harmony for a time. Then they began to quarrel.

The cause is not told—the lovers themselves probably didn't know *exactly*—but the quarrel must have been long and tedious, for ...

At last the woman left and started off to the Sun Land in the East where the Sun, being female, would likely comfort her.

The man followed, alone and grieving, but the woman kept steadily ahead and never looked back. The Provider (Creator) took pity on the man and asked him, "Are you still angry with the woman?"

He said, "No."

"Would you like to have her back again?"

He eagerly answered, "Yes."

The Provider doesn't ask the cause of the quarrel. Blame and punishment are not the concern. Healing is. In essence, the Provider asks the man, "Is your heart still hardened against the woman?" A crucial question, for a hard heart blocks reconciliation and abets mental and physical abuse. Only after the man has affirmed his good intent does the Provider give help, using gentle persuasion.

118

The Provider caused many things to spring up in the woman's path:
- *A patch of ripe huckleberries. But the woman passed them by.*
- *A clump of blackberries. The woman refused to notice.*
- *Other fruits and then some trees covered with beautiful red service berries. The woman kept steadily on.*
  - *Last came a patch of large ripe strawberries, the first ever known.*

The woman stooped to gather a few to eat, and as she picked them she chanced to turn her face to the west. At once the memory of her husband came back to her. She sat down, but the longer she waited, the stronger became her desire for her husband. At last she gathered a bunch of the finest berries and started back along the path to give them to him. He met her kindly, and they went home together.

Reconciliation. Healing. Acceptance of the human tendency to quarrel. A pattern for restoring harmony that involves mutual responsibility and restitution. This is Cherokee Eden, the powerful medicine of the strawberry.

The medicine will not work out of context, however. To experience the myth fully, one must understand its resonance—the ways of the people who gave it voice. The classic Cherokee culture was matrilineal. It was organized around the concept that the gender who bears life should not be separated from the power to sustain it. There were seven mother clans. In marriage, the man took the name of the woman's clan, as did their children. The woman owned the house. In divorce, which could be initiated by either party, the man returned to his mother's clan.

Women also planted, harvested and cooked—not as "squaw work," but as a crucial service to the people, for women were thought to have a special affinity for our Mother Earth. They also sat on the council and made their views known through the Beloved Woman, who shared the place of honor with the war and peace chiefs, both male. In matters concerning hostages, her word was absolute and she was believed to bring messages from the Provider to the people. It is thought that, like her distant Iroquois relatives, who were also matrilineal, Cherokee women trained prospective chiefs. It is certain they helped shape government, which was collaborative rather than adversarial. Only in time of national emergency did the chiefs make arbitrary decisions. Otherwise, they guided by persuasion, and decisions were made by consensus.

When a Cherokee chief squared off with a chief from another tribe, a delegation of women often functioned as intercessors. At its zenith in the mid-eighteenth century, the Cherokee nation extended into eight southeastern states. Although towns were widely separated and independently governed, they never warred with each other, for each town contained families from the seven clans. It was sternly forbidden to make war on relatives.

In the mythology of such a society, women naturally had an important place. Selu, the Corn-Mother, for example, brought the first corn to the people, a cardinal physical and spiritual gift. Kanati, the Lucky Hunter, her husband, was the mythic father of mankind and brought hunting and woodlore to the people. Other myths explored the strengths and weaknesses of both genders, giving women as well as men prototypes for wholeness. If ideas of the Eden apple variety ever rolled in this culture, it is safe to assume the women quickly made cider of them.

In 1817, this classic way of life officially ended. For two hundred years the Cherokee had tried to work out a harmonious coexistence with European settlers, adopting many of their ways. Periods of peace alternated with broken treaties and bloody battles. In a final effort at reconciliation, the Cherokee changed to the patrilineal, republican form of government. The sound of the rolling Eden apple drove matrilineal ways underground. Twenty years later, the Removal began and decimated the nation. Many people in the dominant culture predicted, "In a hundred years, there will be no more Cherokee."

But roots held fast: the Cherokee now number about sixty-five thousand. Both Wilma Mankiller, chief of the Cherokee Nation of Oklahoma, and Principal Chief Ross Swimmer believe in collaborative government and in leadership through persuasion rather than coercion. Matrilineal ways are greening again. They have strength and endurance, like myth. Both have been kept alive by two concepts the Cherokee share with other Native Americans. One is the view of time as a continuum, a fusion of past, present, future. Related to this concept is the oral tradition. By *speaking* their ways and myths, the people keep them immediate and relevant. The *sound* of the words themselves makes them live in the present.

For that reason I suggest you do something outside the Western tradition of the essay, which usually is read silently. So that you can *feel* the powerful medicine of the strawberry myth, ask a friend to read it to you—just the italicized part, not my asides. Quiet your mind. Listen. Note where the resonance of the words causes your thoughts to vibrate. (I'll do the same, then share my thoughts with you. In the meantime, share yours with your friend. When we come together again, the medicine will be alive and at work.)

... I feel good—so good that I toss the apple over my shoulder. In Cherokee Eden there is respect for the female, her intelligence and her rights of choice—and for the male, too. Neither gender is put down or cast in an adversarial role. Competition is removed.

What a resonant fruit, the strawberry! It touches many other places in my mind:

... *A quarrel with my companion*: Neither of us knows the cause, exactly. After thirty years together, it could be almost anything. I've kept "steadily ahead" for three days. I ought to sit down, gather a few berries ...

... *Notes for a talk on race relations for the National Conference of Christians and Jews:* I think I'll tear up my notes, just read the myth (without my asides) and let it resonate. Whatever our races or religions, we all have in common similar teachings about forgiveness, reconciliation, restitution. A Cherokee myth might provide a neutral stimulus for consensus.

... *Rape case in this morning's newspaper:* "She was asking for it," the defendant says. The Eden apple—still rolling, still powerful. Depressing, how little cider we've been able to make of it.

... *A quote I heard at a lecture entitled "Urban Problems: A Holistic View"*: The speaker, an expert from MIT, gave a fine presentation. He then opened discussion by saying, "Adversarial modes of thought are breaking down. But when we look around for collaborative models, we can't find any."

I suggested we stop looking only at patriarchal European-American traditions and try Native American ones, adding, "The Founding Fathers based much of the U.S. government on the Iroquois pattern."

"But," countered the speaker, "we're having problems with it."

"That's understandable," I said, "because the Founding Fathers left out a basic component the Iroquois always included—women."

The words from the myth that touch me most deeply are "alone and grieving." In the communal Cherokee culture, the worst curse one person could call down on another was not death, but loneliness. Perhaps it is the worse curse in any culture. "Alone and grieving ..." As I travel about the country, how often I hear that feeling expressed. It is part of the modern, fragmented life. Surely we should draw from available sources to heal this condition.

Like earth and air, powerful medicines—the fruits of thought—cannot be owned by anyone. They are for sharing. Even the pain-dealing apple plays its part in the whole, which may be to spur us on in the evolution of the human spirit. Each of us carries in the basket of our mind the myths and symbols of many cultures. It would be unreasonable and unwise to suggest we shake them all out to make room for others. What we can do is lay alternatives among them. I offer the Cherokee strawberry, the healing myth of a people who, like our Mother Earth, have refused to die.

In *Walk in Your Soul*, Cherokee scholars Jack and Anna Kilpatrick correct Mooney's translation of the Cherokee word *une:hlanv:hi*, which aboriginal Cherokee most commonly used to designate the Supreme Being: The Provider. Mooney translated this word as "the Great Apportioner," equating the Supreme Force to the sun. This is a common error in Western thought—and not just among ethnologists. What impressed me the most is that the Kilpatricks made the correction in a good spirit, with respect for the sincerity of Mooney's heart and for the overall excellence of his work. The ability to deepen understanding without disparaging is admirable—and rare in American society today. In my mind I marked this footnote, "food for thought."[21]

It was comforting ...

It was comforting to realize that even Selu and Kanati got out of kilter sometimes—comforting not only in my relationships with others, but also in my relationship with myself. I was learning, as Chief Youngdeer had counseled at Red Clay, to "remember the past and look to the future."

OUT! CHILDREN AT PLAY ON THE ATOMIC FRONTIER (1945–1950), OAK RIDGE, TENNESSEE

A Memoir

"Can you come out? A tree's down in the woods! A big one! The storm last night must've done it." Wayne jiggled from one bare foot to the other on the porch steps of our B-house, which were griddle hot in the July sun. "It's the biggest tree you've ever seen. Goes from one side of the hollow to the other! Let's walk the log."

"I have to ask Mama."

Since she was nearby in the kitchen, Mama asked first, "Have you finished your chores, Marilou ... made your bed, run the vacuum, dusted?"

"Yes, ma'am. All but the dusting."

"Hm ... " It sounded like "no," but she was smiling, probably thinking of times she'd told me about when she was ten years old and played in the trees. "I guess the dusting can wait," she said. "Go on out."

Out! Out! Out! The place to be. Children in the neighborhood of South Tampa Lane (and there were dozens of us) played out as much as possible and wherever the whim took us—tree-studded yards, unpaved streets, deep woods. Mama said we sometimes looked like schools of fish swimming around.

As I bolted through the back door, she called, "Remember, dares go first!" The words tied onto me like ribbons on my long, black braids, bumping gently against the back of my mind as Wayne and I ran through my yard, then by the Smiddies' house. Our feet were summer tough, so we hardly faltered as we crossed the gravel-packed dirt of Tabor Road and made our way down the rough path where the woods began, to the boardwalk, just below the lip of the hollow. A different world here—shadowed, cool, alive with rustle, twitter, hum and the succulent odor of moist loam and growing leaves. From the direction of the tree we heard shouts and laughter.

"Wayne, do you think anybody's walked the log yet?"

"Bet not. Too high."

The boardwalk carried the sound of our running feet ahead of us, and a girl's voice rang out, "Hey, y'all. Somebody's comin'!"

We arrived. And stopped short.

The tree was awesome. Its trunk, immense and straight, reached across the V of the hollow—perhaps twenty feet high over the deepest part. On the far side, the wide, heavy limbs had taken smaller trees with them as they crashed down. Here and there a branch shook where some of our friends were exploring the damage. On the near side, where we stood, was a crater, smelling of deep earth—the biggest hole I'd ever seen. Upended at its edge was the tree's vast wheel of jagged roots. The great taproot—which had held longest and snapped off clean—stuck straight out for about four feet, showing its might. Yet the wind, which we had never seen, had been stronger. The tree, though felled, was still alive and would be weeks in dying. The mystery of it all was irresistible.

Down in the crater, Janice and her cousin Linda stopped rummaging long enough to shout hello. Freddie, who had ventured a little way out on the trunk, jumped down and said to me, "I dare you to walk it!"

I gauged the danger of the tree. Slowly pulling the end of my braid through my hand, I weighed the advantages of being the first to walk it.

I looked back at Freddie and said, "Dares go first."

Freddie shook his head.

But Wayne jumped onto the trunk, near the base. The most wiry and agile of us all, he could have climbed the tree even if it had been upright. He moved around, getting the feel of the log. Freddie yelled, "Wayne's gonna walk it!"

Heads popped up through the fallen branches; two boys and a girl began climbing down. Out of sight, someone wading in the creek called, "Wait for me." From farther up the hollow came the snap of twigs as other kids rushed toward the log. When about fifteen of us had ranged ourselves below it to watch, Wayne gripped the bark with his feet, took his mark on the fallen branches, lifted his arms for balance, and slowly began to walk.

We held our breaths, thinking of him: *Steady as you go ... Steady ... Keep your eyes on the mark ... The highest part now—don't look down ... Steady ... Don't hurry ... Almost safe ... Keep going ...*

"He made it!" We hollered and cheered. Above us Wayne beat his chest and gave a Tarzan yell.

Then Linda said she'd try. And Freddie said, "Me next."

We whiled away most of the afternoon with the tree. On the way home, three of us stopped by Mary Jean's house to play on her rope swing. It was the best one in the neighborhood because it hung from a high limb, had a sturdy knot on the end of it and a wide clearing around it. You could get a good running start and swing in a soaring arc without risk of braining yourself on another tree.

The rest of the day went as usual. Since most of our fathers worked at the plants (doing what they weren't allowed to say) and left work at the same time, everyone had supper between five-thirty and six-thirty, then drifted out again, most often to South Tampa Lane, which was a dead end and flat. During twilight we played Red Rover, Crack-the-Whip or Hopscotch. (When the street was finally paved, we also rode bicycles and roller-skated.)

Hide-and-Seek and Kick-the-Can were our favorite games after dark, when the woods seemed to draw closer to the small houses, bringing the scent of honeysuckle, and street lights cast soft, white circles on the road. Hide-and-Seek was fun, but the problem was that those who were caught were likely to tell on those trying to make "home-free." In Kick-the-Can, the "caughts" were helpful because the clatter of tin set everyone free.

We learned the wisdom of mutual advantage and also of knowing your adversary. Having played together so much, we knew the ways of anyone designated "It": who ranged far, who tricked you by pretending to be out of sight, who hugged the base. Each of us created a strategy accordingly. Scattering wide during the count—when It's eyes were closed—we maneuvered back to the base, creeping along the edge of the woods or around the houses, darting from bush to tree. Strategy plus speed, silence and surprise were the keys to success. In France, in the mid-1960s, when I was an interpreter for the U.S. Air Force during the NATO withdrawal, I would adapt the skills I'd learned in those games to power politics, which are Hide-and-Seek and Kick-the-Can on a grand scale—and the stakes are higher.

An important element of our summer was going barefooted. "School's out, shoes off!" was our motto around home. From the first of May, the persistent question to our parents was, "Can I go barefooted?" Some said yes right away. Others like mine, who were Appalachians of the old school, insisted, "Wait 'til the ground warms up. It's hot on top but cold underneath. It's not good for your bones. It'll make you have rheumatism later in life." Now I appreciate my parents' wisdom, but at the time I said, "Other kids are doing it." And the next day I asked again, "Can I go barefoot?"

We didn't need books to tell us the earth is a living organism. We knew it through our feet, and we wanted that connection as soon as possible. Also, because we lived on the atomic frontier, where change and flux swirled around us, we intuitively reached toward Mother Earth to help us feel rooted, grounded, centered. Mama suggested an even deeper meaning of going barefooted, which she said I would some day understand:

Mother's Advice While Bandaging My Stubbed Toe

If you go barefoot in the world
you have to take bad stubs in stride—
or hide in shoes. "Be plucky, like an Indian,"
that's what my papa said to me.
And always test the "seems" of things.
Briars may lurk in dew-drenched grass
and jagged glass in heaps of leaves.
The toughest sole can't bear these
without a wound.
Bare feet can't tease nature. So
choose your path with wary eyes
and do likewise with humans too.
Be wary, but run on …
Go barefoot and feel the joy
and when pain comes, bind up your toe
and go your way again.
"Be plucky, like an Indian."

Good advice. As children, however, we weren't often thinking of deeper meanings. We were concerned with ourselves and what to do next.

Our choices were governed not so much by seasons as by weather and availability of playmates. In fair weather, we played out. In foul weather, we stayed in the house or on the porch, reading, listening to the radio or amusing ourselves with checkers, Parchesi or jacks. Most friends came from the neighborhood, which followed the contour of the hilltop—North and South Tampa Lane and the upper portions of Taylor and Tabor roads. Except for two flattops, the houses were prefabricated cemestos (similar to sheet rock)—A's, B's, or D's—and in every house were two or three children. (Oak Ridge had a young and prolific population.)

Gender in playmates didn't matter much. Age did. Little kids (age eight down) rarely played with big kids (nine to thirteen). (My sister Adele was in the first group, I in the second.) But the groups often played close to each other—"school-of-fish style"—and the main cause of fussing was someone trying to butt in where he or she didn't belong.

Although our mothers usually were at home, they answered most of our pleas for peacemaking by saying, "Go straighten yourselves out." Except, of course, in near tragedies like the Joan of Arc play, which the little kids staged down in the woods.

Lee Ann, who always whined, had begged for a leading role. "You always make me be a dog or a cat," she said. "This time I want to be *somebody*." The directors, Cleo and Joyce, who were sisters, said, "Okay, Lee Ann, you can be Joan of Arc." They made a pyre of branches at the foot of a tree, stood Lee Ann on top of it and lashed her to the trunk. Then Joyce held a match to the pyre. At the first curl of smoke, someone ran to get the nearest mother (as Lee Ann knew would happen). Tragedy was averted, but everyone involved had to stay in for the rest of the day, except Joan of Arc.

Imaginary stories were popular with all of us. Plots began with an idea: "Let's pretend that you're Tarzan, he's Boy and I'm Cheetah" (my favorite role) or "Let's play house" or "Let's play war" (World War II had just ended). From there we improvised the script, sometimes with odd results, such as when Cleo and Joyce suggested, "Let's play the Crucifixion."

Joyce said, "Cleo, you be the Virgin Mary, I'll be Jesus, and Lee Ann you be the Roman soldier who gives me a drink of vinegar." An oak sapling in our yard was selected for the cross, with a stepladder propped against it. Joyce climbed to the top, held out her arms and dropped her head. The Virgin Mary knelt at the bottom. For want of a long-handled sop, the Roman soldier was given a bucket of water.

When Joyce cried piteously, "I thirst! I thirst!" Lee Ann doused her with the whole bucketful.

"God damn you, Lee Ann!" Joyce charged down from the cross and beat her up before anyone could prevent it.

Aside from the atom, Oak Ridge had two things that made our childhood different from that of most children from other places. One was the fence. It encircled the whole area, about ninety-four square miles. When I tell non-Ridgers about it—the barbed wire, watchtowers and armed guards—they look worried and say, "Didn't you children feel *oppressed?*"

I laugh when I remember how free and safe we felt to roam at will. "Where are the children?" "Out and gone," was a frequent exchange among our mothers. Of course, we had to tell them our general direction—"the woods" or "Jackson Square to the movie" or "around home." But other than that, nobody worried. Everyone knew that to molest a child on government property was a federal crime. The FBI would be after him—fast. Whether or not this was *legally* accurate, it was commonly believed to be, so it had the same effect.

Which brings to mind the second difference in our Oak Ridge environment—FBI men. We spotted them easily—by their dark suits, white shirts and neat ties, usually blue—and they were very polite. I made a jingle of our attitude toward them:

Honey, Run Answer the Door

Is it Fuller Brush, Jewel-T
or the cleaner passing by?
Oh, no ma'am, it's none of them,
it's just the FBI.

If there was nothing else to do, Adele and I sat in the living room with Mama while the FBI man asked her questions about the neighbors. (A family could be moved out overnight for breaking security.) Mama was always polite but noncommittal. Once, when Adele was about four years old, she was cuddled on Mama's lap sucking her thumb while the FBI man was asking the usual, "Do Mr. and Mrs. C talk a lot?" (meaning "Do they mention his work?"). "Are they loud?"

Adele took her thumb out of her mouth and said indignantly, "She yells at her children!"

In her mind this was grounds for arrest.

At Elm Grove Grammar School, which was at the bottom of the hill, we students had a favorite guessing game: "Who is the secret agent?" We'd heard that the FBI had them in unlikely places, and we decided that the one at our school was the custodian, who ambled around the halls pushing his broom, listening. I wonder if he knew we thought he was a secret agent. Or if he *was* ...

At recess the playground offered a creek, a few swings and seesaws and a field. One end of the field was used for softball and the other for the ever-popular Boys-Chase-the-Girls, followed by Girls-Chase-the-Boys. Mary Jean was my best friend, and we were the two fastest runners in the school. She was a bit faster than I and had the longest hair—thin, honey-brown braids that came to her hips (mine were thick, blue-black and shoulder length). Usually Mary Jane won Girls-Chase-the-Boys and she would have won Boys-Chase-the-Girls too if she hadn't loved the way her braids flowed out behind her as she ran. A boy always grabbed one of them. I tied mine under my chin.

On the surface, the playground—like our childhood—seemed open, unsophisticated, carefree. But hidden from the casual observer, between the edge of the field and the sheared-off side of a pine-topped hill, was The Ditch—deep, rocky and vaguely menacing.

We were living in the Cold War era. Since Oak Ridge was considered a prime target, scientists had warned us of what could happen in an atomic attack—about the death-light, fireball and fallout. School disaster drills were frequent. At the blast of the horn—more startling than the fire drill bell—we lined up in the halls, then hurried through the double doors and ran to The Ditch.

Huddled there, with our hands and bare knees pressed against sharp rocks, we waited for the "all clear" to sound. Little kids giggled and punched each other. But many of us big kids were silent, forced back into the terrible ditch at the edge of our minds that we tried to keep out of sight: World War II. Memories of it jabbed us: *Pearl Harbor ... War ... Will Daddy have to go? ... Air raid drills ... Convoys ... Dreaded telegrams—"We regret to inform you" ... Images from radio and newsreels: guns, bombers, tanks ... Men dying, children crying in rubble, Dachau survivors looking like skeletons ... and always, always, the fear that the enemy was nearby, just over the next hill. Then Hiroshima, and the end of war forever. Or was it? What if ... ?*

"All clear!" The siren brought us scrambling out of The Ditch, out of bad memories. Out! Out! Out! Free to wander hill and glen and be safe as if our own kin patroled the fence. We recovered joy quickly, regrouped, flowed away. Sometimes loners drifted off slightly disoriented, as if seeking direction—then drifted back again. We were children at play. We were also children who, like the "earthquake goldfish" of Japan, responded to the first harmonic tremors of an upheaval we felt but could not name—the Atomic Age. We were going to need all the lessons of our childhood, especially, "Keep your eyes on the mark ... don't look down ... steady as you go. ..."

I did walk the log, in the fullness of my own time. Weeks after the great tree fell and I'd become well acquainted with it, I gripped the bark with my feet, took my mark, lifted my arms, and walked the log ... alone.

As my life turned toward my fourteenth year—and puberty—I spent hours by myself, roaming the woods, listening. By that time the branches of the tree had moldered, the crater silted in, the trunk settled lower in the hollow. Washed clean, dried and tough, the roots were my favorite part of the tree, the comforting part. I felt the wind of change rising in my own body and in Oak Ridge. It was 1950. The fence was down. Long-time neighbors were moving away, some to different towns, some to different parts of town; new families were moving in. Technology was gaining power. The era of the atomic frontier and of my childhood was drawing to a close. Although the change seemed good, somewhere deep in my mind I was anxious, sensing perhaps that one day the wind would reach gale force and threaten to topple me by loosening my roots. One thing would save me. The great taproot of my Cherokee/Appalachian heritage would hold fast.

We women have a lot of unlearning to do ...

"We women have a lot of unlearning to do. ..." Chief Mankiller's words set me to thinking about my own season of unlearning. The season of gale-force winds that had led to it was still too painful to contemplate publically in speech or print. But I was able to recall in a positive way the fall day of 1969, when I first realized where I was out of kilter and began to unweave my life to where the error was made.

WRITING LESSON FROM THE IVY

Television, the National Storyteller, brought the Famous Poet into my living room. "Women cannot write," he said. "They are not biologically suited for it. They bear children. They can't think in the abstract. And they can't maintain the discipline to write, as a serious writer must. I myself work eight to five every day," he said, without a glance at his wife and butler in the background. And he pulled his brocaded vest down emphatically by the lower tips.

Why did I even listen to him? Because I was used to such talk. For years my formal education and society had given me the same message. And because I was "great with child"—my third. No one has ever surpassed this phrase of Luke, the poet-physician; "pregnant" doesn't approach its precision. I trudged to the back stoop and sat on the top step, resting my feet on the ground and my head on my stomach. The baby moved against my cheek. A baby is not an abstraction.

I knew the Famous Poet was wrong. Everything he said was wrong. But I was too tired to argue, even in my mind. From the corners of my eyes I watched my two daughters, Aleex and Drey, romping with the corgis. Small tennis-shoed feet and short white paws running back and forth. Laughter, barks.

As for my writing, I'd published many articles in poetry journals, trade magazines and church publications. Most of them had been commissioned. But I'd never been able to write my heart, my deepest thoughts. I didn't know how to begin to do it. How to find a publisher. How to find readers who were interested. How to find the time to do any of it. From every point of view, I was out of balance.

Slowly my eyes focused on something beyond the romping feet—English ivy on a moldering sixteen-foot brick wall. Months earlier the ivy had been at the bottom. Now it was at the top. How had that happened without my noticing it? I raised my head, contemplated the dark, shiny leaves. Millimeter by millimeter—that's how the ivy had reached the top of the wall. Sturdy and tenacious, it grew where it had opportunity. It did not worry about the how's. It just advanced one tiny clasper root at a time.

I resolved to do the same. And my mind went back to my own roots. When I was young and said, "I want to be a poet when I grow up," my mother had always replied, "That's good. And what will you do for the people?" That was the direction I wanted to go—create poems and stories and essays that would be comely and useful for people, like baskets or patchwork quilts. To make such things, both Cherokee and Appalachians have traditionally used the materials at hand. I would do that, too. Write about what I knew and develop my own model for doing it. In the context of the 1990s, when many women do this, it doesn't sound especially difficult. But this was the 1960s in the Deep South, four hundred miles from my home ground. I'd chosen a lonesome road.

After Andrew was born and well on his way, I began unlearning. The Famous Poet's tradition and work mode were appropriate for him. He had the support of Western literary tradition, of male entitlement to function in the public sphere, and of society's approval. What he did not have was the authority to impose his values on me.

I needed the Grandmothers, the traditions and work modes that were appropriate for me. My first movement in the quest for a path was to reach out and touch my great-grandmother's hand, the strong woman in the mountains of Kentucky. Her son became my grandfather, the one who first told me the story of Selu.

Coal Field Farewell
Great-Grandmother's Song

"Mama, I'm goin' now … to church."
His quiet words trailed smoke-like
and curled around her at the stove.
She watched the heating skillet—
black as the mine's mouth, black as
her man's face when they'd brought him up,
black as a rotten lung.

The silent ritual had begun and her
son stood by the door—skin so firm,
hair with raven's sheen; tall he was and lean.
She'd told him before, "A man earns his own way."
And now the day was here—he was fifteen.
She remembered him at four saying,
"If I was bacon in a pan, what would you do?"
"Why, son, I'd tend you careful-like
and lift you out. I'd lift you out for sure."

"… to church," he said and knew she'd seen
the suitcase cached among green laurel.
"Mama …?" Their eyes met.
"Go along now," she said. And then
his step was on the path. Too tired for tears—
with ten children more to rear—she laid a strip of bacon
in the pan, watching it careful-like
and listening to the deepest hollow of her heart.

With this poem, my spirit attached its first tiny clasper root to my birthright, as a woman and as a poet. Millimeter by millimeter, I unlearned inappropriate modes of thought and relearned the ones my parents had taught me. Formal education had given me some excellent tools, but heritage told me what to do with them. I listened to the "deepest hollow of my heart"—my Cherokee/Appalachian taproot. Celtic ancestors in my family had also loved the land deeply, called Earth "Mother," practiced the law of respect—and upheld the maxim of "mountainers are always free." First loyalty is to ties of blood—family. Through the centuries, this powerful mutual bond between the two peoples had undoubtedly nourished relationships of friends, lovers and families. And it would nourish me.

Since I was sixteen and read *Marie Curie,* she had been my ideal. She cooked roast on the stove and radium in the yard—food for the family and food for the people, through science.

But neither education nor contemporary society had given me a model for combining family and writing in a holistic way, so I followed an old Appalachian maxim: Do for yourself or do without. Discarding the "boxed" Western pattern exemplified by the Famous Poet, I developed my own. The first stage in the process took seven years. A basket was the model. (And I was too busy to notice that on a deeper level the crosswind from childhood, after a season's lull, was beginning to pick up and put a strain on my roots.)

The four "ribs" of my being have always been family / spiritual faith / writing / community. I fixed them in my mind like this

and began trying to weave my life and work among them. Needless to say, the basket was often out of kilter, out of balance, and I had to unweave to the place I'd gone wrong and begin again.

Although Selu and her story were still dormant in my subconscious, her practical philosophy had been part of my upbringing: Confronted with a dilemma, use your common sense and get the job done. (Selu's injunctions to her grandsons about how to plant and harvest corn are very down to earth and explicit.) These are some of the ways I thought out and put into practice.

Balancing a nine-to-five work discipline with the needs of a growing family was impossible. Instead, I organized a "weaving discipline." I set a perimeter of how much work (articles, poems, stories) I wanted to finish in about a four-month period. Then, I divided the work into types: notes, research, first draft, polishing, final manuscript. (Five or six pieces would be in process at the same time.) Then I adapted my daily writing in balance with the other ribs of my life. For example, for me, writing a first draft requires several uninterrupted hours. Sometimes I would get the children off to school, settle in to write the first draft of a story ... and the school secretary would call to say that one of the children was sick and needed to come home. Getting into my car, the child would invariably say, "Mama, I want my sick tent"—the code for being tucked in bed, given hot tea and hugs, stories and medicine, tending throughout the day. I would put the rough draft of the story aside and take up research on an article, which does not require sustained concentration. Gradually, my weaving rhythm and skill improved. I think most of what I learned about being a woman and a poet can be summed up in one poem.

On Being a Female Phoenix

Not only do I rise
from my own ashes,
I have to carry them out!

My basket was in a doublewoven pattern: the outer side was the writing; the inner side was my life with my husband and children. The two sides were becoming distinct but interconnected. My weaving was uneven and seriously flawed in a few places but coming along. And I was learning to maintain a "continual" mental discipline instead of a "segmented" one (nine to five).

Then I had a severe setback. No doubt the crosswind had been weakening my resistance and the Disdain Virus, which had been riding in my blood all along, jumped me and took me down. It did not abate until the day I sat quietly at my desk and wrote "An Indian Walks in Me." It's mysterious—when one's energy begins to center, things happen. Phyllis

Tickle, of St. Luke's Press, called. "Do you have a manuscript in progress?" she asked. "No, but I have a poem."

Later, we talked. She read the poem. "What would you like to write a book about?" "About how the Cherokee, Appalachia and the atom are interconnected." "That's the craziest thing I've ever heard! They're not at all connected." "They are," I said. And she said, "We want the book." That was the beginning of *Abiding Appalachia: Where Mountain and Atom Meet.*

As a new season of my life began, I realized I needed more "injunctions" from the Grandmothers, more explicit instructions. And in the next year, I found both in an unexpected way.

LIVING IN THE ROUND

What Maria's Bowl Teaches Me ...

"Clay remembers. ... "

Barbara, Maria's great-granddaughter and heir, says this. "Clay is like dough. It is special. It has character. If you don't knead it properly, it may not rise." She laughs. "Likewise, your masterpiece could explode in many pieces in the firing. We learn that a pot doesn't forget where it was ignored. It is pretty much the same with people." She doesn't add, "Clay remembers where it was loved." Maria's bowl speaks for itself ...

> in perfect roundness
> in texture smooth as baby-skin
> in black carefully tended to bear
> the warmth and not the scars of fire.
> Clay remembers ...

I first saw Maria's bowl in 1978, in a photograph. The accompanying text gave facts about the potter: "Maria Martinez / Tewa Indian of San

Ildefonso pueblo, New Mexico / born in 1880s / with husband Julian recreated ancient black pottery / developed striking innovations / is one of the greatest potters of this century / a legend in her lifetime."

The bowl spoke more than facts: to create so truly in the round, Maria must *live* in the round. I was certain of it. And I needed to know *how* she lived. I'd just written my credo as woman/poet "to seek the whole in strength and peace," to live and work in the round. Yet, I was hemmed in by the dominant culture, which insists that everything be squared, boxed, separated. A culture that says, "Art is for Art's sake" (the artist's life is irrevelant); "The true artist lives for Art alone" (relationships are irrelevant); "Form is superior to content" (substance is irrelevant); "Education is learning *about* life" (participation *in* life is irrelevant). How long before life itself becomes irrelevant?

I reached for Maria's bowl, for an artistic and aesthetic tradition that stretches back thousands of years, a tradition in which the potters have been women. They have passed the secrets of how to mold pots by hand (not by wheel) from mother to daughter or to some other female relative. They have also passed wisdom:

> "Clay is like dough is like people."
> —Art / daily life / relationships are one.
> Clay remembers ...

The Cherokee in me remembered, too, for like the Tewa, my mother had always taught, "All paths of life join." But I was isolated in the "square" urban environment of Memphis. As I tried "to seek the whole," I needed the reinforcement of a woman artist working in the same tradition. Rather than go in search of Maria, I centered the image of her bowl in my spirit and waited ...

Gradually, word of her flowed in. From friends. From my husband, Paul, who saw her bowl in Albuquerque. "I wanted to bring it to you, Awiakta, but it cost five thousand dollars!" We laughed. "Show me what it looks like," I said. He cupped his hands, and I felt the space, imagining. ... By and by, the Virginia poet Parks Lanier sent a pamphlet about Maria and the ISBN number of a book, which Paul later gave me for my birthday, Susan

Peterson's *The Living Tradition of Maria Martinez.*[22] At last! I savored it. Absorbed words, pictures, rhythms. Maria and Barbara became as real to me as if they lived next door.

One day I shared the book with my long-time friend, Sonia. Her heritage is African-American, and she continually balances family with her work as a television executive. Like me, she has three children. Sonia is tall and honest and zesty. I knew she'd appreciate Maria.

With the book between us, we sat on my living room sofa, studying the first set of color pictures. We touched Maria's hands as they worked the wet clay, traced the seams of her face—a joyful countenance, strong and humorous.

"Wouldn't you love to have a face like that some day, Awiakta?"

"I sure would. It takes lots of living and lots of spunk to earn that kind of face."

"Don't you know! With her big family ..."

"... everything's happened that could happen."

"And more besides!"

We laughed, thinking and talking, as usual, in tandem. In most of the photographs, there is someone with Maria—husband, sister, son, grandchild. So many to care for. "Imagine all the work!" I said.

"Just keeping body and soul together would take most of your time."

"We know how that goes ... !"

We followed Maria through some of her daily rounds: baking bread for ceremonials; making pottery at home with her great-granddaughters; boiling wild spinach for the black dye (the family dinner was probably simmering on another burner of the same stove). We saw her small great-grandson applying a slip to the pot, her son Adam and his wife Santana digging clay. At the firing of the pots, we counted four relatives helping. "That's part of her secret," Sonia said. "Keep everybody doing everything."

"It takes so much energy to do that. Mine gives out sometimes."

"Mine, too. ... Amazing, how many thousands of pots they must have made!"

"They've had to sell most of them. The first ones went for $1 or $1.75 each. By 1947, they were getting about $20 each."

"What percentage of the collector prices do they get now?"

"Evidently not much."

"The same old story ..."

"The same," I said. "I don't see how they've kept going all these years."

When we came to photographs of the finished pots, we were silent. The light of the fire was in them. They were beautiful. Perfect. Alive.

After a time, Sonia said quietly, "I have one of Maria's bowls. I got it in Albuquerque years ago before she was famous. My family thought I was crazy to pay $50 for it, but I said, 'Listen, I don't know anything about the potter, but that bowl speaks to me ...'"

I nodded, remembering ... "I'd love to hold it. I know your schedule's hectic ..."

"We'll make space, Awiakta, we'll make it."

And we did. A long, flowing afternoon in Sonia's living room, where the colors evoke my native Smoky Mountains in autumn—bronze-gold, bittersweet, crimson. On the coffee table, in a place of honor, was Maria's bowl. We sat in a circle around the table—Sonia and her son Aaron, my son Andrew and I. Both in their mid-teens, the boys shared a love of music (Aaron for percussion, Andrew for piano) and a quality of spirit that drew them to contemplate Maria and her art. We talked, gradually quieted our thoughts. When Andrew played Bach's *Two-Part Invention in D Minor* on the piano, we followed the steady, circular, soothing rhythm to its final harmony. Silence.

I hold Maria's bowl. For me this time is always in the present. Smooth, luminous black, the bowl just fits the cup of my hands. Its voice is the voice of Maria, teaching me ...

"I kept taking care of many—my mother, my sister ..."—also husband, children, grandchildren, great-grandchildren, friends.

"... kept taking care of the pots, choosing the best clay, the best dye, the best ash for firing.

"... kept taking care of bread and house and ceremonials.

"... kept taking care to work in harmony with the clay, to coil and shape it into thin, balanced forms.

"... kept taking care that the family shared in everything, each according to his or her own way."

Art and Life, coil on coil. Blend the seams, apply the dye, fire the whole to bear the warmth and not the scars. ... The rhythmic spiral of the round. I understand. But it's difficult for me to do. So much explodes ...

My hands tighten on the bowl, then relax in its incredible smoothness. "I never saw anybody polish clay the way we do," Maria says. "We get better and better! Ours is so smooth ... it is our long, hard polish—we work very hard—that makes ours so pretty." I hear the sound of a round rock touching a pot's rough surface on only one point, burnishing slowly. Patience. I must learn more patience.

I touch the mat design around the top of the bowl and turn to the signature on the bottom: "Maria/Santana." Barbara's grandmother has done the design. Maria always includes the designer. (In earlier times, it was often Julian or their son, Popovi Da, both now deceased.) She also shares her knowledge with her family and with other potters of her pueblo, so that all can profit. She never takes without giving, this one they call *Kea-e-Kque-yo*, Lady of the Hill. Yet, although she sometimes goes to the outside world to share her talent, there is a large measure of seclusion in Maria's life that protects her core. She is wise.

I raise the mouth of the bowl to my nose. Inside, the unburnished clay smells faintly of our Mother Earth. It is then I feel an almost imperceptible dent in the outside of the bowl—a small flaw left on purpose to show that humans are not perfect. I call it "the chuckle." Mark Twain said, "Humor is the saving grace." Maria has it in abundance. So does Barbara. Sometimes, in spite of all you do, things go awry—pots explode, dough falls, relationships rupture. But we can begin again. That is the great thing, *to keep taking care* ...

I claim this round tradition: True art creates harmony and healing. Its substance *is* its form.

"When I first started potting again," Barbara says, "I asked Maria to make us a large piece because we didn't have any. This is what my great-grandmother told me then, 'When I am gone, essentially other people have my pots. But to you I leave my greatest achievement, which is the ability to do it. It is not weighing material values that is important.'"

All I will ever have of Maria's work is the image of her bowl. I carry it in my spirit. Clay remembers. Like dough. Like people. Like poetry.

What destiny is biology?

"Biology is destiny." I realized that the problem lies in the predicate nominative—not in the verb. Never again would I enter a debate, even in my mind, without first assessing the definition of terms. The Famous Poet's concept of female "destiny" and mine were at opposite poles. Having Maria's bowl in my mind and spirit as a paradigm made me more adept at interweaving family and work. When the children were young, Paul had told them, "Your mother is a writer. I'll do my part; you have to do yours" (which then included helping with chores and being quiet at times when I needed it). When they were older, Aleex, Drey and Andrew helped with the writing, too—assembling paper and carbons, proofreading. The whole family went with me when I did readings or other public events. At home the children also patiently listened to poems and essays in progress. They were honest in their criticism, the most candid being, "Mother, that doesn't make sense." During those years, on the rare occasions when I went out of town, part or all of the family was with me. And I had major responsibilities for them, chiefly cooking and "taking care."

This is one reason that I connect so strongly with Selu now. In every story, the First Woman is cooking and taking care of her family. When she needs to do her private work, she goes into the smokehouse and shuts the door. Her example is strengthening to me. Unlike Eve's. I don't relate to that First Woman. Instead of taking care of Adam and the boys, doing her own work in "a room of her own" and helping her people, she hung out with the serpent. Or so the story is told. Maybe if Eve had cooked the apple before she gave it to Adam, the battle of the sexes would never have begun. Western history might have taken a different course.

During my struggles to bring my life into balance, Selu's story remained dormant in my mind. What I needed was a Native teacher. A person from a matrilineal culture who was trained in both traditional and Western thought and who would understand the kind of balanced weaving I was trying to create. Ideally, this teacher would be a poet and storyteller who was also balancing art and family. I didn't know where or how to find such a person. Since it wasn't yet the season of my life for journeying, I kept close to home and, remembering the lesson of the ivy, worked on the tasks at hand. For some reason, I was sure that in the fullness of time, the appropriate teacher would cross my path.

In 1982, an Abenaki poet and storyteller from New York State came to Memphis. After listening to his reading and talking with him, I knew he was the teacher I'd been expecting. His name was Joseph Bruchac. Along with about twenty other writers, I studied at his week-long poetry workshop. For years I had been struggling to clear a path through the morass, and he showed me a trail that was clearly marked. In a language and a worldview that were familiar, he explained Native writing in terms of the past, the present and the future. I could see that my path would be arduous, but I felt inspired to attempt it. I was forty-two. My formal education should have provided this study opportunity, but I was thankful to have it at last—thanks to a generous teacher. I resolved that in the future I would do all I could to see that all children have an opportunity to see their cultures and themselves in their educations.

HONOR TO THE FOUNDING ELDERS OF OAK RIDGE

In Celebration of "Tennessee Homecoming '86"

> *I spend a lot of time with the elders. They've lived long enough to move beyond the ego to the calm. I need their counsel.*
> —Chief Wilma Mankiller
> Descendant of Outacite (Ostenaco),
> "Mankiller of Great Tellico (Tennessee)"

Chief Mankiller's words make me think of you—the Founding Elders, my parents and their contemporaries. Because of you there's an Oak Ridge to come home to. Thank you for homemaking—and for what you continue to do, homekeeping.

I remember you in the frontier days when we all came to Oak Ridge— in the 1940s and early 1950s, the time of my childhood and youth. Most of you were in your thirties then. Although atomic energy was the keystone of our community, even the word *atom* was new to the public mind. Looking at Oak Ridge from the outside, many people considered it a dangerous, futuristic place, as remote and alien as a space colony floating in the blue-hazed billows of the mountains. To us it was home. While we children played, you worked. Worked hard, creating the root system for dwelling, school and church, for laboratory, society and city government. And all of it "from scratch."

I don't see how you did it, especially now that I'm doing the same kind of work. I didn't have to start from scratch. When I married and moved to Memphis in 1957, the city was flourishing like the green bay tree, its "rooting" six generations in the past. However, in researching my second book, *Rising Fawn and the Fire Mystery*, I went back to 1833, when Memphis was a pioneer town, a gateway to the West—to the future—as Oak Ridge was a gateway to the Atomic Age in the forties and fifties. I discovered that whether it has a population of one thousand or seventy-five thousand, a frontier in any century is a raw place—a hurly-burly, physically primitive, dangerous, invigorating, lonely, freewheeling, "do-for-yourself-or-do-with-out" place. For a family to survive, the parents and other elders must have courage, stamina, shrewdness, faith—and an earthy sense of humor. When I tell you what I saw in Memphis in 1833, you'll know why I often smiled and thought of you and our early days together:

• Dirt streets—mud if it rained—and holes in them big enough to drown an ox (or swamp a car).

• Small, look-alike houses, mostly of logs.

• A few stores, a hotel: rough-hewn, square or shoe-box shaped, strictly utilitarian. Overall, a drab-looking place, except for close-drawn woods and the Mississippi River.

We had woods and the Great Smokies, but structurally Oak Ridge was drab too, with its ash-gray houses and barrack-style public buildings that were painted such a boring green color that we all made fun of them.

Federal ownership. A big difference from privately owned Memphis. Humor in both places, but in Oak Ridge, government bureaucracy was a major target. You made jokes like these:

"How many men does it take to pick up the garbage?"

"Ten. Two to take the top off the can. Two to carry the can to the truck. Two to dump it. Two to carry it back. Two to put the top back on!"

"How long did they take to paint the inside of our house?"

"Long enough to raise a litter of pups. First the 'ceiling crew' came. Two weeks later the 'wall crew' came with flat paint. Two weeks after that the 'spotters' came to touch up the walls—with enamel!"

"Wait a minute. That's only four weeks. Takes six for pups."

"Well, it took me two weeks to get used to the shiny spots!"

"The red tape around here is so bad that if you want to make a baby, you have to fill out a form—*in triplicate!*"

"Humor is the saving grace," Mark Twain said. And you had it in abundance. In the midst of hardships, you created fun (as your Memphis counterparts did) with laughter, dancing, plays, picnics, parties, music, clubs, and visiting with relatives and friends. By example, you taught us children not only the value of work, but also of the "saving grace" so necessary for perspective—for survival.

You were good horse traders, too. And Tennesseans have always admired the ability to cut a shrewd, fair deal. The government needed you for the Manhattan Project and you laid the terms on the line—among them, the best teachers for your children. And we got the best. Never mind that the buildings were rough in the beginning, the education going on inside was second to none. And you supported the work as parents, teachers, counselors and interested citizens. Also, federal ownership was an advantage for education—money poured in; whereas in Memphis, the pioneers had to begin with a privately funded class (for boys only) in a house and build from there. On that frontier I would have grown up illiterate.

Pioneer churches were freewheeling, building-wise; people had to use available structures, which led to some funny situations. For example, Memphis Methodists, whose favorite axiom was "Whiskey leads to dancing," had to meet for a while in the Blue Ruin Saloon, so-named because its gin gave regular customers a blue tinge to their skin. In Oak Ridge, after an ecumenical period of taking turns using the Chapel-on-the-Hill, religious groups found other quarters. We Methodists went to Sunday school in the high school above Jackson Square, then hurried down the hill to the Ridge Theatre for church, where it was dim and cool and the seats were soft. This state of affairs shocked some "hard-pew" advocates, one of whom I quoted to my father:

It's a Sin and a Shame

"It's a sin and a shame,"
said Miss Mabel Travain,
"these children are churched in a movie.
With those billboards they'll sink
and grow up to think
that God looks like Clark Gable!"

Daddy laughed when he heard,
"Why, the woman's absurd ...
You can think better than that.
How much worse it would be
if you grew up to see
that God looks like Miss Mabel!"

As you did elsewhere, you elders "Kept your eye on the mark ... steady as you go." From watching you, we learned to walk in balance, which included the ability to cope with the swarm of different people.

Memphis had "the swarm" on a small scale—less than one thousand residents—but a constant flux of people with different origins: Native American, European and African-American. They came to trade, unload cargo, settle or head west. (Some also came to raise Cain.) Since material resources were few, inner resources had to be many.

Oak Ridge had a *big* swarm—people from all over the United States came to settle among Appalachian families, like mine, that had lived in the area for generations. Oak Ridgers had a common purpose—to work on nuclear energy. And fortunately, government security kept many of the worst "Cain-raisers" at bay. But the fission of the atom in the laboratories was mirrored in the community. There was high energy and high confusion. Life had to be sorted into an orderly pattern. It was up to the elders to create the pattern.

One of the best parts of it was that everyone had a smilar lifestyle, regardless of occupation. Our neighborhood on South Tampa Lane was typical: families were involved in science, construction, city government, cafeteria management, the ministry, teaching, accounting. A business entrepreneur lived in a D-house next to a grocer who had converted a school bus into a "rolling store." When it wasn't en route, the bus was parked in front of the family's flattop house. Needless to say, the rolling-store kids were the most popular on the block.

Neighbors worked and played together—kept each other company. In hot weather everyone was outside a lot, for we depended on mountain air-conditioning. In cold weather, tending the fire was a constant family chore, just as it had been for Memphis pioneers. While their major heat came from a fireplace, ours came from a coal furnace. Remember how the coal was dumped in a closed bin near the furnace, just inside the house's back door—which faced the street (always confusing to non-Ridgers)? Almost everyone came in through the back door and tracked coal dust through the kitchen into the living room. Fire was a *presence*. It had to be fed regularly in daytime, banked at night, stirred up in the morning. Parents taught children its ways, and every family member old enough to be responsible took a turn firing the furnace, as we took turns with other chores.

Our pioneer life was a hands-on, communal experience that included the joy of just being alive. After years of fear and horror, World War II was over. The dark clouds had rolled back, the breeze was tonic-fresh, the sun full on our faces. For a season we rejoiced and were glad.

Then the wind changed. As it seems to do on every generation's frontier.

In Memphis, the change came in the late 1830s, when the federal government shoved the natives (Chickasaw Indians) out west to make way for Big Power, Big Money—the cotton industry. The city grew past its sapling stage and branched into "good" (wealthy) and "bad" (low-income) neighbor-hoods, into divisions of class and race, into the "we's," who had power and money, and the "they's," who didn't. Some elders thrust to one side or the other. But as Memphis leaned in the wind, the wisest elders found their counterparts among the newcomers and began shoring up the roots of the community in every sector. Only a few elders, however, recognized and warned against the deadly borer making its way toward the city's heart—slavery. It caused damage that Memphis leaders of today are still working to heal.

The primary segregation in Oak Ridge was of a different kind—what we had was a season of high and bitter crosswinds, when the city swayed with change. It corresponded approximately to my youth, 1950–60. When the fence came down in 1949 and real estate gradually transferred to private hands, the city began to take on color—literally, in paint and construction, and figuratively, in business and political patterns. Slowly, the population stratified, neighborhoods changed. Private wealth was not the catalyst. Science was. Federally, and therefore locally, the push was for scientific research, education and development. As one high school student put it, "Science is *it* in Oak Ridge." The change in the wind was good in many ways, but there were drawbacks.

Some elders noted the change away from an egalitarian climate by saying, "It was more fun in the old days when we were all in the same boat." Children younger than I complained that they had lost their "roaming grounds." Property lines often extended into the woods, which were formerly communal areas; some people put up fences. It was becoming difficult to play in the hollows and hills without trespassing.

As a teenager I felt a bitter edge to the crosswinds, a bitterness that through strands of family, education, business and politics webbed out from Oak Ridge to the surrounding area. One wind came from the direction of "outsiders" (mostly scientists) and the other from "natives" (mostly nonscientists). They sounded like this:

Outsiders: "We've done everything for these people and they're still backward."

"They're so uneducated they don't even know what the word 'science' means."

"They don't articulate properly."

"They don't have any 'culture.' Just listen to that Grand Ole Opry stuff they call music."

"As for the University of Tennessee, who ever heard of it?"

"Bunch of fundamentalists."

Natives: "They're looking down on us, but we're not looking up to them—and it gets their goat."

"You have to have three degrees to get them to sit down, much less listen."

"They're all book learning and no sense. Show them a rock slide coming down the mountain, and they'll show you a map that says there's no rock there."

"They come in telling us who we are and what to do like the world began with them. But I'm here to say different."

"They talk about our university like it was nothing."

"Bunch of atheists."

Extremes from both sides. Not from everyone, certainly, but from enough to create the kind of root-loosening crosswinds that no tree, no community and no individual can long withstand without severe damage. Someone had to shore up the roots while the wind blew its course.

The wisest of you Founding Elders did just that. You had already begun a network of cooperation between outsiders and natives, between the laboratories and the University of Tennessee and between neighbors. You strengthened those ties by years of patient work—by homekeeping. You explained to the young that not all people in any group are alike, or as one native put it, "One braying jackass don't make the herd." You said that in time the season could change for the better. And today in Oak Ridge, who could deny that you were right. At least on the surface, many institutions reflect mutual cooperation and understanding, among them the Museum of Science and Energy, the Children's Museum and its Regional Appalachian Center, Oak Ridge Associated Universities and various service groups. I have no way of knowing about that vast labyrinth beneath the surface, where politics, history, religion and human relations intertwine and where traumas from seasons past reverberate for generations.

I only know that for me the damage took twenty years to heal. In the "time of bitter crosswinds," I was a sapling. Unlike the elders, I didn't have the girth and tough bark, the far-flung roots and spreading branches to hold me to balance. All I had was my long, tenacious taproot of highlander heritage that my parents kept packed tight in the earth of my homeland.

My shorter roots were tearing loose. I swayed one way, deeply angry at the disdain poured on my people and our culture. Then I swayed to the other, defensive of friends and elders—so called "outsiders"—who were not as some natives described them. Adding to the degree of sway was the fact that I was born in Knoxville and living in Oak Ridge, a child of the mountain growing up with the atom. Could such opposties ever meet in peace?

Exacerbating the conflict of loyalties was a conflict of worldview and communication. Appalachians and Cherokees—my relatives—are symbolic peoples. We view the world in cosmic connection, where the tangible is a reflection of the intangible, of the spirit. We speak of this connection in images. Science, on the other hand, is based on facts that can be demonstrated and proven. It tends to create an objective mindset, which speaks literally and views imagistic thought as subjective, primitive, unreal and romantic. What I was experiencing was the basic conflict between the intuitive and the analytical mind, but at the age of sixteen I had neither the knowledge nor the power to define it as such. I only knew it was painful—a stone blocking my way, for the path I had chosen was poetry.

I asked advice from Papa, my maternal grandfather. A Methodist minister with a live-and-let-live philosophy, he was six feet tall and square-handed. Earlier in his life he had mined coal, then taught Greek and Roman history at Hiwassee College to pay for his education there. He listened sympathetically as I described the bitter crosswinds. "The government and some outsiders make the natives feel shoved out," I said. "And they *literally* shoved out the old pioneer families in Wheat, Scarboro, Robertsville and Elza to make room for Oak Ridge. Some of the tombstones in the Wheat cemetery go back to the 1790s."

"And back then," Papa said, "the settlers were the 'outsiders.' This was Cherokee country ... had been for hundreds of years. Chota was their capital, over at Tellico. The settlers called the Indians 'uncivilized' and 'heathen.' The government made them walk the Trail of Tears to Oklahoma. But the Cherokee knew a secret. The settlers had to learn it. And these new folks in Oak Ridge will too, if they want to last. *The mountains have been here a long time.*"

I took his meaning. "People come and go ... seasons come and go. Mother Earth abides and heals. Hold on ... work patiently ... wait ..."

But I wanted action. I wanted the stone out of my way. "In that case," Papa said, "you'd better be like water. Flow around it. Or vapor yourself and rain down in another place."

Which place? The French teacher at Oak Ridge High School, Margaret Zimmerman, suggested the answer, for she gave me a vision of the land of Pascal, where "the heart has its reasons that the reason knows not of." A land linked to Appalachia through Huguenot immigrants who intermarried with the Scotch-Irish and Cherokee. Historically, the French, Scots, and Native Americans have been drawn to each other by their similarities: devotion to family, a cosmic connection to the world, imagistic language, fierce independence—and a humorous pragmatism based on the "long view" of events. A fusion of these genes runs high in my blood, and when Margaret Zimmerman said, "the heart has its reasons ...," every cell in my body demanded, "Go to France!"

From that moment I was outward bound, driven by the need to find an equilibrium between heart and mind, mountain and atom, art and science— and a language to express the balance. Eleven years later, in May 1964, I stopped in Oak Ridge to take my final bearings for France. Dr. Margaret Mead, the distinguished anthropologist, was also in town to give her critique of the community. I heard her describe the need for balance in Oak Ridge in much the same terms as I defined my own.

But what I felt as "bitter crosswinds," she called "a vast gap between intellectual scientist and uneducated native ... eggheads and fundamentalists ... those highly educated for the modern world and those culturally deprived." She said, "You [scientists] are 'missionaries to the natives.'" Never once did she suggest that natives might have valuable knowledge to exchange, although with her on the stage was one of our wisest elders, Dr. William G. Pollard—physicist, Episcopal priest, director of the Oak Ridge Institute of Nuclear Studies—a man reared in Knoxville. Beside him, representing the wisdom of non-natives, was Alvin M. Weinberg, humanitarian, director of the Oak Ridge National Laboratory. Dr. Pollard's face was calm, unperturbed. Maybe he would tell her, "Margaret, the mountains have been here a long time."

I couldn't. I had to pack. I was traveling with our two daughters, who were under five years old. Paul had gone ahead to his duty station at Laon Air Force Base, which was in the middle of sugar beet fields ninety miles northeast of Paris. The only housing available for us there was a small government trailer with a lean-to built on it. And I would be flying the

Atlantic alone with the children, not in a luxury jet, but on a government transport. It all sounded like another frontier to me. But now I was responsible for the homemaking and homekeeping. It was heartening to find my parents and other elders spinning the web of life as you always have— with courage, stamina, shrewdness, faith and humor. Unchanged also were the mountains, the Ancients who, from generation to generation, teach the art of survival to those who will listen.

I carried my strand of the web to France, where thanks to you elders and the knowledge coded in my genes, I remembered how to spin my part of the pattern. I discovered that stone and water are one of Nature's most beautiful combinations. By its weight and mass, the stone alters the course of the water. And water, with its patient flow, changes the shape of the stone. Together, they sing magnificently. As Science and Art once used to do. I also experienced being the "outsider" and came to bless the "bitter crosswinds" for all they had taught me about human relations. Most important, I finally understood and could say to myself, "I am a Cherokee/Appalachian poet. To find the 'eye of my work'—the center—I have to come home."

You elders were there to meet me, in the summer of 1977, sharing your wise counsel and support as I began to write *Abiding Appalachia*. Because you had been honest with me as a child—telling me exactly what the atom can do to help or to harm and what our responsibility is for its use—I found the point where mountain and atom meet.

Now it is 1986. I've just returned from the Cherokee National Holiday in Tahlequah, Oklahoma, where the mountains are so much like ours in East Tennessee. Seven generations after the Trail of Tears, as elders at that time foretold, the Cherokee are strong again—sixty-five thousand in the West and eight thousand in the East. Twenty-two thousand relatives and friends came to Tahlequah for the Holiday, which had the theme, "Honoring the Cherokee Family."

At the powwow, held on the athletic field of Sequoyah High School, Chief Wilma Mankiller called for a dance to honor a distinguished elder of the nation, saying, "Without his counsel through the years I would never have become chief." Paul and I joined the throng of people circling the slow, steady beat of the drum in rhythm with an ancient song. Children mingled with elders, matching their steps to the pattern. I thought how mysterious the web of life is, how real the strands that connect us all. No matter how wide the web spins, circling round and round are children and elders of the present, of pioneer times, of centuries when none but native people lived on the land. I danced in honor of them all.

But especially, I danced for you.

SECTION IV

Our Courage Is Our Memory

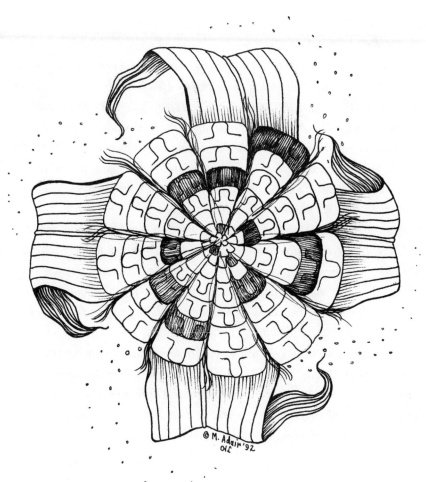

IN THE BELLY OF THE STORY IS LIFE FOR THE PEOPLE

Story as Knowledge

(Note: This essay was adapted from a presentation given at Tufts University Conference: "A New Model for American Studies: Using Black, Ethnic, and Feminist Perspectives to Integrate the Sciences and Humanities," June 1988.)

You asked me to say a few words first about myself ...

In the mountains of East Tennessee, where I come from, stories and the oral tradition are a way of life. Whatever one's individual heritage—Cherokee, Celtic, African, or a combination of the three—we all live by stories. And not only those that humans tell. The Great Smokies and their foothills, themselves, are Story—older than the Rockies, older than the Andes. Veiled in blue haze, whose source remains a mystery, the mountains were never covered by the Ice Age. Their root system of plant and forest has been continuous for millions of years. Mountain people see this ancient web of life with our eyes. We feel it beneath our feet. We know we are part of the Story.

In the 1940s, we learned to perceive the web—and the Story—in a new way. Scientists brought the atom to our mountains—to split it and release a force older than the earth, older perhaps, than time itself. An atom has a photon, made of the same material as a star. So, in a sense, on the subatomic level, everything is composed of atoms—"minute millions," far-flung and bright.

Within the tangible, which manifests in such physical differences, a shining web of light unites the universe. For centuries the Native American has called it spirit. The scientist calls it energy. The major difference is that Native Americans consider the web sacred. But both they and the scientists agree that the web is real. Here, where mountain and atom meet, is the still center of my life and work, the place from which I speak to you.

A Native American Perspective

The circles of life are mysterious. In 1620, when the Pilgrims arrived in Plymouth, Massachusetts, American Indians met them and offered corn and stories. The Pilgrims took the corn. "In the belly of the story," the Indians said, "is life for the people, a way to live in harmony with this land." But the newcomers didn't want such stories. They had plans for the land—and for the Indians. Now, I have been invited to the vicinity of Plymouth to tell stories: I offer you each a corn seed—a grain of hope—that we can begin again ...

I am asked to speak as a working poet and storyteller on the topic "The Story As Knowledge." At first these two perspectives seem antithetical and impossible to reconcile. As the Native American culture values wisdom and experience, the dominant culture values knowledge and facts. For centuries this difference and related ones have been an unbridgeable chasm. ... And yet, "in the belly of the story"—in its essence—the word *knowledge* regains its verbal root, a root that encompasses wisdom, as in "Be still ... and know."

We'll create the experience of the Story together—you and I—using my poems, your story, and the Native stories, which are old and powerful, especially once a human voice sets them in motion. I speak to you directly, in the traditional way of the storyteller.

Like an individual, America can be whole only by going back to its roots—all of them. My premise is this: The Native American story—and the holistic mode of thought it embodies—springs from the original root in our homeland. The story is designed to move among the strands of life's web both within the individual and within the community, to restore balance and harmony. Its ancient ways offer a helpful pattern in making new connections among our different people and academic disciplines.

Instead of considering this premise by the Western method, which reasons from outside in, from a collection of facts to a conclusion, we will use the American Indian way. First we settle quietly into common ground. Then we go to the heart of the matter—the definition, or "being"—of the story. From there we spin strands of thought outward and in ever-widening circles to a parameter of understanding, where the story itself can be told. In short, we will follow the pattern of the Native American story and weave a web where we can be still and *know* that in the belly of the story is life for us all.

Common Ground

Think of a story that has helped shape your life. It may be from the classics, from your ethnic or religious background. Or it may be a family story passed from generation to generation. The important thing is that it must be one in whose essence—or belly—you have found meaning. Remember when you first heard the story and in what circumstances you later recalled it. I will not invade your privacy by asking you to tell it. I only ask you to ponder it.

Here is a story from my family. My mother told it to me often, beginning when I was about four years old and asked her, "What happened when you were born?"

"All five of us children were delivered at home," she said. "As each was born Papa would take the others to the woods with him for the ceremony of burying the afterbirth. And he'd say, 'We come from Mother Earth and we return to Mother Earth. We bury this part of the baby with her so that when he is old, he will know where to come home.' Then we'd all go back into the house to be with Mama and the new baby."

"When I was born did Daddy bury my afterbirth?"

"No. You were born in the hospital and they disposed of it."

"You mean they threw it in the garbage?!"

"Yes. Or burned it in the incinerator." Mother softened the blunt words with a hug. "But that doesn't change the truth of the story. We come from Mother Earth and when we are old, we return to Mother Earth."

"Then did Daddy and the rest of the family come to visit us in the hospital?"

"Why, of course they did …"

As I grew up, I asked to hear the good parts of the story over and over. And gradually they moved the insult to me and my afterbirth into the proper perspective of things that can't be helped and, therefore, should not be dwelled upon.

Years later I had my first child, Aleex, in the charity hospital in Memphis. The rule was that the mother touched her baby for the first time on the third day, when she took it home. The hospital's rationale was that this kept down infection in the nursery.

I sat on the bed in my room and looked through cracked venetian blinds at the concrete parking lot blaring in the June sun. Had I really had a baby? My breasts hurt with milk. Otherwise, for all I knew, I might have had a tumor taken out. I stared at the parking lot, feeling boxed-in, bereft. I couldn't find any strands of the web to connect me to being a mother.

Then my mother's birth story came back to me. "The truth doesn't change." Somewhere under the concrete was Mother Earth. Despite the weight of hospital rules, I *was* a mother. My heart eased. Finally, a nurse brought my baby, packaged in a blanket. With a curt, "Baby girl—Thompson" (my married name), she flipped her out nude on the bed. Gathering Aleex up, I bundled her in a white flannel kimono edged with tiny, green briar-stitches—a gift her maternal great-grandmother, Marilou, had made. My husband came and we went home to the family circle, where love began mending rents in our web of life, especially mine. I'd expected having a baby to be so different.

Later, when Aleex asked, "What happened when I was born?" I told her, weaving her birth into the story that began with my grandfather's ceremony. My daughter is grown now. If circumstances ever appear to have torn up part of her web, perhaps she will remember the story … and begin to weave again.

Whatever our ethnic backgrounds, we all have stories that work similarly in our lives. Beneath surface differences, our roots connect and make us part of all that has been in the past and all that will be in the future. We are not alone.

But what can we do to implement a change in American thinking? It is a crucial question. I sometimes think the first step should be that we stop talking and start dancing—dancing a traditional Native American ceremonial that evokes the Sacred Circle—the unity of the All-Mystery, nature and humanity. Although we can't do such a ceremonial dance here together, we can join in a poem that, on a much less profound level, evokes a similar feeling of continuance in the midst of change and of unity in diversity—primary dynamics of the universe.

The poem "Boardwalk" (from *Abiding Appalachia*) expresses the joy of playing on a boardwalk—and of the irrepressible life force in each of us. To feel that you have to become part of the poem. I'll give you the beat by alternately snapping my fingers (*) in allegro tempo, like this...

* * * * * * * *
"Boardwalk, boardwalk ... step, step, talk, talk ..."

Give the rhythm back to me and together we'll create the poem. One more thing, give all the variety you want in movement—cross your hands back and forth, move them up and down, or from side to side—any way at all so long as you *keep the beat.* After the second chorus of "Boardwalk, boardwalk ...," I'll stop, you say the next five lines, then together we'll say the last line, *"Won't do for me!"* As we say it, we'll make the gesture the baseball umpire uses for "safe." Let's try it once:

"Won't do for me!"

Please join in. This poem is an oral poem, no more than sheet music on paper. But put it into your voice ... ! You may be alone in your office ... or at home. No matter. And if anyone should peer at you to see what's going on, invite him or her to join you. Playing on the boardwalk is great stress relief.

Here we go ... snap (*), snap (*), * ... * ...

Boardwalk

Boardwalk ... boardwalk ...
Step, step ... talk ... talk ...
You echo every step I take
and tell me steps that others make.
Sometimes I do a little jump
and feel you give beneath my thump.
Or else I skip—ta-DON, ta-DON
and send you shaking farther on.
You're mighty onrey when you're wet
and throw me down—how mad I get
and stamp my foot against your planks
(you give me splinters for my pranks).
Dryin' out you smell so good
I like to lie against your wood
and wonder what you think of us
who tread with such a noisy fuss.

Boardwalk ... boardwalk ...
Step, step ... talk, talk ...

Concrete
won't talk to me
won't give to me
won't play with me
won't fight with me
won't do
for me.

Creating this poem together gives an inkling of how the ceremonial
dance makes mind/body/spirit flow as one. If we danced it together in the
stillness, we would *know* that we are one people, one universe. The web of
life *is* real, and its imprint is in the racial memory of us all.

"In the belly of the story is life ..."

... and death, if other people take your story and distort it for their own
purposes. The following poem is about one such distortion. It was told to me
by the Navajo woman who experienced it.

The Real Thing

For Bernice

"We're the most exclusive
Indian shop in New York City.
We only sell *the real thing*."
Coyote-smooth, the man
lured a covey of customers
to where he held up a weaving
three feet by two.
"This rug is genuine Navajo.
You know it by the tiny flaw
they always leave
to let the evil spirit out."

"Ah ..." sighed the covey
and leaned closer.

Behind them a buckshot laugh
exploded
   scattered thoughts
    turned heads
toward a black-haired
four-square woman.
"I am Navajo," she said.
"My family makes rugs.
When I was a child
I herded our sheep,
helped Mother clean the wool.
Grandma spun and wove it.
We don't leave a flaw
'to let the evil spirit out.'
We leave it to show
what's made by humans
can't be perfect.
Only the Great Spirit
makes perfect things."

The covey stared
  blank
    silent
then closed back
to their smooth comfort—
"As I was saying ...
This rug is genuine Navajo.
You know it by the tiny flaw
they always leave
to let the evil spirit out."

My friend laughed when she told me this story. I laughed too. "Evil spirit, indeed!" But the laughter was wry. Because the customers not only refused to see their mistake, they refused to see the Navajo woman—and her culture. This attitude of disrespect and disdain takes many forms; it sickens and kills the human spirit. The experience of this truth is perhaps our deepest common ground, the reason for our convening at this conference. I agree with Sylvia Wynter, who spoke earlier, *"that the core of Western thought must be changed; it must be inclusive of the values of the peoples who live within it. "*[23] If the core remains as it is—boxed, labeled and stacked in a pyramid—with dominance and control as its aim, the people will continue to get sick in their spirits. Many will die.

The Heart of the Matter

Through poetry, we make a quantum leap into the essence of the story, as defined by the storyteller in the opening pages of Leslie Silko's novel, *Ceremony*, in a poem of the same name.[24]

> I will tell you something about stories,
> [he said]
> They aren't just entertainment.
> Don't be fooled.
> They are all we have, you see,
> all we have to fight off
> illness and death.
>
> You don't have anything
> if you don't have the stories.
>
> Their evil is mighty
> but it can't stand up to our stories.
> So they try to destroy the stories
> let the stories be confused or forgotten.
> They would like that
> They would be happy
> Because we would be defenseless then.

He rubbed his belly.
I keep them here
[he said]
Here, put your hand on it
See, it is moving.
There is life here
for the people.

And in the belly of this story
the rituals and the ceremony
are still growing.

Even though we've settled into common ground, this definition of the story may still give the sensation of a web against your face, startling and vaguely disturbing. Startling because it is outside the Western literary tradition. Disturbing because you know the inhabitant who spun it is alive. For as the spider spins a web from its own being, so the story spins its essence into the lives of the people.

Is this pattern of creating really as foreign as it seems?

Science tells us that all nature is alive, sensate, that life begins in the invisible. Through the eyes of powerful machines, we see the story of the universe. The heart of matter resembles thought and is a mystery that no conceivable research is likely to dispel. From this source comes the primal "spinning" of quarks into particles, particles into atoms, and atoms into the tangible world … into things like the corn seed. The corn feels solid. Yet it is almost impossible to touch it without thinking, "In the belly of the seed is life. …" In the invisible, its atoms are moving, whirling. (Could they be dancing?!) Depending on how we *observe* the seed scientifically, it is matter or energy. But the truth is, it is both. And with elegant symmetry, the seed's sprouting and growth will repeat the primary process of nature.

So it is with the Native American story. And our perception of it depends on how we *experience* it. On the tangible level it is literature. But, "See, it is moving. … In the belly of the story the rituals and the ceremony are still growing." I received my grandfather's ceremony of burying the afterbirth as story. Later, in spite of the concrete rules of the hospital

("Concrete won't do for me"), the ceremony began to move in my spirit and thought: "We come from Mother Earth and we return to Mother Earth. The truth does not change." As my heart eased, I spun the ceremony into the events of my life. "I gathered up my baby and went home to the circle of the family, where love began mending rents in the web." When my daughter was old enough, I passed this experience to her as story … a seed for her to keep.

Has your story followed a similar creative process in your life? I use the word "process" because in our high-tech American culture, it is familiar. But it is also too detached to convey my meaning. I say instead, "How has your story moved in the ceremony of your life?" I don't expect a reply; your inner life is sacred space. And even if you invite me into it, the story you would tell is yours alone to interpret. Either way, there is a stillness between us—a thread of mutual respect that has the tensile strength of fused quartz, like the spider's silk.

We move along this strand into the heart of the Native American story. In substance, structure, form and function, it has the pattern of the web. This is true of traditional stories and of the best contemporary Indian novels, such as Leslie Silko's *Ceremony*. She weaves the basic elements so exquisitely fine that it is almost impossible to separate them entirely.

Not "plotted" in the Western sense, the story *revolves* around a happening in the life of Tayo, a young Laguna Pueblo man. In the Philippines during World War II, he and his comrades are ordered to execute Japanese prisoners. As the others fire, Tayo does not. His finger freezes on the trigger. One of the Japanese has become his Uncle Josiah! What does this mean? Stricken and feverish, Tayo looks into the face of the corpse and sees Josiah's eyes, "shrinking back into the skull and all their shining black light glazed over by death." Tayo starts screaming. …

His spirit strains against the vibrations. All but a few threads snap. The military hospital is no help. There Tayo is "white smoke" and "invisible." "In that hospital they don't bury the dead, they keep them in rooms and talk to them." After a time, he recovers enough to go home to the Laguna Pueblo reservation. Tayo finds the familiar web of family and tradition, but he is too sick to pick up the strands and weave them into his life. Old Grandma says, "That boy needs a medicine man. Otherwise, he will have to go away. Look at him."

At last Tayo takes her advice and seeks out old Betonie, who gives him stories and a ceremony. "The stories are all we have, you see ... to fight off illness and death." Slowly Tayo begins to weave. About midway in the book the webbed pattern of his curative ceremony—and of the novel—takes shape.

His cure is not important to himself alone. Old man Ku'oosh says, "I'm afraid of what will happen to all of us if you and the others don't get well." According to the old stories, "It took only one person to tear away the delicate strands of the web, spilling the rays of sun into the sand, and the fragile world would be injured."

Some people try to prevent Tayo from completing his ceremony, but he persists until the web is complete and "whirling darkness has come back on itself. ... It has stiffened with the effects of its own witchery." For now, it is dead.

"Put your hand on it. See, it is moving." In the belly of the story is life for the people. We know it is true. From here, the heart of the web, our other knowings extend to a parameter of understanding.

Extending Understanding

Where the Western dynamic is detachment, the Native American dynamic is connection. "Put your hand on it." The story and its people are one. What happens to either happens to both. Without its cultural context, the story sickens. Forced into the "boxes" of Western thought, it may die. Clearly, the crux of the problem is that we need a new model inclusive of other cultural values, in life as well as in literature.

On a table beside me, I've put models of the thought constructs we are discussing: a picture of a web for the Native American and some small wooden blocks for the Western. (You can see my children's teeth marks on them. Maybe the babies were trying to round them off.)

Usually, the Western story (especially if a white male writes it) has organic unity with the thought construct from which it arises (to illustrate, I stack these small wooden blocks in a pyramid). The elements of the story can be neatly arranged. It is written either in prose or (rarely) poetry. It has a category: novel, short story, myth, fable, folklore or some such. The structure of the story separates easily into components. It has a beginning, middle and end. The "story *line*"—or plot—is based on conflict, which progresses step by step to a climax. Just as the protagonist struggles for her or his own sake, the highest standard of the story is that it stands alone, "Art for Art's sake." Of course, the best stories do affect individual lives; they do enter and influence the collective psyche of the people. But, unlike the Native American stories, they are not *specifically designed* to do so.

At these words, "specifically designed," an alien presence vibrates the web of our understanding, a cultural bias that we hadn't noticed because the beauty of *Ceremony* temporarily stunned it and bound it with silk to stop its whirling. Don't touch it! Just be still and listen to its hum, which contains many voices. One Western archeologist (1983) is quoting another (1949) in *Pueblo Children of the Earth Mother:*[25]

> Amsden was of the opinion that (Anasazi) Basketmakers may never have formalized work, just as *Indians of today* generally do not formalize work, art or religion. "They weave them into their daily lives so smoothly that no word exists to convey the idea that they may be separated from the whole pattern of living." He wondered whether, even before the *blessings of civilization* sublimated our *animal instincts*, there were not human societies in which work and play went hand in hand, "as with *happy children* out berrying." (Italics mine.)

In sum, if American Indians weave work, art and religion smoothly into their pattern of living, it is not because over the centuries they have perfected a civilization and philosophy that enable them to do so—it is not by *specific design.* It is because they are uncivilized, immature people who follow their "animal instincts." This bias is reprehensible and in critical need of correction. But its truly sinister implications become apparent when we listen to another voice in the "hum," the voice of the famous French biologist, Georges Cuvier. We have this insight thanks to the research of Anne Fausto-Sterling.[26]

In 1816, having studied the South African bushwoman, Sarah Bartmann, when she was alive, and having dissected her body after she was dead, Cuvier concluded that Bartmann was one step higher in the evolutionary scale than monkeys. "A major purpose of Cuvier's exploration was to place the Caucasian in the grand scheme of human variety." He "focused on proving that people of color did not give rise to Western Civilization."

This idea whirled through Europe, gathering assenting voices and reinforcing the colonial powers in their conquest of indigenous people, who were in need of being "civilized" and taught to sublimate their "animal instincts." In this process, many native peoples lost their dignity, their land and their lives.

In plain terms, when others want what you have, they make up distorted stories about you. To paraphrase the storyteller in *Ceremony*, they also try to destroy your stories ... let them be confused or forgotten ... because you will be defenseless then. "Cultural bias" is a euphemism for this tactic. It is *witchery*, and it is still humming. ... It is still alive.

If we are not careful, the witchery will get loose again. It will whirl down, draw us aside individually and whisper, "The web of life does not exist. You are not part of it. Cut off your roots; you don't need them. If other people are sick and dying, let them go. The world is solid; it will not be injured. Forget the stories ... " or more slyly, "Only the stories of *your* people are important."

We will set against each other then. We will bicker over whose stories are best instead of creating a circle to include them all.

The power of witchery is mighty. But it can't stand up to our stories—yours and mine, the old and the new. We can use them to turn witchery on itself. And gradually, like Tayo, we may "see the pattern, the way all the stories fit together ... to become the story that is still being told ... with no boundaries, only transitions through all distances and time."

Through her origin stories, the Corn-Mother teaches many wisdoms, one of which is cooperation. Just as a single plant cannot bear fruit and it requires a field of corn to bring in a harvest, neither can a person be as strong alone as in connection with one's family and one's people. In developing a new model for American life, each of us alone can do very little. But if we fuse our energies, if we plant together, we can do much. Let us do so. And look for signs of the harvest. ...

DAYDREAMING PRIMAL SPACE

Cherokee Aesthetics as Habits of Being

(Note: This essay is from *The Poetics of Appalachian Space*,[27] an anthology of essays on interior space based on the philosophy of Gaston Bachelard's *La Poetique de l'espace*.[28])

I.

A Cherokee elder told me, "Look at everything three times: Once with the right eye. Once with the left eye. And once from the corners of the eyes to see the spirit [essence] of what you're looking at."

Viewed from the "corners of the eyes," the mountain forest is the round, deep space—immediately immense, intimate, resonant—that the French philosopher Gaston Bachelard calls "the friend of being." It is also the first space in Appalachia that humans inhabited and called home. For centuries, these American Indians sang and danced and lived poetry as a habit of being. They considered themselves co-creators with the All-Mystery, the Creator, whose wisdom spoke through Mother Earth and the universe. In harmony with this voice, men and women spun a web of life so deftly that no limb bent, no flower crumpled beneath its weight. They made each strand strong and elastic, like the spider's, which has almost the tensile strength of fused quartz, drawn out silken fine. The web was an extension of the forest—a sturdy, secure dwelling open to the flow of wind and light and vision. Round living in round space. It gave the people a twinkle in the eye.

When Europeans arrived, they found many such webs among the mountains. The Cherokee had spun the largest, stretching almost the length and breadth of southern Appalachia. Some of the newcomers liked living in the round. Either they brought this holistic ability with them, or they learned it from the Indians or from Mother Earth herself. They looked at everything three times, with a twinkle. For a while everyone lived in harmony.

Other European settlers believed in the perception of the right and left eyes only. Philosophically, their point of view contained the seed of a dichotomy that would bear deadly fruit: God is God; nature is "the other." They feared the wilderness, the "savages" who lived there, and the amorphous power of the intuitive both represented. Out of fear and acquisitiveness they responded. "This new land needs to be squared up," they said. "Squared, boxed, labeled—*brought under control*. These 'primitive' webs are in the way. We'll tear them down and stamp out the spinners." And they did. Or so it seemed.

But the forest knows better.

That's why we're going there by way of a daydream.

II.

Even in a daydream, no wise person enters the primal forest without looking at it three times. Having taken its measure from the corners of the eyes, we must use the right and the left eye to take clear bearings: our point of departure, the lay of the trail from beginning to end, the experiences we should anticipate.

We are going from contemporary space to primal space, from life on the square to life in the round, and from the line to the curve of time. There are corresponding differences in language and in the movement of thought, which this essay reflects. The language is intimate, for in the primal mind there is *no psychic distance* between the singer and the song; listeners share the web of context and experience. Also, instead of following the conventional Western linear progression (A, B, C, etc.) and reasoning from the outside in, the essay begins with the center, Part I, and moves in a widening spiral to the conclusion, developing the thought from the inside out. This is the traditional American Indian mode that originated in primal space, where everything is connected.

Experientially, it is probably a familiar mode. Imagine you and I are hiking the Appalachian Trail, beginning at Newfound Gap in the Great Smoky Mountains National Park. The deeper into the forest we go, the less we look at our watches. A vast, varied maze of evergreens and hardwoods leads our gaze from mountain to mountain, each more deeply steeped in blue haze, until the last faint curve becomes a wave between sight and feeling. We relax into the flow of wind in branches, of streams rushing over smooth boulders. Our thoughts web out. Peace webs in. Time is seamless—a slant of sunlight on treetops.

The longer we stay in primal space, the more jarring it is to return to what many American Indians call "the other world"—a world not of poetry but of lists:

SQUARED .... THE OTHER WORLD

TIME SQUARED to the clock. LIFE SQUARED to television/ credit card/truck/car/train/jet—to cubicles piled in high rude rectangles. FILL IN THE SQUARE: name/addres s/telephone/sex/age/race/occupation. STAY IN THE LINES. KEEP TO TIME SLOTS: work/play/eat/sleep/love. Box 'em, label 'em, stack 'em up. COMPETE! Claw to the top of t he pyramid. COMPUTE! COMPUTE! COMPUTE! ("No, you can 't have your veteran's benefits. The computer shows you 'dead.'") GET HERESY UNDER CONTROL. The Creation is cle ar-cut: God is God; nature is "the other." Choose you r side. WOMEN, SQUARE your shoulders, starve your bodie s straight. Curves are out. MEN, SQUARE your hearts. P roduce! Produce! Feelings don't raise the GNP. The shu ttle's SEALS are at RISK ...? LAUNCH it! Seven people s meared across the sky translate to the TV monitor, "OBVI OUSLY WE HAVE A MAJOR MALFUNCTION." ... Obviously.

Via television millions saw *Challenger* and its astronauts explode and scrawl a fiery hieroglyph on the curved wall of space. A warning. *"Humans have lost connection—with ourselves and each other, with nature and the Creator."* We do have a major malfunction. We've felt something seriously amiss for a long time. Now, in the blood of seven—a number sacred to the Cherokee and mystic to many of the world's peoples—we have clear warning. To survive, we must set ourselves right and reconnect.

One way to heal the deep slashes that sever us from relationship and hope is to go back to our home ground—our primal space—and find within it the deepest human root. In Appalachia, as elsewhere in America, that root is American Indians. They were the first to call the mountains home, as most Appalachians of every ethnic background continue to do. Perhaps if we study how indigenous people spun their original web, we can adapt their skill to our own time.

But how can we reach our primal space and the people who "sang and danced and lived poetry as a habit of being"?

We cannot see them with the right and left eyes, which only perceive facts and knowledge. We have to *experience* poetic habits of being from the corners of our eyes. To do that we use the phenomenology of the French philosopher, Gaston Bachelard, which reveals the imaginative movement of inner space. In *The Poetics of Space* he says, "All really inhabited space bears the essence of the notion of home."[29] Through thoughts and day-dreams, we bring all our past dwellings with us to our present abode—especially the "original shell" (home) where we were born. This original shell is also "the topography of our intimate being," our soul. Remembering the shell, "we learn to abide within ourselves."[30]

A cross-country trucker from Knoxville put this same idea more plainly: "Wherever I go, I got my mountains inside of me. They keep me steady. Headin' back to East Tennessee, I keep pushin' 'til I get 'em in sight again. When I see that first blue line rise up, I know I'm home."

We're on our way to primal space in Appalachia, to the "spinners" and their web. But we can't get there through Bachelard's paradigm of the house as "the original shell." Although he looks at it from the corners of his eyes, the cast of his gaze—the perception governed by culture—is of the West. It is irreconcilable with the traditional worldview of American Indians and therefore with the model of the web.

For Bachelard, a given is the dichotomy between humanity and nature, between culture and the powerful forces of the universe. Their relationship is adversarial. In the dynamic between human and universe, "the house helps us to say: I will be an inhabitant of the world in spite of the world."[31] This dichotomy is the antithesis of the American Indian belief in the sacred tie to Mother Earth and to the universe as revelations of the wisdom of the Creator, who stands behind. Severance of the tie is basic to Western thought. It ranges God and man together; nature and all identified with it—including indig-enous peoples and women—are "the other."

With this cardinal separation as a base, it is logical that Bachelard derives his idea of the house as a "tool for the analysis of the human soul" from the psychological paradigm of Carl Jung, in which the house is detached from nature and compartmentalized. The attic is the intellect—the rational mind—which polarizes with the cellar, the realm of the irrational and intuitive, where "the walls have the entire earth behind them" and we are afraid. The cellar is the unconscious. It cannot be civilized. To be used, it must be rationalized, dominated, *"brought under control."*[32] In a word, "squared." The other rooms of the house stack up, and we inhabit them one at a time. The mode of the house cannot be applied to the web—an extension of the forest, where the dweller feels the vibration of any one strand as a vibration of the whole.

Furthermore, in the web, the balance of gender replicates the balance of Nature's dynamics and is crucial to communal harmony. "Men and women spun. ..." The power of change and transitoriness (male) must stay in balance with the power of continuance (female). Otherwise, there is discord and death for the people. From this point of view, Bachelard's "oneiric" house is a bird with one wing, which claims to be two-winged. Although Bachelard says he is studying the "houses of man"—that is, of "humanity"—and the experience of inhabiting, all of the dwellers are male. The wing of their experience is powerful and true. But where is the balancing wing of continuance? No woman speaks of her experience—not even in the cellar, much less in the attic. There is no bedroom and no kitchen in Bachelard's house (extraordinary omissions for a Frenchman) and no nursery—no comfortable space for the fecund and regenerative.

Only in a later chapter, quoting Michelet's meditation on birds making a nest, does Bachelard come close to female experience and gender balance:

Michelet suggests a house built by and for the body, taking form from the inside, like a shell, in an intimacy that works physically. ... "On the inside," he continues, "the instrument that prescribes a circular form for the nest is nothing else but the body of the bird. It is by constantly turning round and round and pressing back the walls on every side that it succeeds in forming this circle. The female ... hollows out the house, while the male brings back from the outside all kinds of materials, sturdy twigs and other bits. ... The house is the bird's very person."[33]

Even with so pregnant an opportunity as this, Bachelard does not apply nature's principle of gender balance to humans. Indeed, he cannot. The psychic distance is too great, for the sacred tie that would transfer it has been severed for centuries.

It would seem then that although the process of phenomenology—the daydreaming of images—is wonderfully applicable to primal space and the web, its paradigm is not. However, Bachelard finally dreams his way out of the squared house and into an immense cosmic dwelling, which "is a potential of every dream of houses. Winds radiate from its center and gulls fly from its windows. A house that is as dynamic as this allows the poet to inhabit the universe. Or, to put it differently, the universe comes to inhabit his house." This house expands or contracts as Bachelard desires. It is "infinitely extensible"—a "sort of airy structure that moves about on the breath of time." Unwilling to be enclosed, the space we love "deploys and appears to move elsewhere without difficulty; into other times and on different planes of dream and memory."[34]

Gaston Bachelard is dreaming the web!

Gradually he makes his way toward it, gathering images from nature that have the quality of roundness, like Michelet's bird nest. "When we examine a nest," he says, "we place ourselves at the origin of confidence in the world. ... Our [manmade] house, apprehended in its dream potentiality, becomes a nest in the world, and we shall live there in complete confidence if, in our dreams, we really participate in the sense of security of our first home."[35] The shell, with its "protective spiral," engenders similar confidence and evokes the intimate connection of body and soul. Bachelard dreams on through "the curve that warms"—the curve that is also "habitable space harmoniously constituted"[36]—until he comes at last to the primal forest of his ancestors. Here he meditates on "intimate immensity" and "roundness," implicitly yearning for wholeness, for cosmic connection.

Sharing his feeling and transposing his forest to our own in Appalachia, we ponder the mountains and imagine "an airy structure that moves about on the breath of time," a dwelling that is "open to wind and light and vision." Alas, the webs are torn down, the spinners stamped out.

But the forest smiles. Deep in her nooks and crevices she feels the spinners and the harmony of their web. We will dream our way to them.

III.

Daydream at midnight: We're back on the Appalachian Trail, somewhere in North Carolina—looking for a Cherokee web and "poetry as a habit of being." By the pressure of our toes against our shoes, we feel the trail descending. Flashlights give us narrow glimpses of a rut here, a rock there. It's like a Cades Cove woman said, "You don't know what dark is 'til you seen night come down on the mountain."

As the trail swings into the open along a ridge, we stop. From the corners of our eyes we see the essence of the mountains. By day, clothed in trees and blue veils, they are so beautiful it's tempting to relax in their embrace and forget they are also what we see jetting against the moonlit sky—mass and mystery, immovable. Only a fool thinks of "conquering the mountains." Mountains nurture the reverent. For the irreverent, the consequences are inevitable—and often fatal. If you're born and raised in Appalachia, this wisdom comes with your mother's milk. Mountains teach you to face the realities of life, to "abide in your own soul"—and survive.

Carefully, we feel our way through the folds of darkness. Since our right and left eyes are virtually useless, other senses become our eyes. The roll of a pebble, the breath of dew-cooled pines, a startled flutter in a nearby bush magnify the vast silence of the forest. Wind and stream are the murmuring current of time, taking us back to where poetry is sung and danced and lived. … In the distance a fire flickers—not running wild, but contained, like a candle. The spinners.

Coming closer, we encounter the first strands that define their web: a whiff of wood smoke, the brisk "*SSH … ssh, SSH … ssh*" of shell-shakers and a chant/song that *dips … lifts … dips … lifts.* It's as if, in the still of the night, Mother Earth is making music from her heart. The music draws us on, even shapes our courtesy. Extinguishing flashlights, we approach the large clearing slowly, for it is ceremonial ground, consecrated ground. Around the perimeter of the web, people are moving among the trees. We stop, wait for someone to acknowledge us.

Waiting is part of the poetics of primal space—a silence that allows the gathering of thought, the savoring of meaning. Alternating activity with rest is nature's way. It engenders endurance and reduces possibility of conflict, giving time for stasis to evolve. Even so, the night is chill and to stand in the dark, outside of community looking in, is lonely. The people, the trees, even round Brother Moon seems to be quietly looking us over. Only the steady heartbeat of the web reassures us:

"SSH ... ssh ... SSH ... ssh. Dip ... lift ... dip ... lift. ..."

A woman comes to greet us. Her bearing is confident, kind—immovable. We are respectful. She is the Ghigau, the Beloved Woman, chief of the Women's Council and a principal leader of the nation. Unhurried, she works the conversation around to the key question, addressed to me because of my black hair and high cheek bones. "Who is your mother?" (Meaning of what clan. She would have asked a man the same question.) I answer as my ancestor would have, "My mother is of the Deer Clan from the Overhill (Cherokee) at Tenasi."

With this filament of information in hand, the Beloved Woman begins connecting us to the web. In the forest, as in every town in the nation, the community revolves around seven mother clans. Like protective shells, they ensure the continuance of kin and care in the midst of change. They also keep the peace among the town, for it is forbidden to fight with relatives. Seven arbors, one for each clan, ring the ceremonial ground. In the woods behind them, families have cleared the underbrush and made camp; their small, embered fires are like red stars scattered in the dark.

As the Beloved Woman weaves a path among them, people in the shadows speak or wave to her but courteously avoid looking at us directly. We sense they're taking our measure from the corners of their eyes, intuiting cues for responses. And we do the same. Even by glance, aggression and dominance have no place here.

"SSH ... ssh ... ssh. Dip ... lift ... dip ... lift. ..."

The harmony vibrates every strand of the web, as natural and pervasive as air. Breathing the rhythm, we know we should slowly follow the poetic habits of being to their source. Otherwise, we will be disrespectful, unfit—and unwelcome—in the dance. The primary habit is connecting.

As the Beloved Woman settles us into the Deer Clan, people good-naturedly move over a little—give us greetings, a place by the fire and food from a communal spread nearby—roasted beef, corn, boiled squash and peas, bean bread and spring water, which we dip from a bucket. We take up threads of conversation as they're offered—"Where do you come from? How was your journey?"

Looking at these amenities twice only, we might mistake them for mere courtesies. But the spinners live *poetically*, always moving in harmony with the spirit beyond the tangible. We see the courtesies as they do: the greetings are the first silken strands attaching us to the web. The place by the fire signifies acceptance into the circle. The food and words are tokens of care for us to spin into response. We are entering the ceremony of connecting that originates in the dance. Following its measured pace, we accept what is offered with appreciation—eat slowly, talk with intervals of silence to allow thought to gather and be expressed.

Like an artist's brush, the firelight strokes the spinners only enough to suggest the full life beyond what we see:

- the planes of cheek in the faces close to us and zestful twinkles in the eyes;
- the ebony swing of a woman's hair as she bends over her baby, the smile between two elders who glimpse a young couple edging toward deeper shadows;
- a warrior's arm guiding a toddler away from the fire;
- and slightly apart from the group, the silhouettes of the Beloved Woman and a man walking together, intent in conversation.

"Is that her husband?" I ask the woman beside me.

"No. A chief. The council meets tomorrow."

Societal balances are different here than where we come from, but they generate a peaceful, easy feeling. Gradually we meet other friends and relatives of the clan (and by extension of ours)—a leisurely flow of men, women and children who mingle freely with the adults, not boisterous but *busy*. Conversation and laughter are abundant yet muted. Everyone understands the parameter of behavior at the ceremonial grounds. People gather here to celebrate the oneness of life, to recenter their spirits in the All-Mystery. Although the grounds are inclusive of human needs, there can be no alcohol, no rowdiness, nothing to disturb the harmonies of regeneration and renewal. Do these harmonies translate to twinkles in the eyes? We think so.

They also translate into energy. The dance has been going on for two nights already. When some of the women move, a faint *"ssh ... ssh"* comes from shells covered by their long skirts. Every clan has its team of shell-shakers and male singers, its poetic expression of continuance and change. The leading of the dance alternates among the seven clans, leaving other people free to participate or rest as they have energy and inclination.

"When do you sleep?" we ask.

"When we are tired."

"And when do you get up?"

"When we are rested."

They are amused by our questions as people in the square world would be by someone asking, "What is a clock?" In the web, as in the universe, everything cycles, circles, assumes a round shape, connects to everything else. Our dwelling is an "airy structure," a cosmic house "open to wind and light and vision." The owl glides freely here. The cricket chirps in counterpoint with the dance. The raccoon ambles impudently at will. The spinners address them with familial respect as Grandmother, Grandfather, Sister, or Brother. We are among all our relations, which include the standing people—the vast, staunch company of trees who have seen generations of walking people come and go. Resting confidently against the bosom of Mother Earth, we gaze along the mountains' curve into the dome of the sky, where even the tiniest star has a worthy place—as we do at home in the web.

We inhabit all its parts simultaneously. There is no attic here, no cellar, nothing to keep us from orienting to our whole space and whole being. Instead of cubic rooms, the web has spheres, which—like the auras of a circular rainbow—are distinct and diffuse at the same time. In the outer aura are the campsites, where embering dots signify the presence of perhaps three hundred people. If two hundred more should arrive, the web is "infinitely extensible." Or if that many should depart, it simply contracts. Wind extends the psychic space of our dwelling, bringing scents of deep forest, of distant streams and pollens. From the communal cooking area come aromas of whole beefs roasting on the spit. We know that someone prepares for the morrow—just as looking up at Brother Moon keeping watch over us, we know his sister, the sun, is moving toward the east. Our relatives are dependable—they give us a purring feeling.

In the next aura, people flow continually—visiting, doing errands, or just enjoying themselves while they wait to dance. As comfortable in the night as in the day, the spinners look at everything three times and move easily from the intellect to the intuitive and back again—a habit that many from the "other world" find "primitive and irrational." But in the round world it seems the natural way—in fact, the only sensible way—to move.

The circle of arbors marks the beginning of the web's spiritual center, the aura where meditative energy concentrates. At sundown on the first day of the dance, the spinners had begun the ceremony of connection with special prayers, songs and dances to evoke harmony with Mother Earth, the universe and the All-Mystery. Then they made a great cone-shaped fire of seven sacred woods— to burn continuously until the final day. The ceremonial dance began, a dance so ancient that no one knows its time of origin, a living poem passed from generation to generation. The dancing lasts until dawn.

During the day, although the people move freely in the outer part of the aura, they hold its flaming center in constant reverence. Its sacred meaning is visible at all times from every strand of the web. Because there is no psychic distance between the source, its image and those who express it, the fire is not symbolic in the Western sense. It is analogous to the atom's photon, which is made of the same material as the star. The fire, like the sun, shares the essence of the All-Mystery, Creator, just as the individual shares the spirit of the people. The fire embodies the light of all. To understand its meaning, however, we must experience it in the dance.

We sit among the Deer Clan but withdraw into our inner space ... into a silence that allows the fire's image to deepen ...

"SSH ... ssh ... SSH ... ssh. Dip ... lift ... dip ... lift. ..."

There is ancient magic in the sound. Tuning our ears to the song, we hear predominantly the tonalities of *a*. They seem to resonate from the core of time to a place inside us we feel but cannot name.

Bachelard's voice, soft and discreet, enlarges our thought:

It is impossible to think the vowel sound *ah* without a tautening of the vocal chords. ... The letter *a*, which is the main body of the word *vast*, stands aloof in its delicacy. ... This delicate little Aeolian harp that nature has set at the entrance to our breathing is really a sixth sense, which followed and surpassed the others. It quivers at the mere movement of metaphor; it permits human thought to sing. ... I begin to think that the vowel *a* is the vowel of immensity. It is a sound area that starts with a sigh and extends beyond all limits.[37]

Through their powerful intuitive skills, the ancient spinners understood the vowel *a* and its effect on the sixth sense. They also knew that dance touches the sixth sense in a similar way, making an "Aeolian harp" of the whole body. In combination, the song dips and lifts the people into immensity while the dance holds them secure. This balance repeats in the dance pattern itself, which alternates man/woman/man/woman.

Looking through the web to the great cone-shaped fire and the figures circling round it, we juxtapose on them the image of Michelet's bird, turning round and round, shaping her nest from the inside out. And we understand the cardinal poetic of primal space: The All-Mystery—the source of all light and energy—animates the breast of Mother Earth and turns her round and round, shaping the spinners, their web and their ways to "curve and hold the curve." Man/woman/man/woman. The power of change and transitoriness balanced with the power of continuance—strong shining wings that keep all life aloft. This is the Great Law, the Poem ensouled in the universe. The people sing it, dance it, live it.

Now when we look at the Deer Clan sketched in firelight, we realize the fuller implications of their habits of being:

The Beloved Woman talks with the chief, reflecting the wisdom of both genders active in government.

The warrior *and* the woman nurture the children, who are spread among us like seeds in the forest. Sometimes the woman is a warrior also.

The old couple rejoices in the life cycle of the young, in the assurance that the people will continue.

We ourselves are included in the web through a social interpretation of the Poem. Regeneration and renewal is the theme of primal space. The plane of our cheeks feels stronger. Twinkles well in our eyes.

We are hopeful that the square world we come from can regain its round shape. As we speak to the Deer Clan of problems there, an old man across the fire listens, eyes half-closed. With his forefinger he touches his head and heart, then makes a slashing gesture between them. Nods of agreement around the circle. "Head-severed-from-heart"—disconnection— has long been a source of conflict with European settlers of the two-eyes-only type. Many spinners believe that this unbalanced condition will cause the whites to destroy the Indian webs and, in the end, to foul their own nest.

Although these thoughts are not articulated, the Beloved Woman feels their movement. "There are also whites who *do* keep head and heart connected," she says. "We can learn from their good ways and they can learn from ours. Maybe we can find the balance between ... " Her years of work in this endeavor give weight to her words and a tone of irony as she adds, "... if not in seven years, then in seven hundred."

Her allusion to the medicine man's prognosis—that a cure will work "in seven days, and if not in seven days, in seven years"—is well understood. There is wisdom in it. And stoic humor.

It is time to dance.

People begin to stand up, stretch their legs. It is the Deer Clan's turn to lead. One of the shell-shakers shows me the cuffs that cover her legs from below the knee to the ankle—row after row of turtle shells, with a scattering of pebbles in each.

"How much do the cuffs weigh?" I ask.

"About forty pounds. It takes years of practice to be a shell-shaker."

And, I think, years to build up the stamina. Holding the rhythm of continuance is not a task for the frail.

Neither is singing. The dance is brisk, the songs vigorous and long. It takes the breath of male athletes to sustain them simultaneously. Some of the singers pass near us. They are strong-legged and supple. It is said that they can run for days with only a modicum of rest, and their skill as warriors is well known. Yet tonight they turn their energies to ceremonies celebrating life, which (apparently unknown to the Hollywood of our time) is what most tribal dances are about.

Along with many other members of the clan, we follow the shakers and singers as they cross the web toward their arbor. The closer we come to the center, the more people gather quietly together. In the aura of the arbors, they move very little, and in the circle ringing the dancers they are almost immobile, absorbed in the rhythm. Around the tall fire almost a hundred people jog counter-clockwise in unison—woman/man/woman/man ... round and round ... adults on the inside, children on the perimeter ... round and round ... quick, trotting steps ... arms bent at the elbow ... faces contemplative ... round and round. ...

Vibrations from stomping feet pass through Mother Earth to our own, making us feel part of the dance already; and though we are silent, our throats contract with the a sounds of the song:

"SSHH ... sshh ... SSH ... ssh ... Dip ... lift ... dip ... lift. ..."

The music spirals up, soaring and gliding on perfectly balanced wings. When the shell-shakers cease, the dance ends and the song trails off on a haunting note, like a cry of the loon.

Slowly everyone leaves the dance ground. We wait at the edge ... watching flames ... following smoke as it drifts toward low-hanging stars.

Deer Clan singers file in silently and circle close to the fire. Leaving a space between each pair of them for another person, they begin a slow, rhythmic pace, calling out on every fourth beat, "ahYO ... ahYO ... ahYO ... ahYO. ..." Smoothly, the shell-shakers join them, *"SSH ... ssh ... SSH ... ssh."* As we spiral in with other people, the tempo slowly increases, then holds steady. We settle into a rhythm that has endured for hundreds of years ... round and round. ... The chant lifts and dips in myriad tones of *a* and *o*, synchronizing perfectly with the shells. So intricate is the balance that we cease to analyze and give ourselves up to music ... to warm energy rising within, melting away fatigue and cares ... round and round. ... Shell curves to song and song curves to shell ... the whole moving, moving ... memories come and dreams far beyond our knowing ... membranes dissolve between flesh and leaf and sky, releasing all the atoms' tiny stars. ... They stream round and round ... into the All-Mystery, a radiant cup that holds our spirits in perfect stillness and perfect peace. ...

IV.

Round, deep space
immense
intimate
resonant
the friend of being,
our first home
in Appalachia.

If we really experience its sense of security in our dreams, we can live in our present home with confidence. Whatever our ethnic origins, we have in common our primal space and ancestors who knew how to live in harmony with it. This heritage is the ground of our hope. It holds us steady as we face the realities of our time, a time "squared" almost beyond endurance.

In Appalachia, as elsewhere in the world, the effects of humanity's "major malfunction" are evident. Through lack of reverence for the web of life, humans have upset the balance of nature on a global scale. Poison is invading the ozone layer, the forests, the waters, the food chain—perhaps even the very heart of Mother Earth. *Challenger's* fiery hieroglyph merges with warnings from scientists, theologians, artists and others who "feel it in their bones": we are reaching the point of no return. We must stop the rending of our web and begin to reweave it.

The pattern of survival is in the poetics of primal space. Balance, harmony, inclusiveness, cooperation—life regenerating within a parameter of order. The pattern repeats the deepest heart of Mother Nature, where the atom—with its predictable perimeter—freely makes its rounds to create new life. Continuance in the midst of change, cardinal dynamics that sustain the universe.

The Cherokee have used these poetics for survival. In 1838, after the Trail of Tears, the Nation's web was in shreds. Surveying the damage, the elders said, "In the seventh generation, the Cherokee will rise again." With the wisdom of the spider, the people ingested what was left of their web and began to spin. It was seven generations later, in 1984, that the Cherokee Eastern and Western Councils reunited at the Red Clay Historic Park near Cleveland, Tennessee—on the very ground where the last council before the Removal was held. For three days I lived in the web that the Cherokee wove on the knolled mountain meadow in the same pattern they had used in 1837.

Recently I discussed the reunion of the Cherokee with Wilma Mankiller, principal chief of the Cherokee Nation of Oklahoma. She is a poet-chief, in the classic American Indian tradition. Traditionally reared, she is also a shell-shaker for her clan at the ceremonial grounds, where many Cherokee come regularly to sing and dance and live poetry as you, the reader, and I experienced it in our midnight dream. I asked Chief Mankiller, "In essence, do you think the Cherokee survived because they kept dancing?" "Unquestionably," she answered. "We've held the center. We've maintained connection."

Survival. It *is* possible. A hopeful twinkle glimmers in our eyes as we Appalachians contemplate primal space—our first home, our friend of being. The question is: Do we have the courage to *be* a friend in return? For the sake of renewed relationships, will we unstack the boxes, take off the labels, and open ourselves to the flow of light and air and vision? It will mean giving up the idea of dominance for the concept of harmony with "all our relations." It will mean balancing the power of change and transitoriness with the power of continuance, in every dimension of our society. Most of all, it will mean that we heal the sacred and severed tie between humanity and nature as the expression of the All-Mystery—the Poem, the Great Law ensouled in the universe, which teaches us to live in the round. Looking three times at what lies before us, I chant: *Out of ashes / peace will rise / if the people are resolute / our courage is our memory.*

Smoky Mountain-Woman

I rise in silence, steadfast in the elements
with thought a smoke-blue veil drawn round me.
Seasons clothe me in laurel and bittersweet, in ice
but my heart is constant. ... Fires scar and torrents
erode my shape ... but strength wells within me
to bear new life and sustain what lives already. ...
For streams of wit relieve my heavy mind
smoothing boulders cast up raw-edged. ... And the
raven's lonesome cry reminds me that the soul is
as it has ever been. ...
Time cannot thwart my stubborn thrust toward Heaven.

WOMANSPIRIT
IN THE HIGH-TECH WORLD

(Note: This essay was adapted from an address given at the First National Women's Symposium, held in October 1989, near Tahlequah, Oklahoma, and sponsored by the Cherokee Nation of Oklahoma and Northeastern State University. The theme of the symposium was "Yesterday, Today, and Tomorrow: Thoughts for a New Generation.")

A Time to Give Thanks

I offer you a gift. It's a seed of corn from Tennessee. In the Cherokee traditional story, Selu, the First Woman, brought forth corn for the people from her own body and taught them the law of respectful relationship. "Womanspirit" at work. This gift-seed is a poem of hope and encouragement from Mother Earth. Hold it in your hand, and, at the end, we'll circle back to its full meaning.

I wrote this poem in 1978 for my husband, Paul. Now I say it in honor of our foremothers—yours and mine.

Motheroot

Creation often
needs two hearts
one to root
and one to flower
One to sustain
in time of drouth
and hold fast
against winds of pain
the fragile bloom
that in the glory
of its hour
affirms a heart
unsung, unseen.

The "fatheroots" are equally important. Traditionally, most Native American cultures have emphasized the balance, the complementarity, of the genders and their work, in both the private and the public spheres. The dominant culture has begun to do so. To restore the balance in American society, Womanspirit must be more strongly "sung" and "seen." There are men who are helping this happen. They strengthen my hope that humanity can create a new cooperative spirit, a new harmony—for ourselves and for our planet—before it is too late.

It's heartening to remember that from time immemorial, Womanspirit has woven life for the people and for our Mother Earth, providing continuance in the midst of change. In all ages and among all races, this "woman's work" has been the same. The differences lie in the circumstances of the era and in the ways each culture provides for women to get their jobs done. When women gather to talk and listen to each other, we realize we are part of a long and tenacious root system. We draw strength from knowing that our foremothers coped with the problems of their times (otherwise, we wouldn't be alive to cope with ours).

In my interview with her, Chief Wilma Mankiller said, "Many women internalize the stereotypes of 'the woman's place,' passivity and so on. We need to rethink where we are—there's a lot of unlearning to do—and extend our ideas of home and family to include our environment and our people. We need to trust our own thinking, trust where we're going. … And get the job done."

The first step along the path she indicates is to examine what needs to be done and to *think* about it, think not only with the intellect but also with a fusion of heart, mind and soul—to think purposefully.

A Time to Weep

All around us we see life "dying back"—in nature, in our families, in society. Homo sapiens are literally killing their own seed and the seeds of other life forms as well. One cause of this suicidal violence is greed. And that greed feeds on the philosophy that Earth is not our Mother, but an "it" that can be used and consumed. This philosophy even extends to the "conquest" of outer space. History shows that when the people in power call Earth "it," they consider all connected with her to be its, too—objects to be dominated, controlled, consumed, forgotten. Vanished. They are—*we* are—expendable.

These cause-effect relationships are apparent. But there is another cause for the dying back that is far more subtle. A Choctaw woman revealed it to me. We were waiting backstage for our turns in an event in which she was to dance and I was to say poems. What she said I later wrote down almost verbatim. Like many other people, this woman spoke a poem without realizing it. She is not a writer. Part of my calling as a poet is to listen intently to what people say and send their messages into the world, if they want me to do so. For many years I've prefaced a reading of "What the Choctaw Woman Said" with this explanation of its source, and circled back to the woman who spoke the words how much her insight has helped me and others. From the beginning, I asked her to let me know when it would be appropriate for me to include her name formally on the poem. She says the time is now.

What the Choctaw Woman Said

For Ida

My husband is an alcoholic.
He went to the VA and he told them,
"My spirit is sick. I am dying."
They said, "You need tests. Go to the lab."
He came home.

Later he went back and told them again,
"My spirit is sick. I am dying."
"You need meaningful work," they said.
"Go to the social worker."
He came home.

The last time he went they
sent him to a psychiatrist.
When my husband told him, "My spirit is

sick. I am dying," the psychiatrist
said, "What do you mean by spirit?"

My husband came home. He'll never go back.
My only hope is to get him to a medicine man
but the great ones are in the West.
I don't have the money to take him.

The trouble is, most people look down on
us and our culture. It's harder on a man.
It kills his pride. For a woman it's not
as bad. We have to make sure the children
survive, no matter what.

If I stay with my husband, the children will
get sick in their spirits. They may die.
I have to leave him.

This is the Choctaw woman's story. But it is not unique to the Choctaw, or to American Indians, or even to women. Wherever the story is read, there are men, women and children who say it echoes their own struggles in a society too compartmentalized and too detached to hear their cry, "My spirit is sick. I am dying." Disconnection of body/mind/spirit is death-dealing.

Disdain is a form of disconnection that causes suffering and death in America. "The trouble is, people look down on us and our culture." In Western culture, which is dominant in our country, the roots that feed this disdain go back for centuries, back to the dichotomy that ranges God and man on one side, all other living things on the other.

This disdain concept, this insidious and deadly virus, still runs in the bloodstream of Western thought. Although during the last hundred years activist movements for conservation, women and minorities have mitigated its power, the virus, true to its nature, has changed form, regrouped and continued its attacks. With respect to women, it has even invaded the computer. According to a wry report in *Ms.* magazine (September 1989),

"Thar's a Worm in Them Thar Apples,"[38] the AppleWorks GS software thesaurus gives plentiful synonyms for the word *man*. Included are "Member of the human race, human being, body, creature, individual, life, mortal, party, person, personage, soul, mankind, flesh, humanity, humankind, mortality. ..." The synonyms for *woman* are considerably pared down: "Female partner in marriage, wife, lady, Mrs."

Ms. has started a formal protest through the hierarchy of "boxes" that lead to correction of the error: Claris Corporation, which handles Apple software, will route the protest to Proximity Technology, the Florida company that *wrote* the thesaurus. Maybe by the year 2000 the thesaurus will be revised and all the old editions will be out of circulation. In the meantime, Apple is the "user friendly" computer. It is widely distributed. Every schoolchild, as well as every adult, who punches up "man" or "woman" on the thesaurus will get a dose of disdain for women. The virus is transmitted through other media also: television, movies, advertising, culturally biased customs and conversation, religion. No wonder even the strongest woman sometimes feels her self-image falter.

If the virus still has this much power to attack women, it remains equally virulent toward Mother Earth, indigenous peoples, minorities and others viewed as expendable. For example, southern Appalachia, which includes the Qualla Boundary of the Cherokee, frequently has been proposed as an ideal site for burying nuclear and chemical wastes. Such proposals are never made for Westchester County, New York, or other sites where the affluent are concentrated.

A virus in the mind of a people acts as it does in the physical bloodstream. As we say in the mountains, "It *lays* for you. Lulls you into thinkin' you got it beat. Then jumps you again, meaner 'n ever. A virus'll try to confound you too. Make out like it's somethin' else. You think you got a rash, flu, pneumonia or swellins, and all the time it's AIDS. First you gotta get a virus off to itself, see what it really is. Then fight it." These words aren't standard English, but they are standard common sense. (They are also my mother tongue.) The disdain virus—the "looking down on others"—is, at base, irreverence for the Creator and for the Web of Life. And it is attacking the spiritual immune system of America. The virus appears to be fulminating—replicating so fast that it is unstoppable.

When we women see the damage irreverence has done, and is doing, to our environment, our people, our families and ourselves, we weep. There is a time to weep. Tears relieve the mind/body/spirit. Then comes the time to cease weeping, gather strength, "trust our own thinking. And get the job done." However, before a woman can reweave life around her, she has to reweave her own—center her spirit and make it whole. This is the hardest task, as many of us have experienced.

A Time to Unravel

As a child, I was very happy with the Cherokee-Celtic heritage my parents taught me—namely, that all life is a web and that the deepest reality is the spirit that lies beyond the world we see, hear, smell, touch and taste. I had my feet (bare feet) on my homeground, where my ancestors had lived for generations. I felt very centered until I went to college and began Western education in earnest. To make it through, I had to adapt from the web to the boxes. In retrospect, I realize it was during this period that the virus began its insidious attack and continued over the next twenty years until it finally overwhelmed me.

Everywhere I turned I found a "squared world," a society so compartmentalized that life, including my own, had no room to move around, to breathe.

In the struggle against the Square World, I had unwittingly internalized it, torn my life-web, and stuffed the broken strands into the boxes. In those days, however, I didn't know what was causing my malfunction. Or how to isolate the virus, name it, fight it. I only knew that to survive I had to retrieve the strands, unravel and reweave them. But how to do it? My body was going about its daily rounds—driving the carpools, making meals, writing, and so on. But my spirit was curled up in a dark well. My only hope was that the Creator/Provider would find me. Months dragged by. A year. Then one day this poem came to me.

An Indian Walks in Me

An Indian walks in me.
She steps so firmly in my mind
that when I stand against the pine

I know we share the inner light
of the star that shines on me.
She taught me this, my Cherokee,
when I was a spindly child.
And rustling in dry forest leaves
I heard her say, "These speak."
She said the same of sighing wind,
of hawk descending on the hare
and Mother's care
to draw the cover snug around me,
of copperhead coiled on the stone
and blackberries warming in the sun—
"These speak."
I listened ...
Long before I learned
the universal turn of atoms, I heard
the Spirit's song that binds us
all as one. And no more
will I follow any rule
that splits my soul.
My Cherokee left me no sign
except in hair and cheek
and this firm step of mind
that seeks the whole
in strength and peace.

One quiet line marked the beginning of my healing: "No more will I follow any rule that splits my soul." Not for society or for government or for education or for any power whatsoever would I depart from the traditional teaching of my elders: "All of creation is one family. We are all interconnected, sacred." With this poem as the center of my life-web, I began to retrieve other broken strands from their boxes, to remember what I'd been taught as a child, and to seek other knowledge that my Western education had essentially omitted: the history of indigenous peoples, especially the Cherokee, as well as the history of women and their contributions to every field of study. Unraveling the diverse strands, I gradually perceived a pattern of unity among them, a way to take the positive aspects of my Cherokee/ Appalachian heritage and of the high-tech world and weave them into a new harmony.

Passing years have given me other perspectives of this season when my spirit was sick. My parents have always said, "When animals are sick they have sense enough to seek a dark, quiet place to heal. Humans often don't." I understand now that what I'd perceived at the time as a "dark well" was really the womb of the Provider, of God, a place I sought to be still and renew my life. Healing and recovery came from the time-proven (and joked about) cure for a virus: "Go to bed. Drink fluids. Take aspirin." Rest, flush out your system, relieve the symptoms—give mind/body/spirit time to gather strength and fight the virus from the inside out. For many years I'd been too confused—and too afraid of being called puny—to go through this healing process. Once I did that, I could take up the tasks at hand with a deeper understanding.

A terrible manifestation of society's spiritual illness is violence, especially toward women and children. Women represent the life-force; children ensure its continuance. Any species that damages or kills its life-bearers and its children is doomed. In its earliest stages, the disdain virus is difficult to diagnose. Surreptitiously, invisibly, it begins its work against the life-force by creating an imbalance deep in the soul. From there it invades the mind, then the words, then actions directed toward strands of the web that are attached to the life-force, then women ourselves. Sometimes the virus is at work in the souls of others, sometimes in our own.

Within all that lives, the Creator has instilled appropriate survival devices. One of these is a warning system. Women have the ability to spot the earliest signs of the disdain virus—if we trust our own thinking. Selu, for example, knew immediately that her grandsons had broken the law of respect and spied on her. She probably saw it in their eyes, "the windows of the soul." Although their disrespect was comparatively mild—curiosity— the Corn-Mother realized the implications of letting it grow and nipped it in the bud. In a calm, firm spirit, she taught her grandsons the law of respectful relationship. What women face now is disrespect that has grown unchecked for a long time. It is our duty to see that the law is reinforced.

From history we know that there have been societies in the Americas, in Europe, Asia and Africa where women were reverenced as representatives of the life-force, where their counsel was valued about dangers to themselves, their children and their people. Today, we must be especially vigilant. These two poems are about the disdain virus causing imbalances in the soul. The first concerns a hunter, who unlike Selu's husband Kanati, is irreverent. He does not call Earth "Mother." The second involves young women and advice from the Grandmothers.

The Hunter and His Beloved

She reproached her lover,
"Why do you hunt?"
"Because I love it," he said.
"Not just the killing ...
Nature speaks to me—
tawny fields, sun on leaves,
the silence of the forest,
the smell of loam. I love it!"

"Must you kill to have it?"

He looked away.
"How can I make you see?" he said.
I pick up a deer trail...
The tracks are large and deep.
A buck ... a big one
with a rack like a tree.
I know it.
It's my brain against his
my strength against his
my will against his.
He knows it too
because he moves faster.
He's picked up my scent.

We go all day. He strings me out...
cross ... double-cross ...
a wily bastard.
Up on the mountain
I finally spot him.
I raise my gun ...
He sees me ...
And in the moment I fire
I love him. God, how I love him!"

He grasped her hands.
"Don't you see? Don't you see?"
In his eyes, brown and earth-soft,
she saw the slender, pointed track
of her own face.

Anorexia Bulimia Speaks from the Grave

Young women, listen to me—
I'm talkin' to you.
Don't come down here before your time.
It's dark and cold.
Nothin' doin' down here
but the Grandmothers sayin'

"Anorexia Bulimia!
Tell the young women this for us:
They bound our feet
and our toes busted out—
to travel on, test new waters.
They bound our breasts ...
our nipples busted out,
infra-red eyes to take in
what the other two miss.

When they bound our middle
rib 'n hip busted the stays
    took the waist with 'em—
free as they were born.

But now, young women—*now* ...
They've got your soul in a bind,
    wounded, wound up
in electronic wire and hard paper twine
that cut images into your brain,
    unnatural images sayin'
        'Starve yourself to suit us.
        Starve your body.
        Starve your power.
        Starve your dream—
        thinner and thinner—
        until YOU vanish.'

They want you to do that
'cause if you was to take on weight
you might start throwin' it around.
No way can They handle
a full-grown woman
with a full-grown dream. No way."

Listen young women,
the Grandmothers and Anorexia Bulimia
are talkin' to you—
    Feed your body.
    Feed your soul.
    Feed your dream.
    BUST OUT!!!
                        —For Judy (1966–1992)

A Time to Reweave

The 1990s will be the decisive decade, when humanity will either call Earth "Mother" again or perish. To survive, we must reconnect the Web of Life. People of reverent spirit everywhere are saying it: scientists, theologians, educators, artists, poets, sociologists, the man and woman next door, the kindergarten child who, when asked his greatest wish, said "I don't want to die." It is a time to reweave, a time when women are coming into our own. As Native people often say, "The Grandmothers are coming back."

Whatever our ethnic, cultural or religious roots may be, women since the beginning of time have been "weavers," weavers who work from a spiritual base. We know how to take diverse strands of life and spin them into a pattern. How to listen to the whole web at once and mend small tears that occur. If the web should be damaged beyond repair, women, like our sister the spider, know how to ingest the remaining strands and spin a new web.

We *are* doing that. Consider women across the country who represent major strands of the web: women working in health, history, government, law, literature, family, holistic healing, spirituality, economics, education, art, conservation, and so on. Diverse in many ways, we are unified in our determination to ensure the continuance of life. There are men who support us in our work, as we so often support them in theirs. This cooperative trend among women and between genders is a hope for the future.

But in the world's society at large, people who call Earth "it" are still dominant and still rending the web at a deadly rate. Contending with them, with their disdain virus and the damage it causes, can be very wearying. That's why I've given you a corn seed for remembrance—a gift from Selu, the strong, who fed the people in body and in spirit. Although eternally giving, she brooked no disrespect, not even inappropriate curiosity (much less sexual harassment). When disrespect occurred, she quit cooking and gave the law instead. This is a principle worth pondering for women today.

A Time to Study Law

As women work for the good of our people and move into positions where we help make governing policies, it is useful and strengthening to study the Creator's laws and precedents for their application. Most people now call these laws "natural." Native people have traditionally called them "sacred." In either case, the laws are immutable and inexorable. And they are good guides for keeping focused and centered in our efforts.

My parents used a real spider's web, one that I could see and touch, to teach me the laws. Two that are especially appropriate for women to study are these:

The Creator made the Web of Life and into each strand put the law to govern it. Everything in the universe is part of the web. Stars, trees, oceans, creatures, humans, stones: we are all related. One family. What happens to one will happen to all, for the Creator's laws function this way. They teach us to cooperate and live in harmony, in balance. Ignorance of the laws is no excuse, because through Mother Earth the Creator reveals them continually. If we are reverent toward her and take only what we need, she will sustain us. If we are irreverent and take too much, we separate ourselves from her power and we will die.

A similar law governs all warm-blooded species, including the human. The gender that bears life must not be separated from the power to sustain it. From the eagle to the mouse, from the bear to the whale, the female has the power to nurture and protect her young. A complementary law governs the siring gender, who ranges farther and is more changeable and transitory. Together, the laws make a balance, which provides for continuance in the midst of change—and for the survival of the species.

For centuries American Indians studied the Creator's web and wove the sacred laws into their own cultures, each tribe according to its customs. The welfare of children was paramount.

Imagine that the Grandmothers of these cultures—the female ancestors—have returned to sit in council and consider the dilemmas of American society. Undoubtedly, they would put these questions first on their agenda:

"Who will take care of the children? Who will feed, clothe, shelter, educate, protect—nurture them to maturity?" They would insist that the issue of children's care be resolved before the issue of birth is even considered. To do otherwise is unconscionable. "Children are the seeds of the people. Seed corn must not be ground," is the ancient tribal wisdom for survival.

Suppose we then take the Grandmothers to our cities and show them microcosms of the "grinding of children" that is a national disgrace: physical and sexual abuse, economic exploitation through drugs and the sex industry, the steady descent of women and children into poverty, the violence toward women of all ages. "Although we've had the vote for sixty-five years," we explain, "until recently women have been barred from policy-making bodies that govern life in America. Even now, on a national level, our power is weak: one in nine on the Supreme Court, 4 percent in the Congress and about the same in the state legislatures. We do not have equal representation in making any laws, not even those that affect our children and our own bodies. We are being undermined, disenfranchised, disempowered. ..."

Calm and steady, the Grandmothers have listened intently. "We've heard this story before. Remember what happened then to the people. ..."

Native women, especially, do remember.

I'd thought it would never come to this—again. Seemingly, the women's movement was mending the Creator's law that was broken in the Grandmothers' time. I'd thought my daughters—and surely my granddaughters—would serve with men on the councils of the land, resuming their ancestors' place as "Mothers of the Nation." I'd thought they and my son and their children would live in a society restored to the balance that ensures survival ...

"Seed corn must not be ground."

What can women do to prevent our disempowerment and the "grinding" of our children?

For myself, I am a poet, a writer. I have no political clout, no big money to roll. But I do have faith in the Creator. And I do remember the Grandmothers' stories, especially the Cherokee one. I must *tell* it to my children, for it has been erased from most books. Hearing it, they will better understand the Web of Life and their places in it. Science teaches them the web's pattern, but not that the laws holding it in place are sacred. The story will also help my children realize how crucial it is to keep any issue within its context when making a decision. An issue, too, is part of a web. And many of our society's negative attitudes toward women and children have deep roots in the past.

The story of the Cherokee Grandmothers shows how the people interpreted the Creator's law for the female—making the welfare of children central—and of what happened when that law was broken. This story was repeated in many Indian nations.

As I have described previously, when the European men first arrived, Cherokee women had been the center of the family and the center of the Nation for about two thousand years. When the Cherokee men asked, "Where are your women?" the Europeans said, "What are your women doing here?" To their minds, it was "pagan" and "uncivilized" to have women in places of power. Besides, the Europeans followed the laws of property, and the property they wanted was the land. To get it, it was evident they would have to upset the tribal balance. A primary way to do that was to undermine the power of women. No rocks at first. Just steady pressure for decades. They refused to deal with women in treaty negotiations. They called the Cherokee system a "petticoat government" and insisted on their own way. They introduced alcohol to the people. And within the wholesome teachings of Christianity, which the Cherokee found familiar and sound— God is Creator of all, love God and your neighbor as yourself—many missionaries also brought the concept that woman is unclean (because of menses) and the cause of the fall of man. This teaching alarmed the people, for it was well known that "a people cannot be conquered until the hearts of its women are on the ground." Meanwhile, on diplomatic and military levels, the men fought losing battles. Word came back along the great trade routes that the process was everywhere the same in Indian country.

But there was hopeful news from the Iroquois in the North. As a primary model for their constitution, Benjamin Franklin and his colleagues were studying the League of the Iroquois and its Great Law of Peace, which by the late 1700s had united five, then six nations for centuries. Based on equal representation and balance of power, the Great Law had been codified long before European contact by Hiawatha and the Peacemaker, with the support of Jikonsaseh, the most powerful of the clan matrons. The Iroquois system was (and is) spirit-based. The Council of Matrons was the ceremonial center of the system as well as the prime policy maker. Only sons of eligible clans could serve on the councils at the behest of the matrons of their clans, at the executive, legislative and judicial levels. Public and private life were inseparable and the matrons had the power to impeach any elected official who was not working for the good of the people.

But when Franklin and others incorporated the Iroquois model into the U.S. Constitution, they omitted women *as a gender*, as well as men of color and men without property. Within fifty years, indigenous people were forced onto reservations, declared "alien and dependent" by the U.S. Supreme Court, decimated.

In the time of crisis, bereft of political power and disenfranchised in their own land, the Grandmothers felt their hearts sink low. But they did not allow them to be "on the ground." Instead, they took them *underground*, where they joined with wise men, Grandfathers, who accepted women's power as a complement to their own. By restoring the balance of the Creator's law for survival as well as by keeping faith with other sacred laws, American Indians have slowly and patiently rewoven their lives and are emerging with renewed strength.

In most other surviving cultures, deep below the turmoil of historical events, there have been counterparts of the Indian Grandmothers and Grandfathers who, according to their customs, have found ways to ensure that the gender that bears life is not separated from the power to sustain it.

Many institutions in America are trying to bring gender balance into their structures—churches, synagogues, universities, corporations. The U.S. Congress is not among them. Two hundred years have passed since the U.S. Constitution was adopted, fifty-one years since the Equal Rights Amendment was first introduced for debate. Congress remains adamant in refusing to mend the Creator's law, as well as reluctant to make complementary, *enforceable* laws for the siring gender's responsibilities for children.

In some other sectors of society, also, the attitude toward women coming into the public sphere is, "What are you doing here?"

We know why we're here. We're doing our part to get the job done. Keeping our government and our society in balance requires the minds and energies of two genders. The more America is in harmony with the Creator's laws, the better off our people will be.

You and I are sisters but different. Yet we have common ground in an old saying, "There are many paths up the mountain." If we take the mountain to be Womanspirit rooted in the sacred, there is honor to your path and honor to mine. We are one in our calling to bring Womanspirit into balance with Manspirit in our world. We must continue in our paths and resume our rightful places on the councils that govern our land and its people. Otherwise, our Mother Earth will die. And all the lives will die with her. Peace to your path and peace to mine. On our way up the mountain, we'll call to each other: "Keep going. We'll make it. We'll make it. Sure we will. ..."

Womanspirit is coming back!

A corn seed for remembrance.

LITTLE DEER AND THE SELU CONSERVANCY

A stranger called.

It was early September 1989—the traditional time of the Green Corn Ceremony. The caller was very courteous. "My name is John Hargrove Bowles," he said. "I'm calling from Boston about a matter concerning my family, or—to be more specific—my deceased grandmother, who was a native of southwest Virginia."

Roots first—blood and land. A "purposeful-thinking" man. "Some mutual friends, Seymour Bellin and Clare Hilliker, gave me your name," he said. "They heard your poetry reading at Tufts. When I mentioned my present predicament to them, they told me about Little Deer and Rising Fawn, and what Rising Fawn's grandmother said about the wisdom of the corn. Before I ask your help with a project of mine, there's a background story I'd like to tell you, if you have time."

We talked for an hour on that day and on several other days. The following letter, written on September 22, tells the story:

Dear John:

I'm in "The Dwell," my study on the second floor of my house. On two sides the windows open onto the branches of old pin oaks. Walls and ceiling are papered with gray-green pine boughs on an ivory string-silk background. In the play of sun and shadow the boughs seem to move. I'm once again in the East Tennessee forest of my homeland. My brother-by-affection, Robert Michie, who is a poet, calls this room "a web suspended in time"—I thought you'd like that image of where I'm musing on the wonder of your call and the honor of your asking me to help seek a name for your great gift of conservancy land to the people of Radford, Virginia, and beyond. With Radford University and the good folks there as your partners in the conservancy, blessings are sure to flow to all. There is a spiritual energy in the Radford area. It is in the land and of ancient origin. Perhaps the Cherokee who left long ago invested the land with prayer and vision. I do feel that all of us involved are strands of a web that was spun in the mists of time.

Although you were unaware of it when you called, my heart is very connected to Radford. My mother and her sisters used to change trains there on the way to see their grandmother in West Virginia. Half a century later, an English professor at the University, Parks Lanier, read *Abiding Appalachia*—a book given to him by Jean Speer—and understood immediately what it was about. Then his colleague, Dr. Grace Edwards, invited me to teach a writers' seminar at Radford in 1984, and my association with both of them and the other folks at Radford has continued ever since. Totally unconnected (or is it?) from all this, Clare and Sy give you *Abiding* in Boston ... and you call me. This is a "Little Deer" event—a movement of spirit in the psi dimension of your mother's research. Wonderful. I feel a profound excitement, the kind that only comes when "the deep" is on the move. Your vision of the conservancy is that.

Meditating on the name, I've laid out the strips of thought you gave me, as if I were preparing to weave a basket, with primary attention to their spirit:

- Mother Earth herself in Radford—mountains, valleys, water.
- The nurturing care of her elderly cousin Solace Peters by your grandmother, Kelly Bess Moneyhun—and his gift to her of the land.
- Your wish to continue her nurturing, generous spirit in the conservancy, which you see as engendering cooperation, harmony, peace and respect among diverse people and among academic disciplines. Thus your hope that the chosen name be as "all inclusive" as possible.
- Your wish that the conservancy in its name and purpose acknowledge the Cherokee heritage of the area and that that heritage be a continuous component of the conservancy. Your intention of "giving back with respect" is why I am glad to help you with the naming.

I wove these strands together at the base, where they gave radial support to other, circular strands. Primary among them, and the major motif, is Grandmother Corn, also called the Corn-Mother. (I sent you Joseph Bruchac's version of her story in advance and I'm remembering our conversation concerning the spirit of nurture and cooperation.)

Other strands of my thought: You prefer not to have a hunting connotation in the name; you want it to be short and pronounced as spelled. And most of all, you want it to encompass your vision and to evoke it.

I add a thought of my own. Your vision is part of a great movement to restore balance and harmony in our society. Wallace Black Elk, grandson of the great Sioux shaman, Black Elk, recently put the problem that confronts American society succinctly:

> Today, people talk about their "Heavenly Father," but they don't know who their mother is. And we [Indian people] have a spirit that is with us here ... we know who our mother is. Because we talk about the wisdom which encompasses the knowledge, and the knowledge is a woman we call "Grandmother" or "Mother Earth." We were called fire-tenders and were earth-ruled. Our body is made of fire, rock, dirt, earth. Because we drink water and we eat green, we are part earth ... that's how come we are earth people.

I have been weaving all these thoughts together and a pattern emerged, a name that perhaps is in your mind already, and that I believe will call up your vision, your grandmother's nurturing spirit and our Mother Earth herself, as well as the Creator, who is the source of all. I use a simple Cherokee word, one that's pronounced in the Eastern Band in North Carolina as it is spelled. A word that means both "corn-the-grain" and "Grandmother Corn." The word is pronounced say-loo.

THE SELU CONSERVANCY

How does this sound to you? What images and possibilities do you see emerging from it? Could there be a cornfield at the conservancy where people could walk to feel the oneness of all things and the spirit of Grandmother Corn and of your grandmother? Will people begin to know "who their mother is" as a result and come to a new balance? I look forward to talking with you and to seeing if our minds are moving in the same direction. It would not be surprising to discover that it is so.

Again, John, thank you for asking me to help with this project. I am honored to do so and look forward one day to seeing your vision come into being in the spirit of Grandmother Corn: "One alone cannot bear fruit, but together we can bring in a harvest."

We will meet again.
Peace.
Awiakta

May 1993. The Selu Conservancy has been the catalyst for new ventures at Radford University. In 1991, with the English Department and the Appalachian Writers' Association as sponsors, Dr. Parks Lanier founded the annual Selu Writers' Retreat, which offers "time, congenial space and kindred spirits." This year a new Appalachian Regional Studies Center has been established on campus, in conjunction with a future retreat center and living history museum on the 376-acre Conservancy. The Studies Center's first major initiative will be an academic, interdisciplinary program, "Corn and Culture," to be held throughout the academic year 1996–97. Other plans are growing apace—for other academic programs as well as community ones affiliated with the University's Department of Social Work. True to her nature, Selu has set people singing and working for a bountiful harvest.

Dawn Birth

Sitting in the mountain's cold dark
I watch the horizon soften, dilate slowly
water-pale. Astral veins distend
flow violet   peach   labia rose
well to red, as the sun crowns
in the cleft between earth and sky.
I breathe deep ...

... am drawn back in the womb of space
where we two suns once
turned side by side
warm ... close ...
until pain cut through—
a passing star that pulled me out
alone ...

... I pant, breathe deep again
push with the silent rhythm
that brings forth the crimson face
the lusty cry of light.
I bend into the shine
open my arms
to my sister
my spirit-twin.

WEAVING II

Selu,
Spirit of Survival

© M.Adair '92
OIL

I Offer You a Gift

Still of the night …
   moon on the wane
   sun deep in sleep.
Cricket, bird and wind lay low
as rhythms of earth and sky
   suspend
   prepare to turn.

Awake in the dark
   you know
   I know
We may not make it.
Mother Earth may not make it.
   We teeter
on the turning point.

Against the downward pull,
against the falter
of your heart and mine,
I offer you a gift
a seed to greet the sunrise—
   Ginitsi Selu
Corn, Mother of Us All.
   Her story.

THE RIM OF THE BASKET

Selu, Our Mother, She Who Sustains, Our Life

When Siquanid' told Selu's story, he said he'd found it interesting from his childhood. After a decade of seeking her wisdom, I understand why. The Corn-Mother came into the world as a mystery, and she remains a mystery in many ways, even to science. Just as you think you know something about her, you realize it's only a beginning.

This is a story of Ginitsi Selu in America and of her continuing relationship with We-the-People. Directly with American Indians. Indirectly with others, or so it seemed at first. I share what I've thought through so far about applying the Corn-Mother's wisdoms. If I recounted all this to the elders, they'd probably listen attentively, then with a twinkle in the eye say, "You're coming along." The elders know that with wisdom, most of us "come along" to the end of our days. I think the twinkles in their eyes reflect the sunrise.

You and I have now reached the rim of the basket that is this book. Here the ribs/themes are turned inside: Wounds, Mother Earth, Healing, Selu. Thoughts devoted to the Corn-Mother and her wisdoms weave through them … over … under … over … under. Within the weaving rhythm are the words of Okanagan medicine man and Elder, John Kruger. Referring to his tribe's myths and legends—the stories that embed the wisdom, the laws—he spoke in Okanagan at a winter ceremony and gave this last message to his people: "We have made a mistake in saying these stories are coming from the past. We are the stories. What the story does is speak in the present and bring the past forward, so we can have a future."[1]

GREETING SELU AND THE SUN

"This thing they call corn is I. ... I will be the Corn-Mother. Don't ever forget. ..."

If we could actually go into a cornfield with Selu's story in mind, as my grandfather and I did so long ago, the Corn-Mother's wisdoms would be clear and unequivocal. We can't do that. Distance and time prevent it. But "the spirit always finds a pathway. ..."

Just before sunup, the deer trail brings us to a knoll at the edge of a narrow valley. A ripe cornfield stretches toward a horizon that's deepening from rose to crimson. Row on row of sturdy stalks, long curving leaves and ears plumed with brown silk glisten in the light, rustle in the morning breeze. Selu is singing. Her song carries the scent of moist earth and green corn, the scent of strength and regeneration.

Waiting silently for the sun, we commune with Ginitsi Selu and send gratitude to the Creator/Provider who gave the gift and to the indigenous peoples of the Americas, who received the whole corn and cultivated the grain and its spiritual meaning to share with others. We are grateful too for all of creation, for our families, our people, our own lives—and for the new day.

On the horizon crimson intensifies. We feel the coming of the sun. Mind/heart/soul open to the light. Sunrise.

Beauty. Peace. Hope.

We begin again.

The stories begin again.

As the sun climbs and warms to her task, we make our way into the midst of the cornfield, as humans have done from time immemorial. The Corn-Mother's wisdoms are all around us. In stalk, leaf and ear, we see her strength, balance and harmony. Hear them in the rustle of the plants, scent them in the air, touch them as we gather a few ears. Taste them, as pulling back the shucks on an ear, we nibble the tiny, milky-sweet kernels near the tip. Like deer and raccoons, we find them irresistible. We also contemplate implicit wisdoms: How the Corn-Mother adapts as well to this mountain

209

valley as she does to a plain. How we cooperated in the gathering, as others must have done in planting and tending the field. And no matter what the variety of corn is, we observe how each kernel respects the space of those on either side. Although diverse in size, and perhaps in color, the kernels are one in their nourishing power: Unity in diversity. From the many, one. Ginitsi Selu is a spirit of survival and her time-tested wisdoms are interconnected, a web with the law of respect at the center. Speaking of one wisdom, such as balance, calls up all the others. If we humans do our part, the Corn-Mother's blessings are manifold—for the body and the spirit.

It makes common sense to put her wisdoms into practice, but applying them to life is the hard part. Before trying to do that, we'll refresh our memory of the Corn-Mother as a spirit being, of her qualities revealed in the compass-story. Selu practices the respectful relationship she teaches. Discovering that her grandsons had spied on her, she could have told them the bottom line in four words, "No respect, no food." But that would have been inappropriately blunt. The grandsons had broken the law out of curiosity, not willful meanness.

Instead, Selu reminds them of their "good minds," their integrity—by using one of her most useful survival qualities. Siquanid's version of the story is the only one I know that backlights the Corn-Mother's wisdom with humor. The cream of Cherokee humor is scintillating satire, couched in dry understatement and accompanied by an almost imperceptible twinkle in the eye. Looking closely at this scene, we see the twinkle in Selu's eyes when she notices that the grandsons aren't eating her food. She teases them gently.

> "What's wrong? You're not eating very much. Don't you like me?"
> The young men said, "No. We're just too tired from walking so much in our hunting."
> "But I think that you don't like me," she said. "Or maybe you learned something somewhere, and that's the reason that you don't want to eat. … "
> At that moment the grandmother became ill. She knew that they had found out [her secret]. The grandmother took to bed, and she began to talk to them about what they should do.

Even on her deathbed, the Corn-Mother has strength enough to lay out about seven years' work for the grandsons. Of course, she knows she's immortal. So do they, because she's told them so three times: "Something will grow up right in the middle of my grave. ... This thing they call corn is I. This corn will have its origin in me. ... I will be the Corn-Mother." And she interlaces these pronouncements with directions so precise you could plant a cornfield of your own by them.

The storyteller says, "That's the injunction that the young men were taught to carry out. They thought about this deeply. ... " As any sensible person would. Clearly this good-spirited grandmother is a *force majeure*. Humor feeds her calm power to stand firm and sustain. The grandsons must mend the broken law of respect, but Selu uses the healing art of cheerfulness to teach them how to do it. "From this beginning there became so much corn that everyone in the world had some."

To this day corn engenders cheerfulness among people. As the Pueblo people say, "The corn will not grow unless you plant with a good mind"— with respect and a willingness to do your part. (That law holds true, even in print—as everyone who has worked on this book can testify. And maybe readers too!) It is not surprising that indigenous people, who have been the Corn-Mother's companions for centuries, also have a lively sense of humor that strengthens their ability to survive.

The Eastern Cherokee of North Carolina tell a version of the compass-story that provides another aspect of Selu's spirit. Although this version has the same essence as Siquanid's, its tone is both joyful and sad and the emphasis is different. For the grandson's age (there is only one boy) and for the ceremonial burial of the grandmother, the sacred number seven is used, which ritually signifies renewal and return; seven also stresses the story's universality. The spirit, the grain and the law of respect are for all people.

Joseph Bruchac tells the story in *Keepers of the Earth*. Because the first half of this version closely parallels that of the compass-story, I have condensed it.[2]

The boy and his grandmother had been living happily together in their mountain home. With a small bow and arrow she had given him, the boy brought in game every day. The grandmother put it with corn she brought from the storehouse and made soup for them. Life went along companionably until the boy became curious and unwittingly looked the mystery in the face.

He waited until his grandmother had gone out for her basket of corn and followed her. He watched her go into the storehouse with the empty basket. He looked through a crack between the logs and saw a very strange thing. The storehouse was empty, but his grandmother was leaning over the basket. She rubbed her hand along the side of her body, and dried corn poured out to fill the basket. Now the boy grew afraid. Perhaps she was a witch! He crept back to the house to wait. When his grandmother returned, though, she saw the look on his face.

"Grandson," she said, "you followed me to the shed and saw what I did there."

"Yes, Grandmother," the boy answered.

The old woman shook her head sadly. "Grandson," she said, "then I must get ready to leave you. Now that you know my secret I can no longer live with you as I did before. Before the sun rises tomorrow I shall be dead. You must do as I tell you, and you will be able to feed yourself and the people when I have gone."

The old woman looked very weary and the boy started to move toward her, but she motioned him away. "You cannot help now, Grandson. Simply do as I tell you. When I have died, clear away a patch of ground on the south side of our lodge, that place where the sun shines longest and brightest. The earth there must be completely bare. Drag my body over that ground seven times and then bury me in that earth. Keep the ground clear. If you do as I say, you shall see me again and you will be able to feed the people." Then the old woman grew silent and closed her eyes. Before the morning came, she was dead.

Her grandson did as he was told. He cleared away the space at the south side of the cabin. It was hard work, for there were trees and tangled vines, but at last the earth was bare. He dragged his grandmother's body and wherever a drop of her blood fell a small plant grew up. He kept the ground clear around the small plants, and as they grew taller it seemed he could hear his grandmother's voice whispering in the leaves. Time passed and the plants grew very tall, as tall as a person, and the long tassels at the top of each plant reminded the boy of his grandmother's long hair. At last, ears of corn formed on each plant and his grandmother's promise had come true. Now, though she had gone from the Earth as she had once been, she would be with the people forever as the corn plant, to feed them.

As Siquanid' did with his story, Bruchac gives a summation: "Grandmother brings both joy and sadness in this story. She is giving in every way. In life she gives the boy the bow and arrow to hunt with and the corn to eat. When the boy discovers her secret, Grandmother dies and gives her greatest gift: corn to feed the people through the generations. But the boy has to help the corn to grow. The land has to be cleared to prepare for the "seeds," his grandmother's drops of blood. Then he has to keep the earth clear around the small plants and care for them."

About coping with sorrow and joy, an ancient poet of India said, "Where there is no shadow, there is no sun." The Corn-Mother encompasses both shadow and sun without losing her equilibrium. The stories tell us so. And in such a familial, friendly way that Selu may remind us of our own grandmothers. It's easy to imagine that we emerge from the cornfield and meet her coming from the smokehouse, with a full basket in her arms:

"Good morning, Grandmother."

She greets us cheerfully—and without surprise (as mountain people have an uncanny way of doing). "I was expecting you. Come on in the house. I'm going to put some meat with this corn and make some soup." (Since there's game on hand, her husband Kanati or the grandsons must be in the vicinity, too.)

We give the Grandmother the ears we've gathered and catch a humorous flick from her eyes. "These ears are good and plump ... but the deer must have gotten to them before you did. Or maybe it was the raccoons."

Soon a kettle is bubbling on the stove and we smell a delicious aroma. Like Kanati on their wedding day, we feel peaceful and content—and even more so later, as we eat the hearty soup.

A spirit-being who cooks! And here we are sitting at her kitchen table, feeling right at home. It's reassuring and comforting. Maybe the country won't go broke and the planet won't die out from under us after all. If only we knew more about what to do to prevent it.

Answering our unspoken thoughts, the Grandmother says, "Nowadays you have a lot to contend with. Killing and violence everywhere—in groceries, schools, on highways and even in families. Violence overseas, too. Fighting in Europe, the Middle East, Africa. And people here at home are getting poorer all the time. Up in the Kentucky mountains, there are families living in caves because they can't find work. Mother Earth is sick and tired of what humans are doing to her, too: destroying forests, spilling oil in oceans, spreading chemical waste hither and yon. She's taking all green into her heart and ... "

What? Our spoons have halted midway to our mouths. How does she know our times?

"Oh, I'm current." The Grandmother taps her heart and her head. "These keep me current. They're better than television or fax. Older. I am the Corn-Mother."

She ladles more soup into our bowls. "You have to keep your strength up. Now here is what you must do first: Stand. When you've done all you can, stand. Think. And thank the Provider you have a day to do it in."

"With respect, Grandmother, we hoped you'd tell us exactly what to do—how to apply your wisdoms."

"Wisdoms don't work that way, you know. I give you the seeds. Then you have to plant, tend and harvest them. There'll be plenty for everyone. I told my grandsons the same thing, remember."

It sounds like seven years of work! We don't whine about it, but we must look disconcerted, for the Grandmother kindly gives another injunction. "Go and ask Native people who've lived the wisdoms. But don't expect how-to's from them either. They'll share what they know, but you'll have to work out the meaning for your own lives. That's the only way to learn wisdom. You can't outrun that law. ... Have some more soup."

As we leave her house, the Grandmother stands on the porch, waving a vigorous farewell. In her long dark hair, streaks of white reflect the afternoon sun. "Head East," she calls after us. "Get the job done. We will meet again. Remember where I am. ... "

Back in the city. Rush hour traffic. Our car is caught in a gridlock at a major intersection. Horns. Exhaust fumes. News spewing from the radio: "War continues to rage in Bosnia-Herzegovina. ... Senate rejects the President's jobs bill. ... In Miami, muggers beat a German tourist to death in front of her children. ... Locally, area sites are identified as leaking toxic munitions, buried in 1946. The army believes there is no immediate threat to human health and safety. No contamination has reached the city's water supply. ... Sports next."

How can we find the Corn-Mother in this chaos? Physically and mentally we're too gridlocked to head in any direction. How can we remember where she is?

From our pockets, each of us retrieves a sturdy corn kernel. "This thing they call corn is I." The kernel is deep red, like a drop of the Corn-Mother's blood. Or like a drop of our own, where genes bring the seeds of memory into the present, so we can have a future. "We are the stories." We have to remember that. We are the stories. We are creating them now. ...

SCENT OF SURVIVAL

Sometimes we encountered such a sweet smell that we stood still, because we did not know what we were meeting.[3]

The speakers were Flemish missionaries who lived on Manhattan Island centuries ago. The "sweet smell" came from cornfields in bloom.

The Corn-Mother's essence and scent—her sweet heart—have been constant since her birth. So have people's reactions. Encountering that aroma "too pungent to be honeysuckle, too fecund for roses," humans stand still. Breathe. The powerful, nurturing odor quickens all senses. Permeates mind and heart. Generates goodness, strength—and memory. "Kanati smelled the most delicious aroma he had ever known coming from Selu's bubbling kettle of fresh corn. It reminded him of the sweetness of his own heart."

Cornfields once overspread much of this land now called America, and winds carried drifts of pollen far out to sea. In summer, many voyagers approaching the eastern coast remarked on what Elizabethan poet Michael Drayton called "the luscious smell of that delicious land":[4] the scent of strength, liberty and hope—and of a native survival food. Corn has always been so much a part of life in this country that a Navajo man recently suggested that America should have been called "Maizeland."

Until industrial times, most Americans breathed the scent of corn's sweet heart often. It wafted from blooming fields or from milky kernels or from meal water-ground between great stones. Modern life has distanced us from this scent. Cities have pushed fields into rural reservations. Ears that can be pulled and eaten on the same day are rare. Most meal has been pasteurized—the sweet heart cut out—because it has no "shelf life." Once exposed, corn's heart must be cared for—like the human heart. The "fast lane" has little time for that.

But some people take time. The sweet heart of the corn is still available. It's just that it no longer stands outside our back doors. We have to go in search of field, fresh ears and meal. But they can be found. And so can people who still care for the hearts of others. These people are not usually sensational enough to be proclaimed through mass media. They don't up the ratings for television, movies, magazines or newspapers. But they do up the life expectancy of our country.

You-the-People are out there. I meet you everywhere I go, and I come away with renewed hope. You've taught me that despite all chaos, the sweet heart of America is still alive. You've encouraged me to contemplate what a Chinese-American elder told me in the early 1980s, "The Corn-Mother has been talking to us for a long time."

Have we lived with her so long that she is a counselor coded in our genes? Can her traditional story help us develop a synapse in the mind, a lens in the eye, a drum in the ear and a rhythm in the heart that will reawaken the whole meaning of her delicious aroma? Breathing it, can We-the-People begin again to "form a more perfect union"? You've inspired me to ask these questions and seek answers. "Selu, Spirit of Survival" circles my thanks to you.

MEMORY BRINGS
THE PAST INTO THE PRESENT

The Corn-Mother Incognito. Or Is She?

Indigenous peoples have always known corn metaphorically in two or more of the four senses, mother, enabler, transformer, healer, that I use throughout this weaving. Although early European settlers took the grain only, there is evidence in America today that the Corn-Mother has taken barriers of culture and language in stride and intimated her spirit to those who will listen, even if they don't know her story or call her by name.

One evening I told the story of Selu to a gathering of mountain people in Virginia, starting with the traditional words, "In the beginning, the Creator made our Mother Earth. Then came Selu, Grandmother Corn. ... "

Afterward a Scotch-Irish man of about thirty, an English professor, drew me aside. "I have a story to share with you," he said. "I live back in the country by myself in my grandmother's old house. I raise a little stand of corn and sometimes I take my hand mill and sit on the porch and grind meal. It's a good feeling sitting there ... looking at the mountains, grinding, smelling the sweet heart of the corn. When anybody drops by, I give them a little bag of meal as a gift.

"Now the young folks, they're used to supermarkets and cellophane. I'm not sure they know what corn means anymore. But the old folks do. They might not use the same words you do about corn, but the words would have the same meaning. It's like corn is a perfect plant—the way it grows, the way it is. As the old folks walk away they carry the meal real careful, almost like it's something sacred."

For a decade I've traveled around the country, talking—and listening— to people in cities and rural areas, in parks, prisons, schools, shopping malls, colleges and universities. Wherever I go to share poems and other thoughts, I welcome each person with one sentence, "I've brought you a gift ... ," and extend a corn seed between my thumb and forefinger. No one yet has failed to raise a cupped hand to receive the gift.

Regardless of their ethnic backgrounds, people in the Four Directions—North, South, East and West—respond in similar ways. Some ponder the seed quietly, already knowing, or sensing, its deeper meaning. A few are indifferent (and stay that way). Most ask immediately, "What am I supposed to do with it? Plant it? Cook it? Eat it?"

"Keep it until I tell the story of Selu," I say. "Then you'll see it differently ..."

"I've already eaten mine!"

(Invariably, someone announces this.)

"That's natural. The Pilgrims did the same thing. But don't be surprised if you wake up in the middle of the night to find your hair tasseling out and corn leaves sprouting from your ears!!!" People laugh, josh "the announcer." A good-humored, comfortable feeling moves among us.

Humor usually surfaces immediately also in Native American audiences, where the spiritual meaning of corn is a given. For example, I was a speaker at the Governors' Interstate Indian Council, which is composed of two tribal leaders from each state. They were sitting in a hotel dining room at round tables in groups of ten. Before the session got underway, I circulated with my corn seed gifts, beginning with the group at the first table.

As I laid a kernel in one chief's palm, he said, straight-faced but with a twinkle in his eye, "What's this for?"

"Oh ... you know how corn grows—one stalk alone can't bear ears. In my talk I'm going to work around to the fact that one of us alone can't do much, but if we all plant together, we can bring in a harvest."

His twinkle spread into a smile. "You remember, don't you, that you have to plant seven seeds in one hole—that's the Indian way?"

"Sure I do."

"Well, when have seven Indians ever agreed on anything?!"

He laughed, we all did. People at the next table took up the joke and good humor preceded me all around the room.

The Corn-Mother and humans have been companions for thousands of years. Even in the seed—detached from Mother Earth and surrounded by sheetrock walls in a hotel—when the Corn-Mother touches people she creates conviviality, a feeling of community and well-being, as she always has done. This feeling is the common ground for Americans of all races, the place to consider what corn really means to us.

In the dictionary, English may relegate corn to an "it." But in the hearts of the people, corn is more than a food. Just to name a few dishes calls up thoughts of home and heritage and comfort:

Corn on the cob, steaming on the family table … roastin' ears pulled from the campfire, singeing fingers too eager to get at the kernels … succotash, hominy, grits, polenta, tortillas, chips … thin piki bread baking on a hot piki stone … cornbread rising fat in a cast-iron skillet … hush puppies and fish fries, popcorn and movies … Cracker Jack (with a prize in the bottom) … corn in pudding, soup, soufflé … in dressing with turkey, especially during holidays, when friends and family gather … and, at all times for frying and baking, corn oil to keep our hearts free of cholesterol.

We Americans have corn in our blood—and not only through food and its associations. Corn helped shape our traditional forms of society and government beginning centuries ago with indigenous people. The Corn-Mother also was a guiding spirit in framing the U.S. Constitution. How she did this is incomprehensible apart from the story of the Seneca and the Iroquois Confederacy, which I'll tell later. But how she influenced communities of early settlers—despite their apparent ignorance of her spiritual meaning—is clear.

From the collective experience of untold generations, Indians understood the power of corn to feed the body and spirit. With the settlers, who wanted only the grain, the Indians shared their expertise in cultivation, which included planting instead of sowing seed, cross-pollination, crop rotation and companion planting of beans and squash. They also shared ways of storing and eating corn (most of the dishes we just remembered so fondly are either Indian recipes or derived from them). But for the rest of the settlers' education, the Indians left them to the Corn-Mother and her ways, which haven't changed since humans first gathered her seeds from a wild grass.

Unless the settlers worked hard with her, she wouldn't grow or feed them. But if they did, she would. More than one family survived on wild game and a stand of corn. Especially in eras before the use of machines, there was too much for one person to do. Many hands were required to till soil, plant, tend fields, harvest, shuck, prepare corn for storage and cooking, and make meals. In the course of doing these things, people talked and told stories, they sang, danced, played and "courted." They also feasted and gave thanks for their blessings. Ginitsi Selu's way of gathering people in is as old as she is. She engendered a spirit of cooperation and community, which influenced the way people organized and lived their lives.

This rural communal pattern predominated in our land from pre-European contact into the early twentieth century. Until then even most major cities had the atmosphere of small towns grown large; stands of corn grew in the backyard gardens of many homes. From farmers who raised it as a major crop, to people from other regions who ate it shipped in, corn became—and still is—associated with the earliest days of our country and with the basic goodness of our heritage. For indigenous people this memory goes back thousands of years. Not all of the might of the great "zations"—"industrialization, urbanization, mechanization, conglomeratization, consumerization, computerization—has been able to stop the power of corn from running in our blood, singing to us. And we sing about corn, too. Americans can join in the national classic from the musical *Oklahoma*, "Oh, What a Beautiful Morning." Swinging through golden-hazed meadows and high-standing corn gives us a "beautiful feeling."

The Grain in Gaul

This "beautiful feeling," this singing energy that corn gives is often easy to take for granted—until we're separated from it. Perhaps that's why Americans living in foreign countries often long for corn, yearn to see it growing, smell it cooking, taste it. I thought everyone in the world loved corn this way, until I lived in France for three years. I was in my late twenties. My husband, Paul, our two toddler daughters and I lived in a trailer on a U.S. Air Force Base, which was in the middle of a beet field near Laon. The only place to get good corn was at the commissary, where the manager told me, "Sure we always have corn shipped in from the States. It's the same on every base we've got around the world. You take corn away from Americans and they set up a howl!"

I thought our French friends would be delighted to have a typical American dinner. I outdid myself in making it, even using some of my precious bag of stone-ground meal from the Smoky Mountains in Tennessee to make cornbread. I also had succotash and, as a special treat along with other vegetables and meat, a golden ear of corn on the cob for each person. The French guests sniffed at the corn dishes but refused to eat them.

"In France," they said, "corn is for 'les bêtes ou les paysans'— livestock or peasants."

I took this as a national insult, one step from burning the flag. "It's too bad French soil can produce fine wines but not gourmet corn."

Diplomats that they are, the French hastened to assure me that there were undoubtedly better varieties of *maïs* in America than they were used to. But they still didn't eat the corn.

For courtesy's sake (generations of Cherokee/Appalachian grand-mothers had clapped their hands over my mouth) and also because I love the French, I let their explanation ease an awkward situation. But it didn't ease my heart. Underlying my guests' remark I sensed an attitude more disturbing than a national preference about food. At the time I couldn't get a grasp on the full implications of it. I'd only recently arrived in France, a mountain woman, corn-fed on independence and democracy. I had a lot to learn about the ways of the Old World—and of Ginitsi Selu, who works for the good in the long run of centuries.

Now, after more than two decades of study and experience, I have a better understanding of "Corn is for livestock or peasants." To those with the power to do it, classing certain groups of people with animals—or with being "one step above the animals"—is to render them "its"—expendable. In Europe, linking corn to expendable people is not unique to the French. Nor is it a recent attitude. It has been ingrained in the European mind since the first contact with the plant and with the indigenous people who originally cultivated it.

The Past: Two Memories

The first generally known written record of corn in a European language appears in the log of Columbus on November 5, 1492. He was anchored off Cuba, and two Spaniards he had dispatched to explore the interior of the island reported that the natives made "a sort of grain they call maize which was well bak'd, dry'd and made into flour."[5]

Columbus thought he'd found "India" (that is, Asia), "Indians" and a new grain. What he'd actually "discovered" was the New World, its indigenous peoples and the Corn-Mother.

The Taino-Arawak of the Caribbean, in common with many other indigenous peoples of North America, had a form of democratic government. The people chose their leaders and participated in decisions. Their system evolved from their religious belief, which held that all life was in sacred connection and taught the principles of sharing, cooperation and living in harmony with the environment and with each other. Columbus perceived none of this, because, like most Europeans of his time, he defined government as monarchy—the oppressive control of the many by the few—and religion as Christianity, specifically Catholicism.

As other early European observers were to say again and again of natives on the mainland, the "Indians" Columbus encountered were remarkable for their hospitality and their belief in sharing. He found them "so naive and free with their possessions that no one who has not witnessed them would believe it. When you ask for something they have, they never say no. To the contrary, they offer to share with anyone. ... "[6]

One of the people's offerings was whole corn—the grain and its story, its spiritual meaning. Columbus took the grain only—and ate it. And asked for more. To use and consume was his cultural habit. His attitude may have struck a faint warning note in the minds of the wisest elders, a portent of what would soon happen to their land and their people. If so, the tradition of sharing was overridingly stronger. And the elders had not yet heard about his captives.

Columbus set sail for Spain with corn plants in the hold of his ship, and lying among the drying stalks were seven Arawak Indians whom he had taken prisoner in San Salvador before reaching Cuba. In their ears were tiny ornaments of gold. Here was proof that Columbus could make good on the promise he had made to Their Majesties in the conclusion of his report—that if they would fund his next voyage he would bring them in return "as much gold as they need ... and as many slaves as they ask." He added, "The eternal God, our Lord, gives victory to those who follow His way over apparent impossibilities."[7]

Thus, Columbus sounded the keynote of the attitude of Manifest Destiny: that the powerful of Europe, being superior, had the right to "use and consume" not only the new land but also its indigenous people, who were "uncivilized" and "pagan," that is, expendable. Within a century, the Native peoples of the Caribbean—some estimates say five to seven million—were dead.

The Spanish court was immediately obsessed with the gold and with the idea of slaves to mine it. To the peasants and other common people who were often subjected to hunger and famine, corn was better than gold. Within one generation (about twenty-five years), corn, principally of the dent, or field, variety, spread over most of Europe. Farmers learned to grow it mostly as a food for livestock. Only in certain parts of southern Europe—Italy, Greece, Yugoslavia and Rumania—did people eat it, and then usually as a kind of soupy mush (polenta) that was not associated with royalty, aristocracy or anyone who had pretensions to their powerful circles. The Portuguese took corn to Africa. Within two generations after Columbus's voyage, corn had spread through other trade routes to India, Tibet and China.[8]

When European ships began to reach the Chinese coast, corn was already extensively grown there and taxed by the emperor, a fact that provides a clue to the phenomenally rapid spread of maize worldwide. Many Native people were expert navigators, and there are historic records of their "discovery" of Europe from at least the eleventh century onward. Chinese documents written in the twelfth and thirteenth centuries indicate that Chinese and Arab merchants had visited the New World and acquired corn. A growing body of research establishes that African traders did the same and that corn already had a start in Africa, Asia and Europe when post-Columbian traders arrived there, bringing more of the grain.[9] (Just as you think you know something about the Corn-Mother, she deepens the mystery.) Thus did humans, corn's traditional companions, spin a web of corn silk from the New World out into the Old.

In this process corn apparently was used as a "trade item," not as a gift with a spiritual meaning. However, we do not yet have full knowledge of how it was *received*. To common people —whom I call hereafter "the folks" (because that is what we call ourselves)—corn became a physical staff of life. Because the grain was nutritious, economical to raise, adaptable to climate and altitude, and suitable for humans and livestock to eat, the folks rapidly incorporated it into their food cycle. Some of them may also have perceived the presence of the Corn-Mother in the new grain and welcomed her as a kindred spirit into the circle of their traditional stories. If so, they would have done it through the oral tradition; we will not know this aspect of corn's history until their storytellers and poets tell or write about it or until their work is made more accessible.

The nutritional impact of corn is well documented. Apparently incognito, the Corn-Mother nevertheless continued her work as enabler and transformer. Maize did for livestock what potatoes and beans—also "gifts from the Indians"—did for humans. This great infusion of protein into their cycles strengthened populations and the will of the people as well. During the eighteenth century alone, when corn and other Indian crops were being widely cultivated in southern Europe, the population of Italy grew from eleven million to eighteen million, and the population of Spain doubled. On a world scale, the population of Europe, Asia and Africa in 1750 was estimated to be 750 million, reaching a billion in 1830.[10]

From the time of Columbus's first voyage onward, as corn increased the people, it also multiplied their dreams of its birthplace. The poor and oppressed dreamed of a land of their own where they would be free to find their place in the sun, where no one would consider them expendable. Monarchs and the powerful dreamed of territory, more power—and gold.

In centuries to come, people from Asia, Africa and Europe would follow the strands of the corn-silk web back to its center: the Americas. Europeans would come first—the poor and oppressed moving slowly, the powerful with great speed. Columbus had no sooner reached the court in Madrid than Their Majesties set plans in motion to send him back to Hispaniola. In September 1493—the season of green corn—he sailed from Cadiz on his second voyage to the New World, this time with seventeen ships and twelve hundred men.

Other explorers quickly followed in his wake. One of them was Amerigo Vespucci, who sailed to Brazil and southward along the continental coast, a voyage that convinced him, and scholars as well, that the newly discovered lands were not part of Asia but a *mundus novus,* a "new world." In Germany, humanist Martin Waldseemüller suggested that Vespucci's discovery be called "America" and popularized the name later applied also to the new land in the north. For about three centuries, only indigenous peoples were called "Americans."

The *Encyclopedia Britannica* sums up the Eurocentric memory of this growth era: "Corn became the bridge over which European civilization traveled to a foothold in the New World."[11] Indigenous people remember the "foothold" as a "crushing boot" and the "bridge" as one that was built with the grain only. Its spans did not include the law of respect.

With ruthless armies, the conquistadors Hernando Cortez and Hernando de Soto came to search for gold. To keep their armies going, they confiscated native stores of corn, as well as carriers (men), and women—three staples of military supply. Native people fought back. And they have preserved the history of this cruel time in their oral and written traditions. As if it happened yesterday, the Choctaw of Mississippi today tell of de Soto's bloody march through their nation on his way to "discover" the Mississippi River. With an army of six hundred men, he entered Choctaw territory in what is now part of Alabama. Capturing Chief Tuscaloosa, de Soto demanded carriers and women as ransom. Women were promised for delivery at Maubilia, a large Indian town possibly near the site of present-day Mobile. When the Spaniards arrived there, thousands of Choctaw warriors were waiting for them, and in the fierce battle that ensued thousands of Indians died. Their weapons were no match against Spanish guns and horses, but the warriors inflicted such hurt on the Spaniards that de Soto left the territory, leaving behind his baggage and booty stolen from the Indians. The Choctaw rescued Chief Tuscaloosa.[12] Among Native people, this story was repeated many times—only the faces were different. Europeans at the time recorded many of these events in writing, which has made it possible to retrieve the written historic record.

In Florida in 1565—near the place where Ponce de León had stepped ashore two generations earlier to claim the "island" for Spain—Don Pedro Menéndez de Avilés took over an Indian village and renamed it St. Augustine, the first permanent European settlement on the United States mainland. By this time the Taino-Arawak of the Caribbean had "vanished." Only in *History of the Indies* (still available from Harper & Row, 1971), written by Bartolomé de las Casas, who was a priest and an eyewitness, was there a major account of how Spanish politics of conquest and slavery had used and consumed them. "My eyes have seen these acts so foreign to human nature," Las Casas said, "and now I tremble as I write." (This work, which has been called "the most formidable testimony of denunciation in history," has been a chief resource for scholars since its publication in the mid-1500s. Yet, American history books have continued to teach about Columbus and his "discovery" of America as a great and glorious adventure. Schoolchildren still merrily chant, "In fourteen-hundred-ninety-two, Columbus sailed the ocean blue. …")

The fission of energy that fueled these events was generating throughout the 1490s, the cusp of the sixteenth century. In their dreams, most Europeans, rich and poor alike, saw corn gleaming white and gold in the sun. It symbolized for them a land of milk and honey. The land promised appeasement of their hungers. "It" was there for the taking. There were also people like Las Casas, who vigorously opposed this attitude, as well as philosophers and ordinary folks, who saw a great hope in the New World and in native ways. History doesn't often bring these people to the fore, but it is vital to remember they existed—and were at work.

These are the broad outlines of the era Columbus's voyage set in motion—a story passed to us from the memory of those who came to the land they called America and from the memory of the people who had long called this land home. Both memories are part of the story. Both bring seeds from the past into the present. And among the seeds of both is one the people have called a survival food for many centuries—*Zea mays*, Indian corn.

Generating Energy for the Future

Remembering the past, we look to the future. Like the 1490s, the 1990s are a time of upheaval, violence and change—on every continent, in every country and in our own neighborhoods. Whether it is directed toward Mother Earth or toward people viewed as expendable, the attitude of use and consume is incompatible with the survival of the whole. Old patterns of power and society are disintegrating. The ground beneath our feet is shifting, and almost everyone has a sense of teetering on the turning point. The downward pull is strong.

So is the upward pull. Many people are working to create new patterns, new ways of thinking that incorporate the best ideas from the past and give us hope for the future. To regain our national balance, to get the job done, will require strength, determination and patience. By a law of nature, wounds and sicknesses that have developed slowly will be slow to heal. "What wound does not heal but by degrees." As a people, Americans are conditioned to expect fast results, but we can't outrun the law of healing. Wisdom says: slow down, work patiently, steadily—as your forebears have done before you—and move forward. Begin again.

A major difficulty in finding solutions to our dilemmas is that We-the-People have become so diverse that unity is illusive and sometimes seems impossible. Beginning about twenty-five thousand years ago, four races from six continents have converged on this one. We have cross-pollinated into innumerable varieties of Americans. This diversity is causing strife in the nation, in communities, in families and within individuals. It is an appropriate time to remember the survival food that runs generations deep in our blood and reaches back to ancestors in our mother countries.

Americans eat corn every day—in fresh kernels, meal, syrup and oil. What if every time we encounter the grain, we remember the Corn-Mother—the law and wisdoms embedded in her story? What if we connect this law and wisdoms to kindred ones in other spiritual traditions we hold? What if we then create new harmony in ourselves, with each other and with Mother Earth? What if this result was the intent of the Original Donor of the gift, seven thousand years ago?

SEEKING WISDOM
WITH A "GOOD MIND"

Hard-pressed with the business of living and overwhelmed with information pouring in from every side, some readers may say, "Why don't you just cut to the point—give us the wisdoms, tell what the Indians said about them, and let's get on with it."

I understand the feeling. At times when I've felt impatient during the long weaving of this book, I've remembered the words of Asudi, a ninety-two-year-old Cherokee man I met through the Cherokee scholars Jack and Anna Kilpatrick, in their book *Friends of Thunder*. They describe Asudi as being so physically hale that he might be mistaken for a man of sixty and as being correspondingly keen in sensitivity and mental endowment. "Unaffected but wise, devout yet understanding, open yet still reserved, in his green old age he symbolizes the national concept of the fruition of the good life."

This is the way Asudi "cuts to the point": "There are some things I do remember of the days of long ago that they told about, these events (and stories) that they passed down. 'Everything is just as God planned. He made everything the way it is and He planned the way all things should live'— that's what they talked about. ... In their conversations they would come to these jokes and then go back to more serious things. ... That's the way you heard things, and *if you didn't pay any attention, you wouldn't know anything. If you paid attention, you would know.*"[13]

Italicized in my mind, that's the bottom line. I've taken Asudi's words to heart—in writing this book and in living my life. I hope one day to approach the balance he has achieved. His words remind me of Job's in the Bible (12:7–12):

> But ask the beasts, and they will teach you;
> the birds of the air, and they will tell you;
> or the plants of the earth, and they will
> teach you;
> and the fish of the sea will declare to you.

228

Who among all these does not know that the
  hand of the Lord has done this?
In his hand is the life of every living thing
  and the breath of all mankind.
Does not the ear try words as the palate
  tastes food?
Wisdom is with the aged,
  and understanding in length of days.

These are indivisible:
The corn—grain and spirit.
The story and its cultural context.
The wisdoms and the people
who have preserved them.

In seeking guidance from contemporary Native peoples about the Corn-Mother's wisdoms and how to apply them, it is essential to consider the above elements as a whole. Because of respect. And also because the people themselves make no separation.

The speakers and the Indian nations they represent are offered as exemplars of indigenous thought about the spiritual meaning of corn. Among the wisdoms are strength, balance, harmony, adaptability, cooperation and unity in diversity, centered in the law of respect. Like a web, they are interconnected. Although one strand may be contemplated at a given time, the others are also clearly present. These wisdoms have helped indigenous people survive for centuries, especially against the odds of the last five hundred years. And the wisdoms do not change with time. I will give some of the strands that connected to the people's lives before European contact, as well as those that connect in the present. It should be pointed out that not all Native peoples raised corn as a major crop, but they have traditionally applied the unified way of thinking to all of the creation, which is sacred and governed by the laws of relationship.

As a primary source and also as a model for the holistic presentation in "Selu, Spirit of Survival," I have used *Our Mother Corn*, written by American Indian scholars and tribal elders and published by the United

Indians of All Tribes Foundation in 1981. These scholars and elders give what scholars of the West so often miss in writing about Indian peoples—probably because it is missing in traditional Western thought itself—and that is the sacred link between the material and the spiritual that makes of the two a seamless whole. *Our Mother Corn* speaks of the whole corn—the grain and its sacred meaning—in a clear, beautiful way. Careful attention is given to the correlation between the People's reverence for corn and their ways of living. Unfortunately, the book is out of print and rarely to be found even in libraries. I hope it will be reprinted.

UNIFIED THINKING AND INNER BALANCE

What you're handling is very sacred. You've got to put yourself in tune with that spirit of what you're doing ... so it becomes part of you.
—Paul Encisco, artist
Taos Pueblo/Apache
Our Mother Corn[14]

The Hopi say that "Our Mother Corn" has been an integral part of their life and ceremony from "the time immemorial." In their origin stories they tell that she was with them even before the people emerged from the land beneath the earth into the present world. She accompanied them through the millennia of their four great migrations and was with them when they settled in their permanent home—the mesas of what is now northeastern Arizona. The Hopi reservation is located there, and the village of Oraibi on the Third Mesa is over one thousand years old, the oldest continuously occupied settlement in the United States.

In this hot, arid region the Hopi have always cultivated an ancient and unusual strain of corn that grows well in a desert environment. A traditional story tells how the Hopi chose the short blue corn for their own because it was small and tough and would help them endure. They also grow varieties that are red, white, yellow, and speckled.

It takes much hard work to bring a crop to harvest. Corn is planted in dry creek beds, at the bottom of cliffs, and most commonly in sand dunes. Clearing and preparation of the fields is done in February, the planting in April or May. A hole is made in the soil with a pointed stick and four to eight seeds are put in it, sometimes as deep as eighteen inches. As plants grow, they must be protected from wind and excessive dryness. Little can be done about flooding and destruction by mice and cutworms. Perhaps only half the crop survives until harvest. Men and boys care for the corn in faraway fields. Women watch over those near the village.

Planting is done by the men, older boys and children, with families often working together. Each day the planters work in a different family's field. While they work, the women and girls are cooking a big feast to be enjoyed after work is done. Corn in kernel or meal is used in many staple dishes. One of them is the paper thin cornbread, *piki*, which is baked on hot piki stones. Making piki well requires great skill developed through long practice.

The Hopi say that Our Mother Corn was a gift from the Creator, and they express reverence and gratitude for her in many ways. In ceremonies corn kernels, stalks, leaves, pollen and meal are ritually used. In the *kiva* the Road of Life is drawn with cornmeal. Paths of cornmeal are marked for the approaching *kachinas*. Baskets and plaques of cornmeal are common offerings during all rituals. The Hopi greet the rising sun with prayers and offerings of cornmeal.

They bring this reverent attitude into all their relationships with corn, including grinding it. Traditionally, women grind the corn by hand between two stones—the *mana* and the *metate*—which usually are passed from mother to daughter for generations. At a very early age girls learn the art of grinding from their mothers and grandmothers. The first woman cracks up the corn, then passes it to the next, who grinds it into a rough form, which she then passes to the next woman, who grinds it down finer. While the women grind, Hopi men—usually grandfathers or old uncles—sing to them. It is a social occasion also. Stories and jokes abound, and work goes on for three or four hours until there are great piles of cornmeal. A short story about a young Hopi woman grinding corn in traditional times concludes, "There were happy memories in the pueblo, in her grinding stone and in the corn.

Her work today would help insure strength and happiness for her family tomorrow and the days to come. Taiyomana felt peaceful and well as she rocked and swayed, forward and backward to the music of the mana and the metate."[15]

Further insights into how the Hopi feel about corn and the grinding of it are provided in the traditional grinding song and the interpretation that follows it, which are quoted from *Our Mother Corn*:[16]

> *From the corn we gather the pollen.*
> *The pollen that is like gold,*
> *reminds us of the color of anointment of the ancient ones.*
> *Grinding the corn it reminds us of heaven*
> *and it reminds us of earth.*
> *It reminds us that Father Sky and Mother Earth will unite forever.*
>
> *From the corn we learn to live,*
> *we learn the life that is ours,*
> *by grinding the corn we learn the footsteps of life.*
> *We go through a purification,*
> *until we are like dust.*
> *The corn came from the dust,*
> *from Mother Earth,*
> *and it gives life,*
> *life from Father Sky.*
>
> *We are like the kernel that comes from the corn.*
> *With it we bring life,*
> *like the seed of the corn.*
> *Corn is the fruit of the gods,*
> *it was brought to us by the Creator*
> *that we may remember him.*
> *Our lives,*
> *we must remember that they are holy.*
> *The corn is sacred.*
> *We are sacred.*
> *We hold the seeds of the gods to the future.*

Paul Encisco is a well-known contemporary artist and craftsman. A Taos Pueblo and Apache man, he says this about the importance of corn and the grinding songs. His words are a model of unified thinking, of the synthesis of mind/heart/spirit that the Cherokee call "purposeful thinking":

> The grinding song may tell you first of all that what you're handling is very sacred, and that you've got to put yourself in tune with that spirit of what you're doing, so it doesn't become a chore to you but it becomes part of you. You're creating something, you're doing something. And what you must do is master it, so that as you begin and the rhythm begins to flow through you, you just begin with that feeling, and after you're through grinding, then the feeling goes on to the person at the next stone, who grinds the corn down a little bit more, and a little bit more. And a lot of times stories are told that remind you of life itself, how you must go through life, how you must walk, just like the corn has come from the stalk, and also be thankful, not only to Mother Earth and to Father Sky and also to the sun for what it provides, but also to the Creator of All for creating these things. He has prepared the corn for us to one stage, and now we prepare it in different stages for our own use. And this is why we must be thankful. Because eventually what comes from the ground goes back to the ground, and we just keep exchanging, and so it shows our gratefulness for all this, the cycle. The cycle is never broken. It's an eternal thing, and the grinding song makes us part of it.[17]

Even in print, Paul Encisco's words have the same cyclical rhythm as the thoughts they convey. Spoken aloud they deepen one's understanding even more, because the sound itself opens the door, similar to the way a song does. Read the words aloud yourself, or have someone else read them to you. See if this brings a different way of "knowing" how corn interweaves with the lives of the people:

> ... stories are told that remind you of life itself, how you must go through life, how you must walk, just like the corn has come from the stalk ...

Balanced and harmonious in form and substance, corn is born from the union of male and female flowers that grow on the plant. The male flowers grow on the tassel and produce pollen. The female flowers grow on a structure lower on the plant that later becomes the ear. Part of the female flowers, appearing as slender silks, receives the pollen. Kernels begin to grow, to fill with milk until they are ripe and whole. This is the way the Creator designed corn to *"walk from the stalk."*

And the Hopi aspire to walk the same way, in balance and harmony with nature and with each other. Although men and women step differently, their paths intertwine, as we have seen in their relationships with corn. In the family, people are related to each other through their mothers. Children belong to their mother's clan, and men, when they marry, move into their wife's home, which typically is made in the pueblo design. When rooms get too crowded, others are added.

The women own and rule these houses, while the men own the *kivas*, special dwellings used for men's social activities and religious ceremonies. Women have societies also. At the age of about seven or eight, every Hopi child is initiated into the appropriate society.

Although life has changed for many of today's Hopi, they still practice many of the old ways, centering their lives on their centuries-old religion, which includes morning and evening prayers and participation in seasonal ceremonies. Doing these things helps a person stay in balance with nature and within him or herself.[18]

Our Mother Corn gives these principles that the Hopi live by. To live a balanced life a good Hopi is:

1) strong (physically and morally)
2) poised (free of anxiety, tranquil, concentrated on "good thoughts")
3) law abiding (responsible, cooperative, unselfish, kind)
4) peaceful (not quarrelsome or aggressive, modest)
5) protective (respectful of all life, preserving and promoting people, plants and animals)
6) healthy (free from illness)

The name *Hopi* means "peaceful, good and happy." In English they are often called the "Peace People." And they are also very strong. Beginning with the coming of the Spanish to the Southwest in 1540, many efforts have been made to "vanish" the Hopi and their culture. But the Hopi have withstood them and survived. Our Mother Corn is undoubtedly one source of their strength.

Deep Thought: The Door to Inner Balance

The womb is a quiet place, a place connected to life itself. The kiva represents the womb of Mother Earth. Hopi men go there to think. Women have an indwelling womb—physically and/or metaphysically—where they can go at any time. The point is that deep thought is necessary to maintaining inner balance. Life may swirl about, but inside one is "poised (free of anxiety, tranquil, concentrated on 'good thoughts')." Sustaining such a balance requires a quietness within—"Be still and know."

Traditionally, Native Americans place high value on thinking with this unity of heart/mind/soul. The power of such thought to shape the individual, society and events is deeply respected. Central to it is a communion with the Creator and with nature, where the sacred laws are embedded. Intrinsically, thinking also brings joy and pleasure. If you're thinking, you're "doing something." In Appalachia, and elsewhere in America, there are many non-Indian people who still speak of "communing with nature," especially in times when they need to be quiet and think things through. The problem is, how do we find quiet—inside or out?

A Cherokee man who is a scientist and lives in a city in North Carolina told me this story: "A while back, I went to visit my mother. Her front door overlooks the mountains. I was telling her all my woes: How confusing modern life is. How different ways of thinking are pulling me this way and that. How fragmented I feel. I asked her, 'What should I do, Mama?' And she said, 'Why son, just open the door. ....' She's right. I know the harmony's out there. I just keep forgetting to look."

Maybe remembering to "open the door" would help us all. There are social critics who say that as a people, Americans no longer like to think—indeed, that most have become incapable of it—and that flash, dash and superficiality are the mental hallmarks of our times. There is truth in what they say. But I also encounter many people who, like the Cherokee man, are just tired of being told *what* to think—and then labeled for doing it. A high-school girl in Kentucky put it succinctly, "It's got to where people put so many labels on you, you feel like a suitcase gone 'round the world!" (I urged her to write a poem about it. Isn't that a great image—"a suitcase gone 'round the world"?) Knowing how weary people are of being told what to think is one reason I offer my writings to you as "seed-thoughts." That way, you'll feel free to choose the ones that you find appropriate and leave the others.

Drawing the Line

The Hopi philosophy of inner balance and peace gives much food for thought. In writing this section, I often remembered Maria Martinez, the great potter from the Ildefonso Pueblo, who has inspired me very much—the way she lived in the round, combining care for her family, her art and her people. I've also remembered a film I recently saw, which Pueblo scholars and artists made about the post-Columbian experience of their people. Being peaceable does not preclude drawing the line on disrespect, as the Corn-Mother exemplifies.

The film opened with a view of a cornfield singing in the wind. A voice-over spoke about the significance of Our Mother Corn and other spiritual values. From there the story of Spanish oppression unfolded. The Pueblo people bore with it for many years—until they reached the limit of their endurance. On the land at a sufficient distance from the Pueblos, they drew a ceremonial line of cornmeal. The Spanish crossed it. And were defeated. There are times when the most peaceable people must enforce the law. Now as then, the Hopi have the inner balance to do that and to sustain their traditional beliefs—to hold steady in the midst of change. Thought is central to maintaining balance. It would help us as individuals to do it if the dominant culture put more value on thinking, as opposed to an excess of doing.

Listening for Unity

In American society today cultural diversity makes it imperative that we develop deeper ways of communicating with each other, of thinking and listening to each other, because our mind-sets and the language we use to express our thoughts are diverse also. Often, we automatically assume adversarial positions when respectful thought would lead to cooperation.

For example, at a distance too far to make out the exact words of two speakers, language sounds like music. Listening to the rise and fall of voices, the intensity of tone, the rests between phrases, it is possible to pick up the essence of what is being said and the emotions invested in it. At a Cherokee ceremonial dance, I once asked a male singer, "What do the words of the song say?" And he replied, "The songs are from so long ago I don't know what the words say. But I know what they mean." On reflection, I realized that I knew what they meant too. Music is an international language.

Listening in this way is the audio equivalent of looking at something from the corners of the eyes. Sometimes looking at an object only straight-on gives us its literal shape but distorts the spirit of what we're perceiving. In a similar way, focusing on the literal meaning of the words another person is saying, especially emotionally loaded words, may cause disharmony the second they're uttered. In conversations with people from different cultures, maybe listening with a unified mind to what is being said would enable us to hear the essence of what is meant. What would appear dissonant if taken literally may in fact be harmony in counterpoint—two strains of thought running inversely but compatibly—like a Bach fugue. In fact, this idea for listening first came to me years ago while I was accompanying my son on the piano as he practiced Bach on the violin. The following chapter is designed in counterpoint.

HOW THE CORN-MOTHER BECAME A TEACHER OF WISDOM

A Story in Counterpoint:
Two Mind-Sets, Two Languages

Corn is often called "the supreme achievement in plant domestication of all time,"[19] and its diversity probably exceeds that of any other cultivated plant. Native peoples of the Americas are responsible for this achievement. But how did they do it? And how did the Corn-Mother become a teacher of wisdom—one who feeds the people in body and in spirit?

Two versions of the story, told from opposite mind-sets and in languages appropriate to them, deepen our understanding. Science describes the grain's development and history, which answers the objective, factual part of the question, How did they do it? Only Native people can interpret the spiritual component of the question—How were they enabled to cultivate corn? The response encompasses the Corn-Mother as a teacher of wisdom. The contemporary historian Antonia Frazer wisely points out that when studying a people whose land is occupied by others, "The memory of the people concerned is an important element ... an element not always sufficiently regarded." Although science and the people's memory tell different versions, they are complementary and begin from the same point: The precise origin of corn remains a mystery.

I.

Science says that corn (*Zea mays*) originated from "a" wild grass, growing in a warm, wet place in the Western Hemisphere—"probably" in Mexico, "perhaps" as long as seven thousand years ago. Maize was the product of genetic mutation called "catastrophic sexual transmutation" (a term so momentous it makes me chuckle).[20] Studies indicate a spontaneous mutant of inedible teosinte, which would have remained inedible without human intervention. Indigenous peoples took the best seeds of one harvest

238

and planted them for the next. Over time the seeds lost their wild covering and developed a husk. They could no longer drop to the ground and germinate on their own.

Through centuries of keen observation and experiments of trial and error, Indians became expert in cultivating corn. They learned principles of clearing fields, planting seed, companion planting (usually with beans and squash) and field rotation. Through cross-pollination, they created many varieties of corn. Inherent in the grain's genetic diversity was an equally diverse immune system, nature's survival strategy for the adaptation that is so crucial to survival. (Modern hybrids, which are specialized for uniformity, do not have this diverse immune system. In 1978 almost all corn planted in America was of one hybrid type. It was susceptible to a fungus disease that destroyed most of the year's crop.)

The original cultivators carefully maintained the hardiness of the grain. Innumerable varieties of corn seeds and pollens have been found in archeological excavations. Among the oldest findings are fossilized pollen grains in the ruins of the Aztec capital of Tenochitlan, more than two hundred feet beneath Mexico City; maize deposits near the old Inca capital of Cuzo in the Peruvian Andes; and, in the Bat Cave and Tularosa Cave in New Mexico, remains of maize estimated by radio carbon analysis to be forty-five hundred years old. Indeed, corn has been a staff of life for indigenous peoples for so long that science cannot reach back to their first meeting.

However, science does trace what happened afterward. Migrating peoples gradually spread maize over the Western Hemisphere, from 5° north latitude in Canada to 40° south latitude in South America. It grew long ago (as now) in jungles and deserts, in high mountains and on plains below sea level. Ears varied in size (as they still do) from smaller than a human thumb to two feet long. Colors have continued to range from white or yellow to maroon, blue or black. Although most contemporary Americans think of the "calico" or multicolored variety as "Indian corn," for centuries after European contact, all varieties were known generally as Indian corn or Indian maize (to distinguish it from the cereal grains, which the English generally referred to as "corn.") In terms of the original cultivators, these names are most accurate.

The five main types (not varieties) of corn are:

Dent: Usually white or yellow, it is called "dent" corn because as the seeds dry, a dent forms in them. The Indians of the southeastern states grew dent corn. Today most of the corn used in livestock feed is a dent crossed with a flint variety.

Flint: Extremely hard, like the rock for which it is named, this corn grows well in very cold or very hot climates and was the main crop of Indians in the northeastern states.

Flour: A soft corn that is easy to grind.

Sweet: A tender corn, high in sugar. Indians in many parts of the country have grown different kinds of sweet corn since long ago.

Popcorn: This variety is actually an extreme kind of flint corn. Its small, hard kernels contain no starch and explode when heated. This is the type of corn that was found in the caves of New Mexico. (It is said that it still popped!)

From these five basic types of corn, indigenous peoples of the Americas had developed innumerable varieties by the time traders from other continents began acquiring the grain, probably beginning in the 1100s.

They had also created an elaborate cultural complex, which included methods of cultivation, harvest and utilization. According to science, the early colonists in America took from the Indians not only the corn plant but also its "cultural complex," on which modern American corn growing is founded to a large extent. Corn today has three major uses: feed for livestock, food for humans, and use as a raw material for industry. The annual value of the world corn crop is about $200 billion.

So extraordinary is the power of corn that in recounting its history, even the scholarly and precise *Encyclopedia Britannica* is moved to poetic images, calling corn "the grain that built a hemisphere" and "the bridge" over which Europeans came to the New World. Corn also "traveled" so extensively in the other direction that today "a crop of corn matures somewhere in the world every month of the year."

This is as far as science's story can go. The words "cultural complex" mark its limitation. From the Indian perspective, this cultural complex is permeated with the sacred. Early settlers took the grain only—the physical aspects of its agriculture—and passed that knowledge to their descendants, most of whom still think of corn primarily as an it, an enabler in terms of nutrition and industry. For the story of the origin of the whole corn—the grain and its spiritual meaning—we must turn to descendants of those who lived the story, descendants who by ancient custom still refer to themselves metaphorically as "the People."

II.

How were their ancestors *enabled* to make this supreme achievement in plant domestication? And how did the Corn-Mother become a teacher of wisdom?

The essence of the answer lies in what Paul Encisco says about grinding corn, which applies to its cultivation as well:

> ... *what you're handling is very sacred... and you've got to put yourself in tune with that spirit of what you're doing so it doesn't become a chore to you, but it becomes part of you. You're creating something, you're doing something. And what you must do is master it, so that as you begin and the rhythm begins to flow through you, you just begin with that feeling. ...*

From time immemorial, the People have passed along this sacred mode, this unified way of thinking expressed in the language of connection and relationship—a synthesis of mind/heart/soul. Western thought is based on dichotomies, which separate spirit from matter, thought from feeling, and so on. Inherently, its language is detached, and that detachment has increased in a society now geared to technology and the domination of nature. Some readers may consider the language of relationship "romantic" and balk at the idea that "the supreme achievement in plant domestication of all time" was accomplished by using the sacred mode Encisco describes. But the People say it is true. Their traditions say it is true. And every month, somewhere in the world, a field of corn comes ripe.

Even in a high-tech society most of us have moments when we experience unified thinking. It becomes a magnifying lens—like the water of a deep, clear well-spring. Looking through the water, you see what is on the bottom as if it were within reach. Details are vivid—veins of leaves, color and texture of rock, slight stirrings of earth particles. The water draws your mind/spirit into the mystery of their meaning—in themselves, in their relationship to all of creation and to your own life. You become very still. Perceiving with your whole being, you feel part of all that is—a beautiful feeling.

We "just begin with that feeling" and go back about seven millennia to stand beside the People as they contemplate a certain wild grass. How do they know that among all the other grasses in that warm, wet place, this is the one to choose—the one that has had a "catastrophic sexual transmutation"?

They *think* about it. Thinking in unity of heart/mind/soul is the key to the phenomenon of corn's cultivation (as it will later prove to be the key to corn's role in the great genetic discovery made by a twentieth-century scientist).

The People feel the grass, smell it, taste it—and perceive a gift from the Creator. They begin to work with the gift. Putting themselves "in tune with the spirit of what they are doing," they select the best seeds from one crop of grass and plant them for the next. Remembering that what they "are handling is very sacred," they work patiently and with keen eyes season after season. Even before she makes herself fully known to them, the Corn-Mother ingrains a primary wisdom of the Creator: Abundance lies in the balance of taking and giving back with respect. As the people prove they have learned this lesson, the Corn-Mother gradually arrays her seeds in a sheath of leaves—a husk—and entrusts her life to their care.

In the rustle of her fields, she sings (as she still does) while she grows and ripens. The People sing back, planting with a good mind. The rhythm of her song flows through them as they touch her, breathe her sweet, fecund scent, enjoy the fruits of her labor (and their own). They think of what her ways mean for their lives. They see that the Corn-Mother thrives better in a field than in a single plant, as a person grows stronger among family and kin. They watch the almost invisible pollen drift from the tassels and stick to the corn silks that are part of the small bodies below. When a tube grows from the pollen into the silk, a kernel begins to form and swell with milk. As the plant grows, its long leaf cradles the ear, as a mother's arm cradles her child.

Contemplating this pattern of creation, the People see their own—the harmonic joining of the male and female to create new life. And the ear "walks from the stalk" in perfect balance, carrying within it a strong, singing energy. They celebrate this sacred generative power of the Corn-Mother— and of themselves—in ceremony, ritual and art (which usually also includes the deer, the Corn-Mother's counterpart). They create stories to reveal the mystery of her coming and the wisdom of her teaching, stories that embed the law of respect.

Wherever they go in their migrations or in their journeys along the great trade routes, the People take the whole corn with them—the grain and its spiritual meaning. They find the Corn-Mother "infinite in her variety," willing to adapt to their environment and sustain them according to their need. And she is very, very strong.

Over the centuries, the Corn-Mother *becomes part of them* and they *create something*—not only a food, a love of liberty and a philosophy of living, but also a way of governing their society. They learn to cooperate, balancing the rights of the individual with the common good. In their councils they develop the art of discussion and compromise. The Creator's wisdom of unity in diversity—from the many, one—is evident in the ear of corn, where each kernel remains individual, yet plays its part in the whole.

It takes centuries of thought for the People to apply this wisdom, because, like all humans, they are prone to quarrel and fight. ("When have seven Indians ever agreed on anything?") Gradually each tribe creates its own pattern of living in harmony with the creation and with each other. Some tribes extend the pattern to become nations or confederacies. In their relations with neighboring tribes or nations, many of the People learn to temper war from extermination to the reasonable redress of grievances, which involve protection of hunting grounds and food supplies as well as of trade routes, towns and villages. From time to time, there are eras of chaos and destruction, when the People forget the wisdom and have to learn the Creator's lessons over again.

Since they view the whole of creation through their sacred lens, the Corn-Mother is not their only teacher of wisdom. The deer, the buffalo, the caribou, the spider, the eagle, the salmon, water and plants—everything in nature speaks the cooperative laws of the Creator. In July 1992, at the Native

American Writers Festival, one speaker said, "Nature teaches us democracy. For example, women, children and elders run the caribou into the trapnets. We younger men take them down. Then everybody helps prepare the meat—there's plenty for everybody to eat. Nature teaches you democracy. Who can say which people or which jobs are more important?" Because corn is shared by most of the People in the Four Directions—north, south, east and west—corn silk is a common thread that extends through time to the present. We see its continuity in this contemporary poem by Alex Jacobs/ Karoniaktatie, a Mohawk. He says it was inspired by two films: *HOPI: Songs of the Fourth World* and *ONENHAKRENA: A White Seed (Corn and Culture Among the Mohawk)*.[21]

The Law Is in the Seed

The Law is in the Corn
the people of the southwest say this ...
to be there with the morning star in that sacred time ...
to talk to the corn, to hear it talk in the wind
in the language of movement ... what to do.
Out here at the Eastern Door, we say it is
the Original Instructions,
but also that a sacred thing happened when we were
given the Great Law, for we had forgotten
the Original Instructions ...
When crooked men arise and become dictators,
murderers, thieves, cannibals ...
The People would take the seed and move
to plant their Corn in a new place,
once again under the shelter of the Tree of Peace,
this is called Democracy.
It is in the land, it is in the seed.

The Law Is in the Corn
The Law Is in the Seed.

In the relationship of Native people with the whole corn—grain and spirit indivisible—we've contemplated how unified thinking has given rise to a philosophy of harmony and balance. How it has enabled the people to move the Corn-Mother's wisdoms into the web of life—from individual to gender to family to society to government. This is the first tracing of a pattern that will expand as we go along.

We have also considered how two mind-sets and two languages may be harmonized to create understanding about the subject of corn and about the cultures of indigenous people, indivisible from that subject. By analogy, the method can also be used to engender cross-cultural understanding.

Extending Unified Thinking to Technology

The counterpoint mode in this story also suggests ways of creating harmony and of avoiding disaster in areas other than those based on ethnicity. Despite intolerance, strife and violence, there are strong trends in America to work for racial and religious harmony, focusing more on what unites than what divides. A kindred move is being made between the sciences and the humanities. From decades of confrontation in these sectors, American society has many wounds, old and new. Healing them is at the forefront of many conscientious minds, and we're delving into more recent dilemmas.

What is happening to us vis-à-vis our machines? On a recent television program, a Hopi elder assessed the High-tech Age. "If we continue in the way we are going, either our machines will overtake us—or Nature will take over." Originally, technology was envisioned as a means of freeing humanity from drudgery and disease, of providing time for creativity and deepened relationships. Used without respect, machines go out of balance, wounding everything in their range. Along with its benefits, technology has brought dehumanization and destruction on a global scale. In the personal dimension also, machines often become a world in themselves—separating, alienating, time-absorbing. Even the line between human and machine is blurring. Medically, studies already indicate that working constantly with machines, especially high-tech ones, is affecting human health. For example, long hours at the computer create a particular kind of stress that relates partly to body position and partly to mind-set. Long-term sitting in one position is detrimental physically. Apparently, working all day long with an entity that only feeds back to you what you put into it is like gazing into the pool of Narcissus. It tends to enervate mind and spirit.

Paul Encisco's words take on a warning tone when put into the context of technology. Are machines "becoming a part of us?" As they talk more like us, are we talking more like them? Are we becoming more unfeeling? If the future develops into "virtual reality," as some scientists predict it will—in which machines will simulate life, even to the intimate level of sexual intercourse—will all humans become "its"—expendable? Somewhere there is a balance of respect between the tools of technology and those who use them. Where do we draw the line?

Would it help to draw that line in a living substance—in meal containing the Corn-Mother's sweet heart? Would her powerful regenerating scent remind us of our own sweet hearts and the need to take care of the hearts of others? Would we be transported back in time immemorial to our beginning—as Homo sapiens—and to hers as a teacher of wisdom? We make that journey next—and in a surprising way.

SELU AND THE SEX EXPERT

A Healing Principle

The sex act ... is but a minute part of the overall act of love.
—Dennis Banks, Ojibway

From a "catastrophic sexual transmutation," the Corn-Mother was born as an androgynous plant, one that incorporates the balance of genders not only in sexual parts of silken ear and tassel, but also in the forces of nature that female and male represent—continuance in the midst of change. There is much wisdom to contemplate here, especially when we remember how Selu's gift of corn to Kanati helped him remember the goodness of his own heart and regain his balance with himself and with his environment. He stopped killing too many of the animals and took only what he needed—with respect.

It is like walking a circus high-wire to bring up the subject of sexuality in a society conditioned to the "battle of the sexes" and to categorizing men and women according to sexual orientation. In these terms, we have come to a catastrophic sexual confrontation. Many grievous wounds have been inflicted.

The Corn-Mother may provide a balm here also because her story focuses, not on sexual relations, but on the law of respect and on the importance of maturity in the understanding of the law. The relationship between genders is cast between grandmother and grandsons—or as in the following version of the story, between mother and sons. In these and other stories, First Man and First Woman, Kanati and Selu, represent a unity of mature balance. One strain of Selu's story is gentle: the grandsons break the law out of an inappropriate curiosity. In the harsher strain that follows, the sons kill their mother with malice aforethought. Considering the present state of violence toward Mother Earth and women, it is interesting that the next storyteller chooses to tell the latter version, which underscores willful destruction and the harm caused by disunified thinking.

In the following eyewitness account, a contemporary Cherokee medicine man, a respected spiritual leader, employs this version of Selu's traditional story to answer a sex expert's question about an individual, as well as to comment on the general American attitude toward sex, women, and the environment, which are interconnected. The medicine man's response is a paradigm, a model, for moving the wisdom of a story into the lives of the people by creating a synapse in the minds of the listeners.

The Medicine Man and the Sex Expert met for breakfast in a private hotel dining room. I was with a dozen or so Native women and men who had been invited to join them. While the principals exchanged preliminary courtesies, we clustered about the round table, waiting expectantly for the real encounter between them to begin. In the eyes of the other guests, I saw (as they undoubtedly saw in mine) humor moving, like the almost imperceptible flicks of brown trout in dark mountain pools.

In America, sex is a national obsession, an it, a commodity to consume. Sex is used to sell everything from toothpaste to cars. It is also sure to boost profits on movies, books and television programs. Many people talk about it—and probably do it—in the vein of, "Have a hamburger, have a beer, have sex." In this philosophical context, women, children of both sexes and some men become "its," also, available for exploitation and abuse. How to change the attitude? That was likely to be the subject between the Medicine Man and the Sex Expert. And it was brought up rather quickly. He was solid, calm, wearing a tweed sport coat. She was tiny, dressed in pepper red, and spoke rapidly—rat-a-tat-tat. ...

"Tell me, Doctor, when you have a middle-aged client who has sexual problems with his wife, what do you tell him?" She paused, as one would at a stop sign before driving through it, and fixed her pert gaze on the Medicine Man.

He looked at her levelly, considering the question. Then he replied in a resonant, measured voice, "I tell him this:

> In the beginning, the Creator made our Mother Earth. Then came Selu, Grandmother Corn. Her husband, Kanati, was a hunter, and they lived in the mountains with their two boys, a son and a wild boy, who had wandered up from the river to live with them. One evening the boys came home from hunting very tired and very hungry, and asked their mother for something to eat. "There is no meat," she said, "but wait awhile and I'll get you something."

Selu took a basket and went out to the storehouse, which was set up on poles and had no opening but one door. When she came back, the basket was full of corn. Every day when Selu got ready to cook, she did this. The boys got very curious. Wild Boy said to his brother, "Let's go see what she does." Pulling a chink from between the logs of the storehouse, they looked in. Selu was standing in the middle of the room with a basket on the floor in front of her. Leaning over it, she rubbed her stomach and corn fell into the basket. She rubbed it again and filled the basket to the brim.

"Our mother is a witch," said the boys. "Her food will poison us. We must kill her." And they went back to their house.

When Selu returned, she knew their thoughts before they spoke. "I see you are going to kill me," she said. "When you have killed me, clear a large piece of ground in front of the house, where the sun shines bright and hot. Drag my body seven times around the circle. Then drag me seven times over the ground inside the circle and stay up all night and keep watch."

The boys did as Selu told them. After they killed her, they set to work to clear the ground in front of the house, but instead of clearing the whole piece, they cleared only seven little spots. That's why corn only grows in a few places instead of the whole world. [The Sex Expert's gaze remained fixed, but her eyes began to glaze over.]

The boys dragged her body seven times in a circle but instead of dragging her seven times across the ground, they dragged her only twice, which is the reason the Indians still work their crop but twice. Wherever Selu's blood fell on the ground, corn shoots sprang up. The boys kept watch all night. In the morning the corn was tall as a person, and the ears were full and ripe, plumed with dark silks, like their mother's hair. The boys knew that she had returned to them as a plant, to nourish them in body and in spirit.

Since that time, only if the people work hard, with prayers and thankfulness to Selu, does she return to feed them.

And so I tell my client, maybe he is looking at his wife's exterior. Maybe she is not as pretty as when she was young. But he should look on her heart and remember *who she is.*

Stunned, the Sex Expert stared at him for about five seconds, then rat-a-tat-tat: "Tell me, Doctor, how did you become a medicine man?"

Ships passing in the night. That's what those two were, ships passing in the night. It was a wonderful exchange. From the corner of my eyes I saw that other people around the table were looking down, too, trying to keep the "trouts" from leaping out and flopping on the Sex Expert's sensibilities. But the encounter was deeply satisfying.

One of the guests, the Creek Poet who is a true singer of the spirit, said to the Medicine Man, "When I hear you speak, I know I'm alive." Her words seemed to express the thoughts of us all. And we walked out of the room straighter than when we'd come in ... and more joyful. It's a beautiful feeling to understand who you are, why you were created and that you're part of the universal family—Mother Earth and all that lives. As Asudi said about the stories, "If you didn't pay any attention, you wouldn't know anything. If you paid attention, you would know."

Some Reasons That Ships Pass ...

Some non-Native people have an opposite and very negative reaction to this version of Selu's story. Paying attention, listening with unity of mind/heart/soul, is crucial in understanding differences—among cultures, individuals or others of our relatives in the creation, animals, birds, rocks, plants and so on. We have to listen to what the other entity is saying.

In the human dimension, cross-cultural understanding is especially difficult because the givens are different—worldview, mind-set, language, memory. One reason Native listeners are not unduly concerned about what others often consider the harshness of this version of Selu's story is that we know the story is understood as a means of teaching the law of respect. Also, in a subsequent story in the series, the sons come home to find Selu and Kanati, who are immortal, sitting on the porch, as lively and companionable as ever. First Woman and First Man represent an ideal of equilibrium, for the individual's inner life (male or female), as well as for life partners and gender relations in general. The listener is supposed to take the story in the circumstantial context in which it is told and apply the teaching accordingly.

Especially when an archetypical story crosses into another culture, a cardinal mistake often happens. As a river diverts from its bed into a fissure in the land, so a story may flow errantly into a groove already carved in the listener's mind by a similar but different story. If Selu's story is kept in its own river bed, its own cultural context, the flow runs clear and to the point. Blame and punishment are not part of it. In all three versions, Selu simply states the situation: either "Now that you know [my secret], I must die" or "I see that you are going to kill me." The law of respect has been broken, and she matures the understanding of her grandsons or sons by teaching them how to heal the break—restore harmony to the relationship—so there will be plenty of corn for them and for the people. Work is not a punishment. Everything in nature must do its part to keep life going. Even the corn plant must put down roots, unfold leaves and photosynthesize its food. "It's a curious thing," my grandfather used to say, "that human beings get to thinking we're above the law. We're an uppity species sometimes."

This is the way the elders in my family prepared my mind to receive the story, so that is the way I see it. Of course, every family has its own ways. Although versions and interpretations of the story are diverse, they are unified on the central issue: the law of respect. Even so, a listener from another culture may pass the meaning like a ship in the night, as we've just witnessed.

In the Western mind, the general story—or paradigm—of the passivity of Earth and of Woman has also created a fissure centuries deep. Earth and Woman, so it is told, bear all things, believe all things and return eternally to nurture and sustain even those who abuse them. At first listening, the harsh version of Selu's story passes so quickly that one might hear it say that after the sons kill her, Selu simply forgives them and returns faithfully to feed them.

She doesn't.

Without being mean-spirited about it—even when the transgressors are bent on murdering her—the Corn-Mother calmly draws a line in her heart's sweet meal, reminding her sons that to cross it is to separate themselves from their sustainer. The line is the law. To break it will set inevitable consequences in motion. The sons remember the goodness of their own hearts. In a ceremony of sevens, they carry out the Corn-Mother's injunctions and faithfully keep the watch. Only then does she return to bless them. Ginitsi Selu endures all things. But she does not put up with all things.

Mother Earth is drawing the line even now.

The medicine man explained it very clearly—as clearly for those who listened as he would have for a client who was having a sexual problem with his wife. "In the beginning, the Creator made our Mother Earth. Then came Selu, Grandmother Corn. ... And so I tell my client, maybe he is looking at his wife's exterior. Maybe she is not as pretty as when she was young. But he should look on her heart and remember who she is." The flow of connection is unmistakable. Those who paid attention knew something.

Sex and Ceremony:
A Mysterious Twinkle in the Eye

Thinking of sex as an it and women as sex objects is one of the grooves most deeply carved in the Western mind. This groove in the national mind of America will not accept the concept of sex as part of the sacred generative power of the universe—and of woman as a bearer of this life force. The life force cannot be owned as property, used and consumed—or merchandised. Period. For all of its sweetness, the Corn-Mother's line is implacably drawn.

Paula Gunn Allen, the distinguished Laguna Pueblo literary scholar, poet and writer, deepens understanding of the traditional Native American concept of sex as life force through her commentary on a traditional poem, which was published in Brian Swann's *Song of the Sky*.

The Hopi Butterfly Dance

We wrestle for
corn-blossoms ...
We boys ...
playing with
butterfly-girls ...
We shall send upward
the young-girl-corn
thunder and corn
shall grow
together

A simple, vaguely sensual poem, if it is interpreted within the Western literary tradition. But listen to Allen, who speaks of her own people:

At Laguna Pueblo, long ago, the young women would gather to grind corn, and the young men would station themselves at the doorway of the corn-grinding room to play flutes and sing. ... Amid such giggling and blushing ... a specially vital food was created. Corn is the name of the Goddess Iyetiko (Beautiful Corn Woman) and also of one of her sisters. The Hopi Butterfly Dance is another example of the same ritual and understanding. Out in the fields where early corn grows, about the time the butterflies are hovering above the plants, young women go out and dance in the field. Young men go out and vie with one another over the women; sometimes they catch them. Hopi maidens wear their hair in a style called "butterfly whorls," and this signifies their power to attract generative power, unification and blessing.

According to Allen, referring to such rituals as "fertility" rites, as many accounts do, avoids their dynamic of "erotic magic" and distorts their meaning.

The power and connections between the seen and unseen realities which ritual practices are aimed at manipulating is based on sexuality— its expression, repression, focusing and directing. The generation of power is the purpose of ceremony and the sexual nature of humankind is the most direct link between this and other orders of reality available to human beings.[22]

Within this generation of power is the spark of the Creator, a light reflected in the star-like photons of atoms, a light that American Indians perceived in themselves and in every aspect of the wilderness. Such wonder evoked singing/dancing/rejoicing, and it gave the Indians what Marius Barbeau described as "a mysterious twinkle in the eye." A kindred twinkle is in the eye of quantum physicists as they follow the atom full circle to an understanding American Indians have always had: *Everything in the universe is alive and connected!* As this basic assumption takes hold in Western thought, standard form in everything from poetics to corporate structure is slowly changing. Perhaps the attitude toward sex also is slowly changing from compartmentalization to interconnection, from the box to the web, from the square to the round.

Sex Education at Hearth Level

My first memory of my parents instilling the concept of sex as sacred Life Force happened when I was twelve years old and my mother first spoke to me about my approaching womanhood. Mother said, "You'll soon be capable of bearing life. Think of it, Marilou. It's a sacred power, a great responsibility." I thought ... and waited for the power sign. When it came, there was a dinner in my honor and I chose the menu: corn on the cob, green beans, cornbread, fried chicken. I felt wholesome, proud, in harmony with the natural order. (And looked forward to dessert—warm blackberry cobbler with cream!)

As I crossed the threshold into this powerful, mysterious and vaguely frightening sexual realm, Mother gave me injunctions as explicit as Selu's directions about planting and caring for corn. She fed them to me gradually and with a twinkle in her eye, usually while I was helping her cook:

"After hunger and thirst, sex is the most powerful drive in the world. The Creator gave you a brain to keep you balanced. Use it." Or "Mother Nature has one goal and one alone: the survival of the species. That's why the sex drive is so powerful. Many seeds are sown, so a few will survive. That's Nature's way. And that's why as a woman you have to keep a good head on your shoulders. Mother Nature doesn't care if getting pregnant disrupts your life, cancels your education, or ruins your health. She has her overall plan in mind."

I mulled this over. "There must be a way not to get pregnant. You and Daddy just had Adele and me. What about contraceptives?"

Mother laughed. "There's only one sure way. And that's abstinence. Of course, that's no fun. But you have to think of the responsibilities, too. Bearing life is a sacred thing, so you have to temper yourself—and remember who you're dealing with. Mother Nature can break through any contraceptive invented. Why even women going through the change of life—who think they're safe—have turned up pregnant. We call it 'Nature's last stand.' I'm still relieved every time my period comes round. The only sure way is abstinence. That's why it's best to wait 'til you're married, because every time you have intercourse, there's a chance you'll bring a new life into the world. And a baby deserves to be cared for. Sex is good and natural, but it's only part of the whole picture, part of the loving. When all your hormones get to racing, you likely wouldn't listen to me, so that's why I'm telling you now. Self-preservation is a powerful motivator."

Needless to say, in the years to come, I wasn't always totally wise. But as hormones accelerated, so did her explicit advice, which I heeded more than not, because I could see the common sense in it. "You'll meet some boys that don't have the same idea of sex as you do. The more silver-tongued they are, the more you have to watch out. [Beauty is no threat to the wary.] Anyone who wants to separate your mind, body and spirit is up to no good. The minute you get wind of that attitude, draw the line ... but be respectful about it. No sense in making an enemy to no purpose. If you draw the line soon enough (say, at the first sign of inappropriate curiosity), you can maneuver out of the way before it comes to a knock-down-drag-out fight. But if it comes to that. ... Not everyone who presents himself is respectful. But many are. Test them out. Maybe you'll find the right one some day. Or maybe you won't want to. You've always had your own plans."

That was true. From my earliest memory, I had seen the world in poetry and images. I'd made up my first oral poem (Mother said) at age three and a half, and when I was six, I asked her to teach me to print so I could write a story. Being a writer and having a family had always been my goals, and by the time I was sixteen, I was determined to learn to speak French and go to France. Mother said even among good men, there weren't many who would want to deal with all that. Although the epigram in my high-school annual called me "the girl with the removable brain" because I loved to dance and cut up, I found that Mother was right. A big university was different; the boys I danced with weren't in my classes.

I met Paul on my first night at the University of Tennessee. We were both eighteen years old, and he had had a plan for his life since he was eight. We were friends for over a year before our relationship deepened, then grew into commitment. We were married in 1957, on the birthday of the prophet Elijah, whose symbol is a chariot of fire (which has proved an appropriate emblem of our life together, in more ways than one).

What would have happened if my life had taken a different course? If I had married later, or not at all? Or if my sexual orientation had turned out to be different? Or if I were eighteen today? Would I have accepted the law of respect back then? Would I follow it now? In honesty, like the grandsons in the compass-story I might have digressed from it, but I would have—and would now—circle back to mend my ways and be respectful of the sacred power. Principally because of two indelible lessons my parents taught me.

Mother said that energy, all energies—physical, creative, sexual—are one, like a river. "If you get sexually involved with someone," she said, "it diverts energy you could direct elsewhere—on your writing, for instance. A disrespectful man will take your energy and never look back. Instead of dissipating your energy, channel the force. The narrower the river, the deeper it carves—look at the Grand Canyon."

In sum, the idea was ingrained in me very young that sex is an integral power in the Creator's plan. That it is good, I am good, the opposite gender is good, provided the law of respect keeps everything in balance. A sacred power, a great responsibility. Since there was no television then, my only reality check was life around me. For youth today, it's much more confusing to know what is real and what isn't.

From the male perspective, what was my father saying? "Your mother is right. Listen to her." And then sometimes with a sly look he'd tease her. "Of course, when I was young, the old-timers always talked about 'the recipe' [for contraception]. It was made of some kind of root."

"Ummhmm," Mother said. "I heard about that recipe, too. Seemed like nobody would ever come up with it, though." And they would banter off into their own world (like Selu and Kanati). I liked it when they did that. It made me feel secure—probably because it was in harmony with "the law. ..." Which brings up another memory from my childhood—a swinging bridge strung across a river that was rushing and tumbling down the mountain over big boulders. From that perspective, I viewed the river not as a "carver," but as a consequence.

When I was about ten years old, my father and I were hiking in the Great Smokies and came on such a bridge. It was the only way to cross the Little Pigeon River at that point. Made of hemp, a natural fiber, the bridge had a walking space fifteen inches or so wide, and a handrope on either side that was secured to the walkway by single ropes placed at wide—very wide—intervals. Scary.

I balked.

To guide me across, my father used an old mountain way called "fronting your fear." First we looked at the bridge, studied it. Following the mountaineer maxim of "Never take a step you haven't tried or can't take back," my father tested the bridge for soundness (sometimes constant moisture from the water rots the hemp). Then he showed me how to walk in rhythm with the bridge, being respectful of its ways (each swinging bridge has its own because it's made by hand). He walked over and back twice, always waiting between trips for the bridge to quit heaving and swaying. I was more scared than ever. "Can we walk it together?"

"No," he said. "Our rhythms might get crosswise and somebody could get hurt—more likely killed." We fronted my fear for a good while. He'd walk over to the other bank. I'd wait for the bridge to quiet, then venture out a few steps—and freeze. The motion, the rushing water, the spray in my face were terrifying.

"Go back to the bank, wait for the bridge to settle and try again," my father said. "Think. Concentrate. Don't look down. Look at me. Listen to the bridge through your feet. Just go with the rhythm and you'll be all right. Don't step hard and don't jerk the handropes." Finally, I did as he said. When I reached the other bank, I was no longer afraid of the swinging bridge. But my respect for it was profound and would last my life long. Four decades later, I see the bridge as an entwinement of the life force and the law—and the result of disrespect as a fall that will hurt, or more likely kill, especially with the AIDS virus rushing below.

Song of the Swinging Bridge

Mind your step.
I'm alive!
Not steel or concrete—
musky sinew. Sunwarm
yet damp and pliant
in my deepest fiber.
I vibrate to your touch
curve to your shape
undulate, sigh beneath
your weight.
But ...
Stomp me—I fling you up.
Yank me—I break your stride.
Shake me—I swing you
in an arc of fear.
Mind your step.
Blend your rhythm with mine
so I can bear you safely
through the void.
When you reach solid ground
look back.
I sway gently
remembering ...

"Virtual Valerie" and Indian "Love Secrets"

At this exact point in the manuscript, an amazing and mysterious synchronicity of communications occurs. In early evening, I take a break, gather up the mail and turn on the television. An interviewer is introducing a program on electronic sex, which she says is being touted as the "boom of the '90s." I sit down with the unopened letters in my lap.

All but one of the panelists are enthusiastic representatives from the "new industry." Young men and women, attractive, well groomed, personable. They say that with these wonderful new video games, you can indulge any sexual fantasy you want and it will all be safe and won't hurt anybody. Yes, it is true that most of the women are presented as sex objects, but the panelists expect that will change. Eventually there will be more "multiplicity of roles." They emphasize, however, that there is no sado-masochism in the games. "We draw the line there." And electronic sex is creative, because you can invent your own sex partner of either gender and even invent yourself—become whoever you want and do whatever you want anywhere in the world and with anyone.

Sex in the box. Literally, figuratively, metaphorically. "Its" all around. Most of the audience is enthusiastic.

Now the interviewer turns to the sole "opposition" member of the panel— a woman of about thirty. To their credit, the producers have chosen someone whose comments won't sound like sour grapes. This woman also is attractive, well groomed, personable and calm-spoken. She is also wearing red, a wise choice. Given the tenor of the program, it takes courage to "face East." She says that these video games put human relationships at risk because relationships with real people take time and care. Might not these new video games become an escape from responsibility. And what effect will they have on the family— on relationships between the parents, on children's concepts of sex. One woman and one man in the audience agree with her. But the response of the other panelists and others in the audience is, "Oh, it's just a game."

The opposition has been timed for the middle of the program. The emotional load, the real pitch, comes toward the end. A segment from one of the games is shown, featuring "Virtual Valerie." Virtual Valerie is lying on the sofa with her legs spread, a buxom, Barbie-type woman wearing a black bikini. The viewer comes in the door, Valerie looks up and from that point, the viewer can take Valerie to the bedroom and fantasize—take off her clothes ... and whatever. The segment closes with Valerie luring the viewer into the bedroom ... (and to the closest video store). "Electronic sex is the wave of the future," they say. "Big bucks." Then comes the summation: "It's private, safe. You can fulfill all your fantasies with no harm to anyone and no danger of AIDS or pregnancy. Why be lonely? Go to your video store. And remember, it's just a game."

"Brave New World." With a chill I turn off the television. Just as it seems we're making some headway in calling Earth "Mother" again, in restoring respect for women as bearers of the life force, for other people who have been treated as its, and for humanity in general, here comes the disdain virus *again*. It has undergone a "catastrophic sexual transmutation" into an electronic game. Squared, boxed, labeled. A harmless fantasy in which viewers use and consume "virtual" men and women—and undoubtedly children, too—as its. As Encisco said, you "put yourself in tune with that spirit of what you're doing … it becomes part of you. You're creating something, you're doing something." And you pass what you are doing along. … First to yourself, for the attitude put into a video game circles back to the player. Electronic sex commercially injects the dehumanizing disdain virus into the most powerful human drive after hunger and thirst.

Keep this attitude "boxed, private, safe"? No way. We are on the verge of creating a society of virtual hearts, where those who remember their human mothers with love will be called savages. Aldous Huxley saw this coming over half a century ago, but the contemporary Hopi elder who spoke on television in the early 1980s saw an added element. "If we keep on the way we are going, either our machines will overtake us, or Mother Nature will take over."

The Life Force will not tolerate being treated as an it.

I see people crowded on the swinging bridge, respectful and disrespectful alike, caught in the heaving, swaying cross-rhythm. Bodies are falling into the torrent below—men, women, children, the unborn. … In my own community, they are falling all around me. Straight people, gay people, the old, the young. A pediatric researcher who specializes in newborns who are HIV positive tells me that American society is sitting on a time bomb the likes of which we can't even imagine. "Think of these children growing up and becoming sexually active—the proliferation of the virus." What about my children, your children, our grandchildren? What about you? What about me? The future for us all? Many people already have seen loved ones swept away. The "downward pull is so strong, the torrent beneath so swift. …"

To lift my heart, I open a letter from my friend Ginny in Anchorage, Alaska. But it isn't a letter. It's a newspaper clipping from about two years ago, which was published in the "Dear Abby" column of the *Anchorage Times*. In the margin, Ginny has written, "For you and *Selu*." At first glance,

I think she's sent this clipping as a wry joke, for the headline seems in the same vein, though not as extreme, as what I've been watching. It says, "Indians Tell of 'Love Secrets.'" Then I read on:

Dear Abby:

When a reader asked you if Indian men were superior to white men in the art of lovemaking, you suggested that he contact the Bureau of Indian Affairs or the American Indian Movement. As the executive director of the American Indian Movement, I feel it is my duty to respond.

For the Indian, "love" does not begin when the lights go out or when pot or liquor is consumed, and it is not confined to the bedroom or any other hidden place. The way in which the Indian treats his wife throughout the marriage is the key to making him a superior lover. His daily acts of kindness, consideration and respect for her demonstrate his love. While we recognize that the sex act may send man's mind afloat for a few fleeting moments, it is but a minute part of the overall act of love.

The above code of behavior plus the Indian's respect for women have been passed down from father to son. I personally have fifteen children and am an Ojibway Indian.

Very truly yours,

Dennis J. Banks

I reread the letter many times. "The sex act is but a minute part of the overall act of love." This is the "secret," the pearl of great price. Through the window I watch the full moon rising in a black velvet sky. Round. Luminous. Brother Moon, who orders the tides and faithfully keeps the watch so that all his relations may rest and restore themselves. A true warrior. In perfect balance with his sister, the Sun, who just as faithfully will rise in the morning and set life bubbling in leaf and seed and gene, waking Mother Earth—and us—to our creative rounds. The harmony is clear. The law of relationship is clear.

Why are many people wrecking this harmony, beginning with human sexuality? Why has American society reversed the balance, making the act of love a minute part of the overall sex act? Overwhelmingly, films, television programs, magazines, advertising emphasize sex as an it, a commodity. Sex sells. The overall act of love doesn't. Our society is wracked with violence, much of it sexually related, yet the law of respect—and those who support it—is rarely given prime time, on television or anywhere else in the marketplace. It is mostly confined to the private sectors of home, church and family, "hidden" from the media that so influence contemporary life. Are these media reflecting the reality in America or are they creating a "virtual reality" that people emulate and make real?

They appear to be circling both ways, feeding each other. To this point humans and machines have maintained a reasonable, but increasingly shaky balance. Now, we teeter on the turning point. Our machines are on the brink of overtaking us, and if they do, human consciousness as we've known it will be confined to remote enclaves of people who remember the sweetness of having a heart. To hold machines to a creative, respectful use will take all the strength we can muster, both in unified thinking—deep, purposeful thinking—and in drawing the line. Individuals must do this. And so must conscientious people in policy-making positions in the media and other sectors of the marketplace. To espouse and practice virtues privately and make a living by upholding and practicing their opposites is not a process compatible with survival. It sets up an ambivalence, a cross-rhythm, that destroys balance in the individual and in society at large. And it certainly sends mixed messages to our youth.

"In the beginning, the Creator made our Mother Earth, then came Selu, Grandmother Corn. ... And so I tell my client ... he should look on [his wife's] heart and remember who she is."

The interconnection of human sexuality with the sacred, with the life force, with women, with men and with the good of the people and Mother Earth is a line clearly drawn in the heart's sweet meal.

This living substance—these values—are shared by many Americans who from their spiritual traditions have similar teachings. I rarely meet these people through the media. I meet them often wherever I travel in the Four Directions. And although the Sex Expert did not connect with the Medicine Man's meaning because of cultural difference, her ship is a good one. She believes in keeping sexuality respectful. There is enough similarity in what many Americans believe on this subject for us to listen for the counterpoint, the commonality of what we are saying.

What measures should we take to mend the broken law of respect in the area of sexuality. I think the key lies in restoring the balance, in "making the sex act a minute part of the overall act of love," in extending love and consideration to people all around us. The Great Law of Peace of the Iroquois says, "In all our deliberations, we must consider the effect of our decisions on the next seven generations." This philosophy is sound; it strengthens our determination to do our best. Seven generations are expecting us to do so.

By the time I finish handwriting these thoughts in a notebook, the moon is sinking toward the west. I sink into bed. Snuggle into my place by Paul. I am "wore out." Virtual Valerie and Indian love secrets are heavy subjects. I need some brisk and cheerful thoughts on "sex in America." A bird's-eye view maybe. Not from the eagle; he flies too high. A bird who has the overall view from hearth (and bed) level. A recent conversation with a woman in Cherokee, North Carolina, drifts into my mind.

"We've had a good month up here," she'd said. "Eleven flights of the wren. Five '(hunting) bows' and six '(cornmeal) sifters.'" (Five boys and six girls.) The first image connotes Kanati the hunter, and the second evokes Selu, the Corn-Mother. When women ground corn, they were careful to leave some meal for the birds. Each image is complete in itself—and evocative of the place of each gender in the whole. I smile. Grandmother Wren is the one I want to talk with. I'll need a good night's rest for that. She is, as the French say, "small but concentrated." Energy emanates from every feather. She's always kind but too busy to mince words. In the midst of sending her a call, I fall to sleep ...

Sex in America: A Bird's-Eye View

Dawn.

No sooner do I sprinkle cornmeal on the windowsill and put a cup of water beside it than Grandmother Wren arrives. She fixes me with her pert and penetrating eye. "You called?"

"O si yo, Grandmother."

"Si yo. Thank you for the snack. I'm really on the wing today. Lots of babies coming in. You're not having one, are you?"

"No, I'm having a book."

"Same thing, just more labor. Now what's on your mind?"

"I'd take it kindly if you'd give me some of your views on sex in America. Teenage sex and pregnancy, for example. On the one hand we tell young people, 'Don't do it,' and on the other we load them with media of all kinds that say, 'Do it.' What's the matter with us?"

"Primitive."

"Excuse me ... ?!"

"Primitive. The birds and animals have met in a council about American culture. Your problem with sex is that you don't know that intercourse causes babies. If you did, you wouldn't give young people mixed messages. Also, you must be incapable of thinking in the abstract. Otherwise, you'd see the connection between the teenage problem and the products you push on them—and change the products. Hormones are stimulating young people enough as it is. Next question."

I'm still reeling from her first answer, but I'd better push on. She's "on the wing." "As you've undoubtedly noticed in your travels, our society's in a mess. Many women and children are trapped in poverty. One thing is, men and women can't agree on whose responsibilities are whose. I don't mean it's all men versus women. Both genders are on both sides of the question about what 'woman's place' is. And that controversy is diverting a lot of energy from the central issues. How should we begin to unravel this dilemma?"

Grandmother Wren cocks her head, considering. "That's a complex question." She takes a sip of water, raising her head to let it trickle down her throat. "The first step is to think about who you humans are."

"We're Homo sapiens."

"I don't mean your species. Are you warm-blooded or cold-blooded?"

"Warm-blooded. At least most of the time."

Ignoring my wry joke, Grandmother Wren continues her train of thought. "And what is the Creator's law for all warm-blooded species when it comes to keeping life going? Genderwise, I mean."

I have to think about that one. "Well, the female always has the power to sustain life—you know, keep it fed, warmed, sheltered, educated and defended. Birds, mammals, it's true for all of you, I think."

The Grandmother bobs her head approvingly. "But of course, you mammals have a drawback that we birds don't. Most of our mates stay with the mother and help. They work as hard as we do with the young. I understand at least one of your species got wise and took a swan as a mate. What was her name? ... Leda, that's it."

"Grandmother, you're teasing me. That's a very funny thought. But I don't get your point yet about the Creator's law for the warm-blooded and the problem we were discussing."

"The point is, to keep Homo sapiens in balance, you need to follow the Creator's law. Women need to be on councils that make policy, right along with men. All policies that affect the welfare of the people. Otherwise, the society's out of balance. The more you get in harmony with the Creator's law, the better balanced your society will be. And a lot of things will smooth out. The Cherokee had things arranged that way, you know, and a lot of other Indian tribes, too—and look how long they've lasted. I've got a Cherokee family up in St. Louis that's expecting this afternoon, so I have time for one more question."

"This is the big one, Grandmother. There's so much violence against women and children, physical and sexual abuse. We're killing the gender that bears life and grinding our children up with drugs and child prostitution and so much else ... and ... "

"Rabies. That's what all the birds and animals have decided. Why, there's not a species among us that does what you're doing. We'd be finished if we did. Homo sapiens are suicidal. Not all of you. But the majority are. Bound to be rabies that's causing it."

"What can we do ... ?"

Grandmother gives me a very direct look. "You figured out what to do with any other animals that get rabies, haven't you?"

"You don't mean we ought to shoot ... "

"No. I'm just saying that if you can figure out what to do with others, you ought to be able to figure out what to do with yourselves. Trust your own thinking, trust where you're going. ... Keep a positive mind, Granddaughter. Look around you. There's a big move toward balance. Women are on many councils along with men. For the first time you have a First Lady who's been given official power to make policy. Your attorney general of the United States is a woman, and she says her priority is the children of America. Remember, children need hope to thrive. I have to go now. Face East," she calls over her wing. "We will meet again."

"Thank you, Grandmother Wren. Thank you."

I watch her tiny body soar purposefully into the vast sky. On her way to get the job done.

Conservation

An irreverent man
looks at earth
as he looks at woman.
"Feed me," he says.
"Receive my seed
and recreate me.
Soothe me
with cool waters.
Shelter me
then let me soar
as I will."

Earth says,
"Look again."
Woman says,
"I too have wings."

COOPERATION AND GOVERNMENT

Upon the continent of North America prior to the landfall of the white man ... the Peacmaker came to our lands, bringing the message of peace, supported by Ayonwatha. He began the great work of healing the twisted minds of men.

—The Honorable Oren Lyons, 1987
Speaker for the Onondaga Nation

All of these things have to be kept in balance—the listening and the speaking, the male and the female, the clan mother and the chiefs, and all of the people in between.

—Audrey Shenandoah, 1987
Clan Mother of the Onondaga Nation
Recording Secretary of the
Haudenosaunee Council of Chiefs

In all our deliberations, we must consider the effects of our decisions on the next seven generations.

—The Great Law of Peace

How does the balance of genders relate to family and government? And what does this balance have to do with the Corn-Mother and the United States Constitution?

The League of the Haudenosaunee—which was firmly established between 1390 and 1500 and remains an independent nation within the United States—is the oldest continuous participatory democracy in the Western Hemisphere and perhaps in the world.[23] In English it is usually referred to as the League of the Iroquois, the Iroquois Confederacy or the Six Nations. It was the French of centuries past who renamed the people the "Iroquois." They call themselves the Haudenosaunee, "People Who Build." Originally there were five Nations in the Confederacy: the Mohawk, Oneida, Onondaga, Cayuga and Seneca. The Tuscarora joined in 1712. The

Haudenosaunee live in the northeastern United States and their central fire—or seat of government—is at Onondaga, near Syracuse, New York.

From the time of European contact, the Haudenosaunee have drawn non-Indian thinkers to study their Great Law of Peace—including early explorers, especially the French, and many of the Founding Fathers of America, including Thomas Jefferson and Benjamin Franklin. Recently, Sally Roesch Wagner has rendered visible the Iroquois influence on women's rights through its connection with the "mothers" of early feminism: Elizabeth Cady Stanton, Lucretia Mott, Matilda Joslyn Gage and Susan B. Anthony. It was not a coincidence that the first women's rights convention in 1848 convened at Seneca Falls, New York—Haudenosaunee country.[24]

In the fall of 1987, at Cornell University in Ithaca, New York, Native and non-Native scholars gathered for a conference entitled, "The Iroquois Great Law of Peace and the United States Constitution." Sponsored by the American Indian Program at Cornell, the conference created a fission of ideas that through chain reaction of discussion and publication of articles and books has spread into the thoughts of many Americans. *Indian Roots of American Democracy,* published by Cornell's Akwe:kon Press (1992) gives the major addresses and papers presented at the conference.

Indian Roots begins with Alex Jacob's poem, "The Law Is in the Seed," and with a summary of the Thanksgiving address spoken in the Cayuga language by Iroquois elder and chief Jacob Thomas. Ron La France, Mohawk Longhouse Chief, briefly explained the message. "At our gatherings among the Iroquois people this salutation, or opening address, is always given and, in a way, is our preamble to our way of life, our society. The Thanksgiving Address acknowledges the whole universe."

According to ancient custom, the address is given to help human beings living in a society to achieve what the Iroquois call "one mindedness." It takes time, perhaps an hour or more, to acknowledge the people, the gifts of Mother Earth, which include "all the gifts that have been given to us by the Creator." The litany continues with thanksgiving for the "beings above our heads"—such as the spirits of wind and rain—that hold the balance and maintain the cycles that the Creator has created to sustain Mother Earth and the people. "The last part thanks the Creator. In many of our nations we say that all the Creator wants is for us to acknowledge creation, that we try to remain peaceful not only between ourselves and among ourselves, but also in our minds and that we help the creation, that we protect it and that we nourish it."[25]

When the people convened have reached this state of one-mindedness, then and only then, do the Haudenosaunee "get down to the business at hand"—and *think* together. Perhaps American society's general failure to take time to quiet the spirit and unify the mind before speaking is one of the great impediments to resolving the dilemmas that confound us.

Listening to the Great Law

The Great Law of Peace is the heart of the Haudenosaunee. Whenever possible, people should speak their own hearts. The speakers' sequence of thought, the words they choose, the spirit in which the words are spoken—all of these elements reflect the value placed on what is being said. The listeners hear with an understanding that the words of another person writing *about* the subject cannot evoke. In the following passages from *Indian Roots of American Democracy,* Oren Lyons and Audrey Shenandoah speak excerpts from their addresses at the Cornell conference. We will listen with an ear to what is similar to our own experience of family and government. The differences we hear may suggest patterns and ideas for change in American society. The Great Law of Peace is preserved in ancient Wampum Belts, documents of record for the elders, who preserve the Law through a precise oral tradition. To recite the Law in its entirety requires about eight days.

OREN LYONS:
"LAND OF THE FREE, HOME OF THE BRAVE" [26]

I am going to discuss early history, prior to the coming of the white man to this continent. This time receives little attention in the history books of the country, but it was in these early times that the development of democratic processes came about on this land. I would like to give you our history, a very short history, of course, but it will deal with those times. So, I shall begin.

Upon the continent of North America prior to the landfall of the white man, a great league of peace was formed, the inspiration of a prophet called the Peacemaker. He was a spiritual being, fulfilling the mission of organizing warring nations into a confederation under the Great Law of Peace. The principles of the law are peace, equity, justice, and the power of the good minds.

With the help and support of a like-minded man called Ayonwatha, whom some people now call Hiawatha, an Onondaga by birth and a Mohawk by adoption, he set about the great work of establishing a union of peace under the immutable natural laws of the universe. He came to our Iroquois lands in our darkest hour, when the good message of how to live had been cast aside and naked power ruled, fueled by vengeance and blood lust. A great war of attrition engulfed the lands, and women and children cowered in fear of their own men. The leaders were fierce and merciless. They were fighting in a blind rage. Nations, homes, and families were destroyed, and the people were scattered. It was a dismal world of dark disasters where there seemed to be no hope. It was a raging proof of what inhumanity man is capable of when the laws and principles of life are thrown away.

The Peacemaker came to our lands, bringing the message of peace, supported by Ayonwatha. He began the great work of healing the twisted minds of men. This is a long history, too long to recount today in this forum. Suffice it to say it is a great epic that culminated on the shores of the lake now called Onondaga where, after many years of hard work—some say perhaps even 100 years—he gathered the leaders, who had now become transformed into rational human beings, into a Grand Council, and he began the instructions of how the Great Law of Peace would work.

The Peacemaker set up the families into clans, and then he set up the leaders of the clans. He established that the League of Peace would be matriarchal and that each clan would have a clanmother. Thus, he established in law the equal rights of women.

He raised the leaders of each clan—two men, one the principal leader and the second his partner. They worked together for the good of the people. He called these two men *royaner,* or *the good minds,* the peacemakers, and they were to represent the clans in council. Thus, he established the principles of representation of people in government.

Henceforth, he said, these men will be chosen by the clanmother, freely using her insight and wisdom. Her choice must first be ratified by the consensus of the clan. If they agree, then her choice must be ratified by full consensus of the Chief's Council of their nation. Then her choice must be ratified and given over to the Council of Chiefs who then call the Grand Council of the Great League of Peace, and they will gather at the nation that is raising the leader, and they would work together in ceremony.

He made two houses in each nation. One he called the Long House and the other he called the Mud House. They would work together in ceremony and council establishing the inner source of vitality and dynamics necessary for community.

He made two houses in the Grand Council, one called the Younger Brothers, consisting of the Oneida and the Cayuga Nations and later enlarging to include the Tuscarora. The other was the Elder Brothers, consisting of the Mohawks with the title Keepers of the Eastern Door, the Onondaga, whom he made the Firekeepers, and the Senecas, who were the Keepers of the Western Door. Now, he made the house, and the rafters of the house were the laws that he laid down, and he called us Haudenosaunee, the people of the Longhouse.

Now, the candidate for the clan title is brought before the Grand Council to be judged on his merits, and they have the right of veto. If they agree, then he may take his place in Grand Council. But before that, he is turned back to the people, and they are asked if they know a reason why this man should not be a leader and hold title. Thus, the process is full circle back to the people. Thus, the Peacemaker established the process of raising leaders for governance, and, by this process, a leader cannot be self-proclaimed. He is given his title and his duties, and his authority is derived from the people, and the people have the right to remove him for malfeasance of office.

He established the power of recall in the clanmother, and it is her duty to speak to him if he is receiving complaints from the people concerning his conduct. The clanmother shall speak to him three times, giving sufficient time between warnings for him to change his ways. She shall have a witness each time. The first will be her niece, in other words, a woman. The second shall be the partner of the chief in council or the principal leader, as the case may be. And the third and final warning comes with a man who holds no title, and he is coming for the chief's wampum and for the chief's emblem of authority, the antlers of a deer. Thus he established the power of recall vested in the people.

The leader must be free from any crime against woman or a child. He cannot have killed anybody and cannot have blood on his hands. He must believe in the ways of the Longhouse. His heart must yearn for the welfare of the people. He must have great compassion for his people. He must have great tolerance, and his skin must be seven spans thick to withstand the accusations, slander, and insults of the people as he goes about his duties for the people. He has no authority but what the people give him in respect. He has no force of arms to demand the people obey his orders. He shall lead by example, and his family shall not influence his judgment. He carries his title for life or until he is relieved of it by bad conduct or ill health. He now belongs to the people.

At the first council, there were fifty original leaders, and their names became offices to be filled by each succeeding generation. So, it continues up to this very day. The Great Peacemaker had established a government of absolute democracy, the constitution of the great law intertwined with the spiritual law.

We then became a nation of laws. The people came of their own free will to participate in the decision-making of the national council and the Grand Council. Thus, the Peacemaker instilled in the nations the inherent rights of the individual with the process to protect and exercise these rights.

Sovereignty, then, began with the individual, and all people were recognized to be free, from the very youngest to the eldest. It was recognized and provided for in the Great Law of Peace that liberty and equality demanded great moral fortitude, and it was the nature of free men to defend freedom.

Thus, freedom begat freedom and great societies of peace prevailed, guided by the leaders, the good minds. The men were restrained by moral conduct, and the family with the woman at its heart was the center of Indian societies and nations.

Now, the Peacemaker said the symbol of the Haudenosaunee shall be the great white pine with four white roots of truth extending to the four cardinal directions, and those people who have no place to go shall follow these roots back to the tree and seek shelter under the long leaves of the white pine that we shall call the great tree of peace. I shall place an eagle atop the tree to be ever-vigilant against those who shall harm this tree, and the eagle shall scream his warnings to our chiefs whose duty it is to nurture and protect this tree.

Now that this is done, the chiefs, clanmothers, and faithkeepers being raised and the Great Law being firmly established in place, he said, *I now uproot this tree and command you to throw all of your weapons of war into this chasm to be carried by the undercurrent of water to the furthest depths of the earth, and now I place this tree back over this chasm, throwing away forever war between us and peace shall prevail.*

This is what prevailed upon this great Turtle Island at the first landfall of the white man. They found here in full flower, free nations guided by democratic principles, all under the authority of the natural law, the ultimate spiritual law of the universe. This was then the land of the free and the home of the brave. …

From this succinct history of the Great Law and how its tenets apply in governing the nation, we give equal attention—as the Haudensaunee did at the Cornell conference and in *Indian Roots of American Democracy*—to how the Law applies to family and society.

The Corn-Mother, Women and the Great Law

Traditionally, the Seneca say that women and corn are one—the Mother—for both give life and care for the people. The elders also say that a woman's childbearing powers pass to the corn and make it produce young of its own, which in turn nourish the people. This concept of a circle of sustaining power is important to understanding the basic pattern of the Great Law, which as we have seen, begins with the clan mother and the family. Like other Native peoples, the Seneca have always considered corn a sacred gift from the Creator. In *Our Mother Corn*, Chuck Larsen, a contemporary Seneca, gives a liberal translation of a traditional ceremonial song, "A Seneca Thanksgiving." These are selected stanzas: [27]

Now begins the Gayant' gogwus
    This sacred fire and sacred tobacco.
And through this smoke
    We offer our prayers.
We are your children, Lord of the Sky...

You said that food should be placed beside us
And it should be ours in exchange for our labor.
You thought that ours should be a world
where green grass of many kinds should grow
You said that some should be medicines
and that one should be Ona'o
the sacred food, our sister corn
You gave to her two clinging sisters
beautiful Oa'geta, our sister beans
and bountiful Nyo'sowane, our sister squash
The three sacred sisters; they who sustain us.

This is what you thought, Lord of the Sky.
Thus did you think to provide for us
And thus you ordered that when the warm season comes,

That we should see the return of life
And remember you, and be thankful,
and gather here by the sacred fire.
So now again the smoke arises
We the people offer our prayers
We speak to you through the rising smoke
We are thankful, Lord of the Sky.

Women were agriculturalists, the ones responsible for the major crops of corn, beans and squash, which were companion-planted and yielded thousands of bushels. Most fields were owned by the clans, some by individuals. Women managed the farming—cleared the land, planted the seed, hoed and weeded. They organized into groups, choosing a leader to direct the work, and moved from field to field. Their mood was convivial, with much singing, laughing and joking as they worked. In the fall men and women went to the fields to gather the harvest. Afterward, there were feasts and ceremonies of thanksgiving.

John Mohawk, Seneca scholar, says that although each of the nations raised corn, "The Seneca had a reputation without question, even among the Indians of 1687, of being the bread basket of the confederacy." In that year, when the French army invaded the town of Ganondagen in the heart of Seneca country, they found great storage silos, which they estimated held three million bushels of corn. Even if this estimate was exaggerated by three or four times, there was a prodigious amount of corn stored at Ganondagen. In addition, there were hundreds of acres of cornfields surrounding the town.[28]

According to one strain of the oral tradition, it was at Ganondagen that the Peacemaker began teaching the law to the people. Ganondagen, which is just outside of Victor, New York, was dedicated as a New York State Historical Site in 1987, three hundred years after the Frenchman Denonville destroyed the town. People of two cultures have worked to have the site established, but the main board of directors was made up of citizens and scholars of the Haudenosaunee. In harmony with their tradition of commemorating places of peace, the Haudenosaunee chose to remember the site as a place once inhabited by Jikonsaseh, the Mother of Nations—the Peace

Queen. The elders, who have carefully preserved the oral tradition, teach that she played a central role in the formation of the League of the Haudenosaunee. Some say that she was a Seneca; others say she was a Neutral, a tribe later absorbed into the Seneca.

Pete Jemison, a Seneca, is director of the site and interprets this knowledge of Jikonsaseh. According to Haudenosaunee cosmology, she was in a lineal descent from the first woman of earth, the Sky Woman. In the Peace Queen's time the People were involved in blood feuds, and she lived at the crossroads of the war trails. The Peacemaker had already been preaching the Law to his own people, the Huron, when he came to Ganondagen. The first person to accept his message there was Jikonsaseh. The Peacemaker gave her the name Mother of Nations and explained to her that women would have an important role in the peace. She accompanied the Peacemaker and Ayonwatha on their teaching journeys to other tribes and they consulted her in every important detail, for without the approval of the Mother of Nations, the principles of the confederacy of the Five Nations would have been assailed.

At the time the confederacy was being formed, four nations wanted to join, but the Onondagas—through the resistance of one man, Tadodaho—were an impediment to the union. Everyone was afraid of his power. The elders say that Jikonsaseh, working with the Peacemaker, came up with a solution to persuade Tadodaho to consent to the peace. They offered him the idea that the Onondagas would be the central fire (or capital) of the confederacy. They would have more chiefs than any other nation—fourteen of forty-nine—and an Onondaga would be made the head man.[29]

The role that the Great Law specifies for women is in harmony with the Creator's law for the survival of all warm-blooded species, including the human: the gender that bears life must not be separated from the power to sustain it. Women in the Longhouse today mirror the responsibilities entrusted to them over half a millennium ago. By paying careful attention to Audrey Shenandoah's words we can see the practical, day-to-day workings of genders living in balance and carrying out "the overall act of love" for the good of the people.

AUDREY SHENANDOAH:
EVERTHING HAS TO BE IN BALANCE[30]

Being born as humans to this earth is a very sacred trust. We have a sacred responsibility because of the special gift that we have, which is beyond the fine gifts of the plant life, the fish, the woodlands, the birds, and all the other living things on earth. We are able to take care of them. We are able to see, if we live right and follow our own instructions, that they might have a good earth, have good air, good water, a good life, just as we would have if we would follow the instructions of our Creator.

Humans have a sacred trust—men and women. The women within our own society have a special place, a special place of honor. We have the ability to bring forth life to this earth. We are given, further, the sacred responsibility of nurturing that life from the beginning, from the most necessary and important time in a human's life: from the time that they are infants and learning their first things about living, the ways that they must treat one another as humans, the first ways that they are to survive.

In the days past, a long, long time ago, we have all read how the women had such a big responsibility of taking care of the gardens. They did the gardening, they did all that is called hard work, what actually was an honor. The women of the village taught the children, everybody's childen, all the things that they had to know in order to survive on this earth. ... The children up to an age of, let's say, eight or nine years were in the trust, the responsibility, of the women.

The gardening was not specifically labeled women's work by our people. There were always men and male children around who helped and did the harder work, because there were always some men who did not go on the hunts, some men who stayed behind to help the women. ... Today, women still do much of the gardening around people's homes for those who plant.

So when the children became of an age that they went out into mixed society and began to learn whatever their natural talents led them to—some people became singers, some speakers, some dancers, some workers—they just seemed to know how to do all kinds of things. For a while they went about learning these things and practicing them from either men or women, whoever could see what this person was designated to become. And then when it became time to learn the man things—the hunting, and all of those things that took them away from their home, away from the village—they were prepared to meet life in the wilderness. ...

When it came time for a young man or a young woman to be married, to join with another, and to lead a life of their own and make their own family, again it was the women's responsibility; it still is the women's responsibility to give them the instruction. The women were the ones, in the old days, who chose a mate for their young people and still, today, it is the mothers who must give their consent when a young couple are joined together, to lead a life together ...

Taking care of little children is not a job or a chore; it is something people enjoy doing. There is a special bond between the grandchildren and the grandparents or aunts, anyone who has grandchildren knows this. And as life goes on, and now the young people reach an age themselves when they are going to leave this earth, again they are prepared by the women. So, all through a person's life, from the time they are conceived, from the time they are born, until the time they leave this earth, their care is truly in the hands of the women, the mothers of our nations, and that is a sacred trust.

We, the Haudenosaunee, have a matrilineal system among our nations. When they have a family, the mother's clan determines the clan of her children, and so we have a clanmother. ... She must perpetuate the ways of our people; she must be able to teach the ways of our people to the young people. She must be able to look out for large numbers of people because now, all of the clan people are one family. And so, because of the changing of the times, in these days we don't necessarily have the eldest women being the clanmother of certain clans, but the eldest eligible woman. We cannot have someone teaching our children our traditional ways who does not follow the traditional ways themselves and cannot perpetuate this way. ...

The ways of our people are important because these are the ways that have sustained our people from the time of contact until today. Among our ancestors, the traditionals were the strong ones, the ones who kept to the ways of our people. They were the ones who did battle—not necessarily only physically. Our leaders are still doing battle today. They are not armed to the teeth with weapons of war, because of the message of peace that came to our people so many years ago. We know that they were the strong ones, these are the strong ones here today. ... These have to be the kinds of people who are going to be able to sustain, to survive and to teach our young people to survive. *So, a woman who is designated to be leader of a clan must have these feelings and they have got to be intact, otherwise the clan and the nation are in danger.* [Italics mine.]

The clanmother's duties have to do with the community affairs, the nation affairs, but they also have another role and that has to do with the spiritual side. ... We watch the printed calendar like you do now, but we still have those people who must watch the phases of the moon, who know when it is time to call the faithkeepers and the women together to sit, and to set the time for the ceremonies which are held at various times throughout the year. So this becomes another duty of the clanmother—she must watch these times and always be ready to call the people together when it is time for a ceremony. She must be ready to call her clan people together if a person from another clan has suffered sickness, some kind of tragedy or emergency. ... It is our way that we do not leave a family alone in time of trouble. ...

The names within all of our clans are handed down from generation to generation. ... So the clanmothers also have the privilege and responsibility of naming the young babies, the young people in their clans. ...

The clanmothers also have a duty of watching out for the young people. ... The mothers are the ones who bring them with their basket to what is today a marriage ceremony and so if this young couple runs into problems, as everybody does, differences of opinion, many reasons that they would need help and support, the clanmother has the duty again of being there to support these young people. ...

Each clan has a clanmother who has the duty to select the leadership of our nations. In English they call them chiefs; these are the leaders of our nations. Each clan has its own leader, and the clanmother is, again, responsible for selecting a candidate to lead her people. To be a person worthy of that trust, I believe, to be a person who is given all of this responsibility is a very honorable position within our society.

Sometimes our young people become confused. In the last few years it has become a trend for women to feel that they need to do something to become more than a woman, or more than what a woman's responsibilities are. But this is something that we have always had within our society. Women have always been able to do anything that they are physically able to do. There have been, as I mentioned before, no labels to say that this is women's work, and this is man's work among our people. It has always been a balance, a cooperation, and so when I say that the women, the clanmothers have the responsibility of selecting a candidate to lead our people, selecting the leadership of our nations, that is a very honorable position. But, it does not mean that she is now going to be the one who is going to tell him what to do. She must work with him; a balance has to be there. She must work with him and they, together, work for the will of the people. Whatever the people want is what they must work to do, for the good of the people.

There are many duties, probably some that I have not mentioned here. For the cooking of the food at ceremony time, the clanmother has a faithkeeper who stands beside her. She has the duty of preparing food so that her chiefs and her people will always have food, the children will always have food. Some people, I have read many times in magazines, have dared to write that preparing food and looking after food is looked on as some kind of a lowly position. Taking care of the children and keeping house can be looked at by some people as a lowly kind of a position, a lowly kind of a job, not very important. In our way of life, it is very important, one of the most important jobs that a person can have.

Now, I don't mean to sound as if they exclude the fathers altogether. I don't mean to sound as if the men are, let's say, put into a position where they are not as important. Everything has to be in a balance. ... The balance of everything in creation is what allows us to continue to be. The balance is what allows us to continue to live. We breathe the air, we use the water, we share the space and the balance must be looked at very carefully. We must try to keep that balance. Within our society we maintain a balance between the responsibilities of the women, the responsibilities of the men, of the chiefs, of the faithkeepers. All the people in between have a special job to do to help to keep this balance so that at no time do we come to a place within our society where anyone has more power than any of the rest, for our leadership all have equal power. They must be able to listen to one another.

Speaking and listening are two fine arts that are much forgotten in today's society. We do not know how to listen to one another anymore. We don't know how to listen and hear the people who have the good things to tell us. All of these things have to be kept in the balance—the listening and the speaking, the male and the female, the clanmother and the chiefs, and all of the people in between. And so, as a woman within my own society, I have never had the desire or the feelings to join these great big congregations, conclaves of women who are trying to get what I guess they call equal power. They all have the power; they only need to assert themselves. You do not need permission from anyone to do what it is your inner person tells you that you must do. The only thing that people leave out is the spiritual side. That is the guideline that our people must use to choose the leaders, to choose the faithkeepers, to choose the clanmother who is going to look after the clan family. She, in turn, will choose a candidate for leadership, a chief to look after his nation. The spiritual side of these responsibilities that I have mentioned tonight is the most important part. It's the very foundation of everything that would allow this system to work peacefully. ...

I think people learning about other people is one of the most important things that can be happening today because it seems, as I talk to many, many different kinds of people that everybody wants to live in a peaceful world. Everybody wants to look for a way that we might live in peace together. People learning to know other people, to know other people's ways, is one of the ways that can bring that time closer and closer to us, so that maybe our children and our grandchildren can have a realization of people working together and communicating in a peaceful way.

Continuance in the midst of change—women and men carrying the balance of these two great forces of nature into the human dimension. The Haudenosaunee are exemplars of how this sacred law can be applied, and traditionally many indigenous peoples have lived according to the same principles of balance.

As American society searches for new life patterns for the future, it is sensible to study also those patterns that are indigenous to our country and that have proved reliable for the survival of the people. In this study we will undoubtedly find agreeable harmonies—perhaps moving in counterpoint, but harmonies nonetheless. If we listen to each other. ... Many concepts which appear controversial may be rendered less divisive than we thought. When we look at the increasing role of women in the government of America today and the increasing participation of men in family life, we see it not only as a new phenomenon, but as a resurgence of the indigenous roots of democracy.

We now turn to the Cherokee, who in the historical record appear to be separated from the Iroquoian people by thousands of years, with links only appearing in similarities of language constructs and custom. But science and history can go only so far in establishing links. The Cherokee scholars, Jack and Anna Kilpatrick, give a deeper insight in *Friends of Thunder*: "There are truths that defy the statistical apparatus of the sociologist and the comparative powers of the ethnologist. They have their being in the subjective subtleties of turns of speech, responses to stimuli, selections of values. One such verity is the fundamentally Iroquoian material of the Cherokee ethos. Affinity is clearly perceived and cheerfully confessed by people of both the Longhouse and the Sacred Fire."[31]

HARMONY AND ADAPTING

The medicine men and the elders talked to me about how we should be as a people. They showed me the sacred wampum belts that teach the truths of Cherokee life: that we should have good minds, consider everything in the world—including nature—as brothers and sisters. We should not be judgmental but accept all as family. They taught me not to be dragged down by the negative. That divides people.

—Wilma Mankiller

You will recognize these words of Wilma Mankiller from the interview, "Rebirth of a Nation." In the fall of 1979, Mankiller was struggling to survive critical injuries she'd suffered in a car wreck. As healers and spiritual counselors, the medicine men worked to help her restore harmony from the inside out. "They taught me to approach life from a positive, loving perspective," she said. "Your chances of surviving are much better this way than with a negative outlook. I applied that concept to my work, too. What I really wanted to do was rebuild our tribe and our people." This pattern of restoring harmony from the inside out, and of extending that concept from the individual to the community is a classic example of the Native American ability to adapt and survive. It is the ability to think purposefully—with mind/heart/soul—and head East. And it is understandable that corn, which is extraordinarily adaptable and embodies the principles of strength, balance and unity in diversity, became a teacher of wisdom to her human partners. Native people are culturally adept at taking a principle from one sphere and applying it appropriately to another.

Stump Settin'

Why is this principle of restoring harmony from the inside out so effective? And what relation does the webbed concept of the universe—that we are all one family—have to do with adaptability? A Cherokee leader gave me a clue. "The real reality is in the mind—that's what shapes the world we see." For several years, I've been "settin' on a stump," thinking this through.

To mountain people (and maybe to you, too), settin' on a stump means quietly pondering a subject for a long time. Considering what it is, what it has been and what it may be again. Studying the roots of it, their depth and breadth, how they connect. A tree stump naturally leads you to think this way because it has been—and may still be—alive. You don't know what may be going on in the roots under the ground. A stump helps you hatch ideas, which is probably why the old-timers say "settin'" on a stump, as opposed to "sittin'." If you set long enough, your common sense will birth an idea. Here is what has come to my mind from my figurative "stump settin'."

Two thousand years ago, a biblical poet wrote that in the beginning was the *logos*, the Thought. Then came the tangible world. For a long time the Western mind and science swung wide of this idea. Now science has circled back to it, and the Western mind is trailing toward it. Apparently, the atom refines into a process resembling thought. Fueled by energy—and within a given circumference—atoms move around, fuse, and soon up pops a tree— or a corn plant. You and I began with thought—twinkles in our parents' eyes that led to fusions of sperm and egg, and eventually we popped into the world. In a very real sense, the whole universe is the result of thought moving from the inside out, from the invisible to the tangible. Wounds heal that way, too, from the inside out—"what wound does not heal but by degrees?" It makes sense that to restore harmony in a person or in a society, you follow this cardinal law of nature. Another basic law is that Mother Earth is always preparing for tomorrow. Sister Sun always comes up. Being positive and preparing for the future is the best way to make sure you come up with her.

Like other Native peoples, the Cherokees have been "stump settin'" for centuries. And it's easy to see how the Old Ones came up with the idea of governing according to natural laws, which are sacred because of their source in the Provider.

An elegant study of these traditional laws and how the Cherokee adapted them to the legal system of the United States is *Fire and the Spirits, Cherokee Law from Clan to Court*, by Rennard Strickland, who is a Cherokee and Osage Indian.[32] He is now Shleppy Research Professor of Law and History at the University of Tulsa.

With the sacred fire and the ideal of harmony at the center, the law webbed out into every facet of Cherokee life. The contemporary medicine men and spiritual elders were speaking the essence of the law when they said "to consider everything in the world as brothers and sisters—as family—and to maintain a 'good mind,' a positive mind. In the sacred law, love of family and of Mother Earth—of the land—are inextricably entwined.

The stories of Selu, Kanati and Little Deer are small strands of the web that reflect the whole. Individual rights are taken in the context of community responsibility. Family and community are constant themes in the Cherokee traditional stories. "Family first—and that means all my people" is a contemporary saying that reflects a long, long tradition. The Corn-Mother also maintains a positive mind, whatever the circumstances, but there is no hint of a Pollyanna attitude in it. Instead, the circumstances are faced, and the opportunity given to "begin again."

One beauty of the webbed mode is that within a circumference of respect, it allows maximum diversity and expression. Engendering a "both/and," as opposed to an "either/or" philosophy, this mode allows the individual maximum mobility and choice within a circumference of respect and security. A spider, for example, knows everything that goes on in its web, which is literally an extension of itself. A vibration in any strand of the web vibrates the whole. The spider can move around and adapt lickety-split. If the web is damaged, the spider repairs it. If it's reduced to shreds, the spider ingests what's left and spins again. If the web is totally destroyed (and the spider isn't), it can remember the pattern and spin another web. The spider is very like the atom, which moves around within a given circumference, lickety-split, weaving and creating.

Contemplating the symmetry of the law, the atoms and the web is comforting. My parents always said, "Mother Nature is the best teacher. The more in harmony with her laws you are, the more likely you are to survive. … The real reality is in the mind. … " I think I've grasped the idea.

The Web and History

For centuries before European contact, the sacred law had been real in the Cherokee mind. It had shaped the web of their lives, permeating every strand—from individual behavior to family, to government, to religion. Hunting, agriculture, games, art, stories—all were part of the web.

A traditional wedding, for example, included an elaborate network of consultations among the clan elders of the bride and groom. Emphasis was on establishing a solid base of stability for the new couple. In comparison, the ceremony itself was quite simple. One aspect was the exchange of tokens. As a pledge that she would provide the family and the people with food for the body and food for the spirit, the woman gifted the man with an ear of corn. He gave her a ham of venison—a pledge to provide ample game, protection and respect for her and the people. Because the stories of Selu and Kanati were held in common, the tokens resonated many meanings in all assembled.[33]

As we have seen in previous chapters, gender balance was woven into the fabric of Cherokee life from subsistence to ceremony. Women cared for the corn, from planting to cooking and storage. In balance with men, who were hunters, warriors and chiefs, they also brought the sustaining power of Selu (and of Mother Earth) into the family, into the council and into religious ceremonies, such as the Green Corn Ceremony, which was celebrated as summer turned into fall. The beginning of the Cherokee year. Sometimes they went into battle with their husbands and sons. Traditionally, values of assertiveness and nurturing were taught to both genders. Men took many responsibilities for the care and guidance of the children. Because descent was through the mother, no child could be "illegitimate" or without nurture and protection from the mother's clan. The Cherokee devotion to children and family was (and is) legendary.

Achieving harmony and balance was the Cherokee goal in government as well, and they used a confederacy pattern. Although like their distant relatives, the Iroquois, the nation met in central council to consider matters of war and alliance, the central emphasis was on local town councils guided by well-established custom law, which governed and ensured the general welfare. It was an egalitarian system, and the councils discussed matters for a long time until a consensus was reached. Sometimes these discussions went on for days, as the chiefs guided by persuasion and indirection. The influence of this mode and value system strongly marks the Cherokee governments of east and west to this day.

Psyching the System

Ethnologists, sociologists and others who have observed the Cherokee from the outside have often remarked on the people's ability to maintain an equilibrium between two opposing worlds of thought, to adapt without assimilating. What would be the clearest way to express how this is done? When I'm puzzling over something, I usually just wait around for the fullness of time. An answer always arrives, often when I least suspect it.

Last year I was chatting and joking with Evelyn, a Cherokee woman who has a family, a profession and the brisk mind one expects in a Mother of the Nation. We were talking about contemporary life, when out of the blue she said, "I've been telling my sons—and other Cherokee women are telling theirs—we don't want to hear any of this 'The day of the warrior is over.' What did it take to be a great warrior? Persistence. Courage. Psyching your adversary. What does it take to succeed in the modern world? Persistence, courage, psyching your adversary or the system. So, you just take the skills from one era and apply them to the one you're living in."

That's it! Just like the Corn-Mother. Mountain or plain. Hot or cold, dry or rainy. You adapt your form, but never, never your essence. Your spirit sustains the balance. The real reality is in the mind ...

The Cherokee have practiced this survival strategy for three centuries: persistence, courage, psyching the system. From the skillful diplomacy of Attakullakulla with the governors of South Carolina and Virginia to recent reinstitution of the tribal court system, the people have worked to take the best from both cultures and create a new harmony. Sometimes it has been enough to save the people. Sometimes not.

In the nineteenth century especially, times were increasingly harsh. A generation or so before the Removal of 1838, some of the Cherokee moved to Oklahoma. But the bulk of the people—about seventeen thousand—remained in the eastern nation. Realizing that the settlers profited greatly from putting their thoughts into print, Sequoyah, who was born in the Tellico area of Tennessee, invented the Cherokee syllabary in the early 1820s, the first time in history that an individual developed an alphabet. Within two years, the whole nation, east and west, was literate, and shortly a newspaper was published, *The Cherokee Phoenix*. Also, during this period the Cherokee shifted their town governments to a centralized government and in 1827 adopted a written constitution modeled after the U. S. Constitution, which as we have seen, contained a process long familiar to Indian peoples. Many Cherokee became Christians, perceiving no conflict between Christian laws and their own. The Cherokee hoped that these changes would make peaceful coexistence possible and the government would allow them to remain on their ancestral lands.

None of these adaptations saved the nation. In his classic novel, *Mountain Windsong*, Robert J. Conley evokes the peoples' experience of the Trail of Tears through the story of Waguli, "Whippoorwill," and Oconeechee, young lovers who are separated when federal troops suddenly sweep down and herd men, women and children into stockades until they can be "removed" to the West, to Oklahoma. Waguli is in the stockade. Where Oconeechee is, he doesn't know. Slowly, realization of the total significance of what is happening comes into his mind. "It was more than the unhappiness of Waguli and Oconeechee, more than the cruel, needless suffering of the wretches around him in the stockade, more than the thefts and deaths. All of these things were bad enough, but it was more than all of them combined. It was like the crack of doom."[34]

As you read the book, you know that Conley "walked in his soul" to write it and that he is Cherokee, for only one who understands the sacred law in his bones could portray the hearts of the lovers—and the people—as they slowly turned East and began again. Part of what enables them to do this is *to hi ge se s di*, making peace or making peace for the earth—freeing oneself from bitter resentment—which helps heal the soul. East and West, the Cherokee regrouped, reorganized. In the Oklahoma nation, Cherokee clan law was adapted to the U.S. court system, and the first school for women west of the Mississippi was established. When Oklahoma became a state in 1906, tribal structure was officially abolished, the language and culture suppressed, and religious ceremonies such as the Green Corn Ceremony were prohibited, as they were in the Eastern Band.

But the people took many traditional ways underground—and preserved them until the Tribal Reorganization Act in 1934 made it possible to begin again. Today, both in the Eastern Band of Cherokee in North Carolina and in the Cherokee Nation of Oklahoma, traditional values, rewoven with contemporary adaptations, still sustain the people. In Oklahoma, the Cherokee have re-instituted the tribal court system—which combines federal and state laws with custom law—in the same building from which it was evicted in 1906. Under the modern name of Community Development, the traditional pattern of the town council functions as effectively as it used to. People convene, discuss and decide what they need and what skills they can pool to "get the job done." The traditional word for this process is *gadugi*.

Thinking of cooperation versus competition brings to mind another way corn teaches. Corn cannot reseed itself because, when an ear falls to the ground, the seeds fall off in a heap. Kernels expend so much energy competing for space that they don't grow. To thrive, seeds must be planted apart—but close enough for company.[35] Harmony in a family, an institution—or a nation—depends in great measure on giving people room to grow.

THE SWEET HEART OF SELU

Birth Gift for My Grandchildren

The Time of Unknowing

"You never know what lies around the bend" is an Appalachian maxim—for survival in the mountains and in life. Implication: Be alert, be flexible. The mountains reveal a bend coming up. Life often doesn't. For me during 1991, the maxim proved true again. As March began, farmers in Tennessee were preparing the ground for spring planting, mostly corn and soybeans. "Got your fields ploughed yet, Sam?"—"Not yet. Waitin' on the weather."

Our family was waiting, too—for two "flights of the wren," the births of the first grandchildren. One was due in late March, the other in early October. Technology's "probing eye" said the first would be "a cornmeal sifter" (a girl) and the second would be "a hunting bow" (a boy). However, Mother Nature has been known to fool the "eye," so Grandmother Wren would make the definitive announcement. Pending her confirmation, the parents had already chosen the names Chelsea and Gregory.

The first draft of the Selu manuscript was complete. In celebration of the upcoming family events, I had written a "birth gift" chapter, which I then viewed as an "insert," significant but not the crux of the book that it later became. Meanwhile, I was skipping around on the tips of my toes. Here in the South becoming a grandmother is a momentous and ceremonial event. Among family, friends and even strangers with whom one "happens" to share the news, a chain reaction of excitement begins, especially among women. Why is this so? I think it's because three tribal cultures that give high esteem to grandparents have long converged in the South—Native, Celtic and African. They share a similar tradition for a woman's life cycle that Paula Gunn Allen, Pueblo writer and anthropologist, describes for Native American women. The four cycles are childhood, youth, the time of bearing (children and/or career), and Mother of the Nation. In this last cycle, having completed the responsibilities of the previous ones, a woman takes all she has learned and uses it for the good of the people. She is also free to take up a path of her own interest—which she may have deferred—and to savor the harvests of life. Through blood kinship or by affection, this harvest often includes the special bond between grandparent, or aunt, and child.

I could hardly wait to share the joy of my daughters as they became mothers and to hold each newborn, looking into eyes still "trailing clouds of glory." A numinous time. No words for what it means, just the heart's knowing ...

As I wrote "Birth Gift" I was thinking of our grandchildren—of all children who are looking forward to the future, of the generations of the unborn. Filled with the hopeful exuberance that burgeoning life brings, I had no idea what lay around the bend—that these were the last words I would write for a year, that when I came back to the manuscript I would have made a journey with each of my children to the edge of the Darkening Land. Without science and technology, without men and women "of the good," who used modern tools with respect, Paul and I probably would have come to the end of 1991 bereft of our children and grandchildren.

A shadow of anxiety always surrounds a birth. Most of the time, things go well. Sometimes they don't. I agree with Paula Gunn Allen that childbirth is for women what battle is for men: the moment of truth. Modern science notwithstanding, one's life is on the line. The baby's life is on the line. And you know that whatever the outcome—whether the baby lives or dies, is healthy or deformed or sick—this child is part of your heart and soul forever. There is no turning back. As labor begins, you face East and set your whole being into bringing forth a new life. A momentous event that resolves into joy only when you hear that the baby is safe.

For Drey and Aleex, there were more shadows than usual. Both had very difficult labors, and in the end the babies were delivered by Caesarean section. Two generations ago, without sophisticated monitoring equipment and surgery, our daughters or their babies almost certainly would have died. On March 23, when Chelsea was born, and October 6, when Gregory arrived, the words "Mother and baby are fine" were filled with sunshine.

Between these two births, shadows suddenly deepened around our son, Andrew, who was twenty-two. On May 3, he completed final exams at the Memphis Academy of Art. Early that evening, he had a seizure. After many days of testing, the diagnosis was given: a tumor on the brain stem, twined around it like a vine. Specialists debated whether to hazard surgery. A recent advance in technology made it possible—but not certain—that the operation could be done without damage to the brain. The most crucial factors were the skill and judgment of the doctor who would guide the tool and of his partner who would administer the anesthesia. Never had I been more acutely aware of the connection between technology and the hands that use it. And even with the best men and women of the good in attendance, the imponderables were the questions Andrew asked me just after the diagnosis was made. "Mama, will I still be the same person? Will I still be able to create?" And the unspoken question, "Will I still be?"

As we had at the time of the births, the family gathered in. Friends surrounded us with comfort and joined their prayers with our own. Eventually, Andrew was completely healed. Because it was like a rebirth, our son, in a sense, also became our grandson. Our daughters and their children were also safe. Seven months of shadows made the sun more radiant and our gratitude to the Creator more simple and profound. It is good to have one day and be alive to do something for the good.

These experiences had stripped my heart to the bone. For what seemed like seven years, I'd sat beside my children in the bourne between life and death. It was a place of perfect stillness. A place without gender, race or creed. The view was very clear: God, pain, prayer, love. Slowly, slowly, I reached a calm that is beyond hope. With my arms around my children, I faced East, accepting that whichever way their paths veered, they would find a sunrise.

When I first looked deep into the eyes of my grandchildren, I saw dawn's light. An expression of peace and trust and goodness. One pair of eyes was brown, one blue. The expression was the same, the newborn gaze that expects the one who bends near to be good, expects the world to be good. Doesn't every child deserve that it should be so.

When I returned to the manuscript, I was the same person, but different. The themes of the work, including the central one of unity in diversity, were still sound. The basic essays and poems were still appropriate. But the whole had to be deepened and widened and new material added. The form had been a singlewoven basket; I saw that, given the perils of our times, it needed to be doublewoven, and very sturdy. Unweaving what I had already done, I began again.

Of "Weaving II," only the following "Birth Gift" remains as I originally wrote it. After contemplating the Corn-Mother on a deeper level, I saw this chapter as her message distilled to its essence, her sweet heart. For some reason, the very young and the very old understand her heart with the same ease. Maybe because the young have so recently come from the perfect stillness of the sunrise and the old are so near to returning there.

Song Twice-Sung, 1991

I stop weaving my basket,
contemplate the pattern of Selu ...
I reach four hundred miles beyond
to our daughter
who is about to bring forth
her first-born
in the shadow of the Great Smokies
the Mother Mountains
where I myself was born
and ancestors made their home
planted corn
raised children ...

I.

Amazing—the power of the unborn to set thoughts cycling and to suspend a far-flung family in a web of expectancy.

Dwayne the father is beside Drey waiting ...

On the banks of the Mississippi my husband Paul and I are waiting ...

In the mountains my mother Wilma is waiting, remembering when her husband Bill was alive and they were young and I was about to be born and grandparents on both sides were waiting ...

My sister Adele and her children Michael and Michelle are in Atlanta waiting ...

Up near the Kentucky line Paul's sister, Mary Claire, her husband Sam and their children, Sammy and Beverly, are waiting ...

Andrew, our youngest, the uncle-to-be, is waiting ...

In the spirit world Paul's parents, Ruth and Clyde, and my father Bill, are drawing near and waiting ...

Our eldest, Aleex, and her husband Jack are waiting—for this baby

and for their own
who will come in mid-fall.
it's mid-March now—

> time to prepare fields,
> begin the cycle
> of planting, growth, harvest.
> And our family waits,
> as families from time immemorial have waited
> for the mysterious news ...

Meanwhile, we work at the tasks at hand, try to cope with the stress of a world teetering on the turning point. What a comfort to know that in the dark safety of our daughters' wombs, the eternal cycle is continuing: The seed has drawn strength from the warm, wet place of its planting. In the fullness of time, "First the blade and then the ear / Then the full corn shall appear ... "

> In blood and hope,
> in pain and joy
> a child will be born
> a gift from the Creator.
> "Come ye thankful people ... "

And we will come—the whole family. I'll go first, Paul a week later. My bag is packed. My "Grandmother Bundle"—a gathering of small gifts— is ready too, except for the primary birth gift, which I'm still thinking about. And so the whole family will gather in to rejoice and give thanks for the new life among us. As time goes on, each of us in our appropriate way will provide nurture and guidance so the child can grow up safely to sing whatever song the Creator has instilled. This growth cycle will repeat the original one. Paul and I hope that when the season comes for us to depart from this world, we will hear our family singing yet another harvest safely home. And that these great-grandchildren too will have:

> Peace to live
> Peace to ripen
> Peace to be thankful
>   PEACE
> But where is the peace?
> Ensuring it is our task.

II.

What birth gift should I offer
to my grandchildren?
What will help them survive
the teetering of the world?
Looking at my basket
I see what it should be—
Selu's heart
the sweet heart of the corn
so fragile it's cut out
of store-bought meal,
so good that meal
is dross without it.
My grandchildren must have
the whole corn—
the grain and its story.
They will be corn-fed
like all their mountain
ancestors have been.

Mountain babies literally used to cut their teeth on corn—on a ring made from dried kernels. I don't know how to make a safe one. But, as soon as they can eat solid food, these babies will know the Corn-Mother, the sweet taste and scent of her heart—probably in cornbread made with stone-ground meal (no pasteurized pap for them). Maybe we can walk in the cornfields, like my grandfather and I used to do. Then during their tender "blade" years, as soon as they are old enough not to take the dried corn and eat it, I will give them a multicolored ear and trace the first outline of Selu's story in their minds.

In the beginning
The Creator made our Mother Earth.
Then came Selu, Grandmother Corn.
Her children circled round her
like the kernels on her body—

Touch them—
   red, black, white, yellow
   round and round
   no one first or last
   all in harmony.
Each one different
Each one good—just like you.
When the children did their part,
When they helped her
and remembered their manners,
Selu fed them.
When the children forgot their part
She went away until they remembered
   Selu says,
"When you take, always give back.
   Say, 'Thank you.'"

As the children grow bigger, so will the story. Kanati and the grandsons or sons will come into it. But before that, when they are still very small, the children will want to know, as mine did, "Was Selu born like us?"

"No, not like you. Selu was born full grown, the First Woman. I want my friend Mary Ulmer Chiltoskey to tell you this story, because she tells it best. She's from the Eastern Band in North Carolina. In the year you were born she sent me her book as a gift. She calls it *Aunt Mary, Tell Us a Story,* and this is the story Aunt Mary tells about Selu and Kanati."

THE LEGEND OF THE FIRST WOMAN[36]

For a time the man was very happy on the earth. He roamed around and ate the fruits and berries and he visited the animals and he saw all his homeland. There was much to learn and the earth was beautiful. But before long the man grew discontented and he became very unhappy. He didn't know what this disease was, but it was a disease that we still have. He was bored.

When he got bored, he used his mind and his strength differently. He shot arrows at the deer without really needing to. He picked the plants and didn't use them. He tore up the animals' dens just to see if he could do it. And soon the animals became concerned about the new creature.

The animals called a council meeting to try to determine what to do. They said they thought this creature was supposed to have respect for other creatures, that he was given a mind. A little insect said, "Wait, you haven't thought this out. The Great One made him; let's ask him what to do." This seemed to be a good idea. They called to the Great One to help them with the new "superior" creature.

The owl said, "You told us the man has a mind and he is to respect us."

The deer said, "I don't want to be disrespectful, but you told us the man would need more of us deer than any other animal. If he keeps killing us like he is now, very soon he won't have any deer left."

"Oh," said the Great One, "thank you, thank you. I had not thought about something I left out in this man."

The bear said, "Look at him now. He's lying out in the sun with his face up. No animal will sleep right out in the open. We all know to go into a private, guarded place to rest."

The Great One said, "Yes, there is something missing because I was in such an excited hurry to make him. But I know now what is missing."

"Stand back," he said. He made a green plant to grow up tall. The plant grew up right over the man's heart, up toward *Galunlati* (Heaven). It was a plant with long, graceful leaves and then an ear and a golden tassel. Above the tall plant was a woman, a beautiful, tall, brown woman growing from the stalk of strong corn.

The man woke up and thought he was dreaming. He rubbed his eyes and said, "This is not true. In a minute I'll wake up and be just as bored as I was before. Oh, I am so lonely."

The Great One sort of kicked him in the behind. "Get up, you lazy thing," the Great One said. "Be a man for your lady." Now no one had any reason to think this man was a mannerly individual. Recently he had certainly not been acting like a real gentleman. But we don't have to be taught manners: We need someone to expect the best from us and we use the manners the Great One has already given us. So the man got up, brushed himself off, and gallantly offered his hand to the woman, who came down from the stalk of corn.

The woman said, "No, wait a minute." The man didn't argue or huff. He just waited as she asked. She reached up and pulled two good ears of corn to take with her. Then she said, "I'm ready." Do you know why she wanted the corn? She couldn't have known yet that the corn would be an important food. She just knew that she had sprung from the corn and she needed to take something of her heritage with her.

The Great One remembered that although each man will sometimes need to be alone, each man will also need companionship to be his best.

Over a period of time, the man and the woman built a home where they kept the corn for planting. The next spring she planted her corn and it grew into a beautiful plant. It was probably the next year that she noticed a large bird who became sacred to the Cherokees, a large bird who stays usually on the ground. We call this bird a turkey. The turkey became sacred to the Cherokee because they could watch what he ate, and they would then know it was safe to eat.

One morning the woman noticed the turkey eating the tender corn. She knew then the corn was food and it was time to eat the corn. That evening she set a pottery pot of corn in the middle of her cook fire. She covered the pot with a curve of chestnut bark. When the man came in to eat his fish stew, she didn't tell him what she had cooked. She just pulled an ear of corn from the pot and pealed it back so he could smell it. He thought it was the best aroma he had ever smelled and he began to eat the first corn of the spring. (Cherokee women even now never tell their men when they will serve the first corn of the season. They believe if they say it, bad luck will happen. One year not long ago, Aunt Mary's husband overheard her tell a visitor when they would have the first corn of the season. Before the corn was good and ripe, wild hogs ate nearly all of it!)

To my grandchildren, I'll say, "You aren't supposed to spy on Selu or her daughters when they're doing their first private work—not even with your ears." And I'll tell them the story of Little Deer, too, how he is connected to Kanati, the Lucky Hunter. And that will lead to another of Aunt Mary's stories. "When I first came to Cherokee (N.C.) fifty years ago," she says, "within fifteen minutes I saw Selu and Kanati. I was walking along the street by the hospital and there they were—sculpted in wood in a bas relief over the hospital door. Kanati was dozing in the sun. Nearby, near his heart, was a tall cornstalk and Selu coming out of the top of the plant. On either side of her was a leaping deer. I found out that Goingback Chiltoskey, the famous Cherokee woodcarver and artist, had made it. Little did I know that twenty years later, G. B. and I would get married!"

For twenty-five years after Mary Ulmer came to North Carolina, she taught history and was a librarian in the Cherokee schools. She also became a famous storyteller. In 1989 she was named an honorary member of the Eastern Band of Cherokee in recognition of nearly fifty years of service to her Cherokee neighbors.

> *Somewhere in the world*
> *Selu is always singing.*

III.

As I think of my grandchildren and their future, a line from Selu's story circles in my mind: "She knew that she had sprung from the corn and she needed to take something of her heritage with her."

These grandchildren have Celtic heritage also, through their fathers, who are mountain men, and through part of my family and Paul's. From what I see of this teetering world, these children—and others like them—are going to need every root of their heritages to survive. They will learn some of their Cherokee/Appalachian heritage from books at school. But most of it will be passed through the family.

From first contact centuries ago the Celt and the Cherokee got on well together because of what they shared: devotion to family; love of the land; reverence for the Creator and the natural law; the egalitarian relationship between men and women; the sense of fierce independence and outrage at foreign invasions, which both sexes would battle to repel; the love of ceremony and symbol. All of these combine in a quality of soul that relies on the inner life of the spirit to survive.

The Celts who came to the Appalachians took to Grandmother Corn as to an old friend. They were very much at home at the Cherokee's Green Corn Ceremony, which was so like their own. When the contemporary mountain man told me the old folks went away carrying his gift of stone-ground meal "real careful, like it was something sacred," there was in that a way of carrying a racial memory that stretches back to the time before the Roman invasion of England—a time when the Celts called Earth Mother and when the genders were equal.

In 1989, I asked a Scotch-Irish farmer in the mountains near Sevierville, Tennessee: "Do you think corn is more than a plant?" This came, of course, after an appropriately rambling conversation.

He gave me a long, measuring look, then gazed out over his field of ripening corn, weighing the question. He knew from my accent that I was no "furriner" and expected a thoughtful reply. From his good-humored expression, I knew he liked the question.

Finally, he said, "Well now ... you take somebody corn-raised. You can't do nothin' with 'em. We're strong. We're free. We do as we think proper. Folks who say contrarywise have a fight on their hands, don't they ... ?" I laughed. He laughed. We had a perfect understanding. Democracy. The Law is in the seed.

But right on our heels is the corn borer—an insect that lays waste to corn, the "use and consume" attitude so powerful today. How can these two grandchildren safely make their way into a society so highly competitive, aggressive and violent? "The sweet heart of Selu"—the spirit of reverence, cooperation and sharing—is fragile. Without protection, it is easily destroyed. But the heart of the corn has protection—a tough shell that enables the seed to exist until it is safe in the warm earth. "I see that you have come to kill me," Selu said, calling a spade a spade.

So eventually, after they have been well grounded in the positive, the children will have to know and understand other stories of history, the stories of pain and blood, which lead to the birth of hope. Gradually, as their judgment matures, they will hear these stories, which will give them forewarning and patterns of coping with the world. "Beauty is no threat to the wary ... "

I have a plan for Chelsea and Gregory. In 1998, when they are seven years old, they will be "nubbin ears," like I was when my grandfather and I discussed Selu in the cornfield. The three of us will go to Washington, D.C.—just before the millennium begins. In my mind, this experience is already taking place:

We look at the Jefferson Memorial and talk about the Declaration of Independence and the Constitution. Then we go to the Lincoln Memorial and recall the terrible years in the mid-nineteenth century, when the nation was torn by civil war. Brother fought against brother; women held the fort at home, keeping the family—and life—going. In the South, women also faced invading armies, marauders—and hunger. African-Americans were slaves, hunted down if they broke for freedom, and Native peoples were being torn from their lands, killed, herded onto reservations and denied citizenship in a country that was once their own. Those were days of pain and blood for almost everyone, and it seemed America might not survive the violence, as it seems we might not survive today.

Although the words in the speech are big for seven year olds, I tell the children what President Lincoln said in 1858, what he called on all Americans to remember:

> What constitutes the bulwark of our own liberty and independence? It is not ... the guns of our war steamers, or the strength of our gallant and disciplined army. ... Our reliance is in the love of liberty which God has planted in our bosoms.[37]

"President Lincoln said that a long time ago. But it's a great wisdom still. The Creator has planted a seed of liberty and democracy in our hearts. And we have to take care of it. Help it grow. So there will be plenty for all the people. ... We have to remember what is important, especially when times are bad and many people are fighting each other. Remember when you were very little, how I showed you the Corn-Mother with all her children gathered round her—all different colors, but one family? Remember the stories of Kanati and Little Deer and the law of respect?

"Since you know the stories, I can show you the mysterious ciphers here in Washington. They are secret messages for your future. Only people who know the stories can see them."

"Where are they?" they will say. "Show them to us, Grandmother, show them." Hand in hand, Chelsea on one side and Gregory on the other, we will make our way to the ciphers and decode them.

I know what shoes I'll wear for this historic occasion—the "granny boots" I bought when the babies were born, one for each child. Crimson suede and leather. Firmly laced. In these boots I plan to take my grandchildren into the twenty-first century. And I'll be wearing them at the end of this book, when you and I make a journey of our own to the ciphers.

THE LAW IS IN THE CORN

A Story of American Democracy

The Law is in the Corn
the people of the southwest say this ...
to be there with the morning star in that sacred time ...
to talk to the corn, to hear it talk in the wind
in the language of movement ... what to do.
Out here at the Eastern Door, we say it is
the Original Instructions ...
This is called Democracy.
It is in the land, it is in the seed.
                                        —Alex Jacobs/Karoniaktatie

History and Poetry

For three years I've been "settin' on a stump," thinking through this poem and the story of Selu. Around me, violence has ranged from the Gulf War, called Desert Storm, to the recent murder of three seven-year-old boys in West Memphis. They were found floating in a bayou—bound, beaten and sexually mutilated. The suspects arrested are three teenage boys.

Sometimes the downward pull is so great that my heart falters, as yours may also. I say to myself, "It seems like I already heard these stories before … the only thing is, the names sound different." Then I remember Roland's arrow arcing toward the East. I tell this story of American democracy because in the patterns of pain and blood, there is also hope. What has been survived before can be survived again. And in every era of turmoil, now as then, there have been people who work to ensure a just and companionable peace.

This is a story of the parallel journeys the Corn-Mother and indigenous democracy made to Europe and home again, a story of cornfields singing and cornfields trampled and burned. In conventional American history, corn is mentioned so often in connection with peace and war that it becomes a natural metaphor for the rise and fall of events and attitudes. When the grain is united with its spiritual meaning, corn becomes a mother who bears and works with her people, urging us to uphold the Law. Us: We-the-People of the United States.

In the Constitution two concepts of democracy cross-pollinated. One was Native American, which was gender-balanced and egalitarian. The other was Greek and Roman; it was essentially for privileged males. I think of one as Corn-Mother Democracy and the other as Great Stag Democracy. We will look at what happened between them and among the peoples involved, especially the "folks," whom history seldom mentions. In the twentieth century this story is all but forgotten.

The Told Story of American democracy usually jumps from Columbus to Jamestown settlers, the Pilgrims and the Founding Fathers, who for inspiration in creating the U.S. Constitution drew on the work of European philosophers, especially John Locke and Jean Jacques Rousseau. The Told Story is true, but incomplete. Another story—and the people involved in it—

is missing. Fortunately, Europeans who lived it wrote many documents, books and letters. Through their precise oral traditions, indigenous people still remember what happened. Today, scholars among descendants of both cultures are working together to bring the Untold Story back to the American mind. For background, I've used distillations of their work from *Indians and the U.S. Constitution: A Forgotten Legacy* by Kirke Kickingbird and Lynn Shelby Kickingbird (published by the Institute for the Development of Indian Law) and from *Indian Roots of American Democracy,* edited by José Barreiro and published by Akwe:kon Press at Cornell University. (*Akwe:kon* is the new name of the *Northeast Indian Quarterly.*)

Indian Roots was compiled from the proceedings of a fall 1987 conference at Cornell, "The Iroquois Great Law of Peace and the United States Constitution." The book begins with Alex Jacobs' poem, "The Law Is in the Seed." It is significant that every Haudenosaunee (Iroquois) speaker at the conference emphasized that the idea of the Great Law, of democracy, originated with the Creator. Native Americans as a whole say the Law as they interpret it has the same origin. It is sacred. This idea is in harmony with President Abraham Lincoln's admonishment to Americans to remember that "our reliance is in the love of liberty which God has planted in our bosoms."

At this crucial juncture in American history, it is time to correct the mistake made so long ago and accept the whole corn—the grain and its spiritual meaning. And it is sobering to consider that over the millennia the idea of egalitarian government has been sown in many places, including West Africa and the ancient mother-centered cultures of Europe. It is the Creator's strategy to sow seed widely so that some will survive. We must take respectful care of ours so that the people will have plenty.

Cross-Pollination

Several times before 1492, Ginitsi Selu evidently journeyed to Europe; chroniclers noted her presence here and there. After Columbus, she soon was everywhere. When the Corn-Mother and the seven Taino prisoners arrived in the Old World with Christopher Colon, the royals and nobles, who considered themselves "the People," saw a grain and slaves—"its" to use and consume, like livestock and peasants. The Taino-Arawaks vanished. History, which is usually written by those in power, rarely takes note of "its." Because these Taino represent the first indigenous people of the Americas that the Spanish colonists wrenched from their homes and the first of the people in North America to be "vanished," they are a metaphor for the regeneration of Native peoples that is in process now, five hundred years after Columbus. (And the fate of the vanished ones themselves has recently been explored through the research of a countryman, José Barreiro, in his *Indian Chronicles* [1993].)[38]

But the Taino Seven were reborn in another way. Columbus presented the Corn-Mother to Europe with neither her spiritual name nor her story. Shorn of everything but her nurturing power, she passed into the hands of the peasant folks, who within one generation spread the Cornsilk Web over Europe. Ginitsi Selu nourished the folks physically. Also, as they worked in their hot, rustling fields, she enveloped them in the sweet, rich scent of her pollen, sang to them as she grew—stirred their thoughts. They remembered that this grain was a "gift from the Indians" and that Indians came from the New World. Word of this new land began to trickle down. As they handled the gleaming gold and white ears of corn, the folks began to dream of a place where they too could be "the People," with a capital P.

How could this happen? According to the familiar version of the Told Story of democracy, the "masses" of Europe were illiterate, poverty stricken, reduced to "animal instincts" of foraging and mating. Corn should have meant no more to them than it did to livestock. But the Corn-Mother works in mysterious ways—strength of body often leads to stronger minds and spirits.

Also, just as history often fails to consider the element of the people's memory, so it neglects the equally important element of their *ears*. Word passes on the grapevine. As we say in the South, the people—the folks— always know "what's comin' down." Universally, that's why wise leaders have made it their business to ask, "What are the people saying?"

In the time of Columbus, as now, the operating principle of the grapevine was that the powerful—who claimed to be "the People"—didn't watch what they said (or did) around those they considered inferior, which amounted to about 80 percent of the population—among them slaves, servants, peasants, poets, artists, musicians, soldiers, tradespeople, functionaries, children and women. (A popular philosophical debate was whether women were animal or human. Even those who said human doubted that women could think. Early European explorers in America, beginning with the Spanish who came to the Caribbean, repeatedly expressed amazement at how well the Indians treated their women. The Indians made the opposite observation about the Europeans.)

In the spring of 1493, Columbus's arrival in Spain created a great furor. He made a triumphal progress from Seville to the Spanish court in Barcelona, where the king and queen received him with "solemnity and splendor." If from this event we exclude the hero, the royals and nobles and focus instead on what might democratically be called the "support personnel," we see a great host listening and watching—both along the progress route and at the court. It's certain that before the sun rose the next day, each one had told the news to one—or maybe two or three—of their relatives and friends.

This same loquacious human vine twined around the explorers and philosophers who were inspired by the new form of government discovered among the Indians. They wrote about the idea, talked about it and circulated it widely among the other intellectuals of Europe. However, intellectuals must be fed, clothed, brushed and barbered, conveyed when they wish to travel and attended when they are ill. Those who performed such services listened to what was said—and repeated it, perhaps as they sat at supper eating bowls of corn mush. They too began to dream of a government that was "of the People, by the People, for the People."

Though he didn't recognize it as such, Columbus had planted the first seeds of American democracy in the European mind: "Nor have I been able to learn whether they held personal property, for it seemed to me that whatever one had, they all took shares of ... of anything they have, if it be asked of them ... they invite you to share it."[39]

This seed was already sprouting in the thoughts of Amerigo Vespucci when he set out on his voyage. His book of discoveries, *Mundus Novus,* or *New World* (1505), was a tasseled field that released great drifts of pollen into minds where Columbus's seeds were already in bloom. Sir Thomas More, inspired by *Mundus Novus* and by interviews with Dutch explorers who had visited America and the Indians, wrote *Utopia* (1516), which depicted a government operating on the consent of the governed. In the same year the Spanish explorer

Peter Martyr published his *American History, Decades of the New World*, which was translated into English in 1555. To European intellectuals, Martyr's Golden World of the Indian looked like the ideal state described by the Greek and Roman writers and philosophers,[40] a state that did not include women as full citizens. From long habit, the intellectuals were blind to this discrepancy in their comparison with Indian governments.

In France, Montaigne became intrigued. He read the writings of European explorers and interviewed many of them. He also talked with three Indians touring Europe at the court of King Charles IX in 1562, who commented on the injustice of European society, with its classes of rich and poor. Drawing on these interviews and using part of Martyr's history, Montaigne wrote his essay on the New World, "Of the Cannibals" (1578–80), in which he discussed the ideal country and government and scathingly indicted many "cannibalistic" practices in the Old World.

The cross-pollination of thought continued apace during the next two centuries, germinating in the writing of men such as Voltaire, Shakespeare, Hobbs, Locke, Bentham and Rousseau. Curiously, although the intellectual air they breathed was saturated with the pollen of New World government, few would know its American Indian source. Fewer still would inquire. Most were content just to consume the air.

In his *First and Second Treatise on Government* (1690), Locke set forth the idea that the people of a nation contract with a ruler or king to govern them. He had read avidly about the Canadian Huron and cited their freedom of government. However, in Locke's time, intellectual thought confined the "people" to the wealthy class. About two generations later, Rousseau advocated an idea more in harmony with the American Indian concept of democracy. He viewed the basis of government as an agreement by the people themselves to combine the individual will into the General Will. (In the 1960s, when I lived among the French, they assured me repeatedly, "Your American Revolution would never have happened if it hadn't been for our philosophers, especially Rousseau." Since I'd been educated in the Told Story of democracy, I had no rebuttal.) In 1762, Rousseau published his *Social Contract*, which stimulated thinkers on both sides of the Atlantic.

That same year a delegation of three Cherokees made a private visit to the English court, led by the famous warrior and orator Outacite (Mankiller) of

Great Tellico.[41] In 1730, his colleague, Attakullakulla—chief and master diplomat—had led an official delegation to London to negotiate a treaty with the king. In fact, talking with Attakullakulla is what had inspired Outacite to come to London.[42] Back home, they had also exchanged views with many Europeans who came through the Cherokee Nation. In these "olden times," much more traveling and conversation took place than is now commonly supposed. Both Outacite and Attakullakulla knew the story of Selu—the link to "the Law is in the corn." It is possible that contemplating the expanding fields of maize and the growth of democratic ideas abroad, the two men saw the Corn-Mother enfolding the Europeans in a dream of liberty. It is certain they saw her doing so among the colonials in America.

Companions and Corn Borers

As Europeans began to settle on the eastern seaboard, their dual attitudes toward indigenous people were evident. One was the attitude of the Companion, a desire to coexist peacefully, as beans and squash do with corn. The other was the attitude of use and consume, as lethal to the concept of democracy as the corn borer is to the grain. As the story goes on, we will see how first one attitude, then the other gained ascendance.

During the era of the Revolution, the attitude of the Companion was strong in Williamsburg, which was the capital of Virginia and a training ground for the leaders of independence. As letters of Jefferson, Franklin and other Founding Fathers clearly indicate, many of the teachers of democracy were American Indian, especially the Iroquois. About the presence of Indians in general, Thomas Jefferson wrote to John Adams:

> Before the revolution the Indians were in the habit of coming often and in great numbers to the seat of government, in Virginia, where I was very much with them. I knew much of the great Outicité, [sic] the warrior and orator of the Cherokee; he was always the guest of my father on his journeys to Williamsburg.[43]

The *Virginia Gazette* reported visits of official Indian delegations in great detail, giving the subjects under discussion, the full text of key speeches, the entertainments that followed and who was there. Cherokee delegations were often composed of "gentlemen and their ladies," but the gazette was not privy to any counsel the women gave. Conditioned to Great Stag Democracy, reporters would not have been aware that such advice was sought or heeded. Otherwise, their accounts of the Indian presence are excellent, informative and lively.[44]

In unofficial ways, the exchange of ideas about democracy had been going on for a long time. In 1776, the process was described in *The History of North and South America*, published in England. (Indigenous people at that time were called "Americans.")

> The darling passion of the American is liberty and that in its fullest extent, nor is it the original natives only to whom this passion is confined; our colonists sent thither seem to have imbibed the same principles.[45]

"Imbibe" is an apt word here. Used in this sense, it means "to take into the mind and keep." Another meaning is "to inhale." Both are appropriate to the way the colonists absorbed participatory democracy. From the Southeast up along the coastline to the North, they found Native peoples planting great cornfields and governing themselves "by the consent of the governed" in a variety of confederacy patterns, which each tribe had evolved from its own perceptions of the Law.

The colonists, who took the grain only, didn't understand the sacred link between the corn and the Law. Nor did they at first realize that indigenous people even had a Law—a government—because it was so different from the authoritative monarchies of Europe. But colonial communities have been described as "small islands in great rippling seas of corn." Like the Flemish missionaries on Manhattan Island, when the corn was in bloom, the newcomers inhaled the smell so sweet it makes you "stand still" —the scent of liberty. Perhaps many a person set on a stump by a field and communed with the corn, heard it "talk in the wind, in the language of movement" and perceived the Original Instructions. Whether this did or did not happen, no one can say. Corn is a sacred and mysterious gift.

What is sure, is that through trade, conversation, councils and other forms of human intercourse, the colonists were in frequent contact with Indians, who considered themselves the People, with a capital "P," free and independent. Newcomers with the Companion attitude got along well with them and often attended their councils, town meetings and ceremonies.

However, the Corn Borer attitude was also strong in colonial thought. From the first settlers onward, its presence was manifested in their attitude toward corn and the Native people who grew it. The Told Story, which Americans have heard since childhood, is that newcomers to Jamestown (1607) and Plymouth (1620) would have starved without corn—a "gift from the Indians." The Told Story is true. But the Untold Story is equally true.

The Europeans in Jamestown and Plymouth already had a century-old attitude toward corn—it was for "livestock and peasants."

Among the people at Jamestown, the majority were "well born." The others, like most of the Pilgrims at Plymouth, were "poor born." When the Indians offered them corn—the grain and its story, its sacred meaning—the Jamestown settlers took the grain only ... and ate it. They were hungry. No doubt the well born detested being reduced to eating such a food as much as did the poor born, who had counted on getting away from anything associated with being "its"—the expendables.

Eat corn they would—but work to grow it? Let the peasants do it, the "heathen savages." Few colonists wanted stories that insisted they must work hard and with respect in the cornfields. Consequently, their crops were meager, while those of the Indians were abundant. Other solutions presented themselves. Some newcomers went where the corn was and lived with the Indians. Some stole the Indians' crops. Some planted their own.

Trade was another option. After Captain John Smith took over the direction of Jamestown, he made a journey of more than one hundred miles to see Powhatan, chief of the confederacy of the Chesapeake Bay area. Because of previous experience with the English in Virginia and through the "moccasin telegraph," brother to the grapevine, Powhatan and his people already knew much about European encounters with other Indians along the eastern seaboard. Reports brought along the great trade routes boded ill for the people.

Nevertheless, Smith and Powhatan worked out a tenable relationship that continued for a time, then became uneasy as the colonists created difficult pressures through stealing corn or desperately insisting that the Indians sell it. Slaves from Africa were brought in to do the field work, and, with the rise of tobacco as an export crop, the colonists increased demands for land to grow tobacco. The situation became explosive and deteriorated quickly after Powhatan's death. Four years later, in 1622, the Powhatan confederacy attacked Jamestown. This first major colonial war lasted twenty years, with great loss of life on both sides. The result was destruction of the Powhatan confederacy as a military and political force.

The first thing the Pilgrims took from the New World was corn. It was not offered as a gift. In fact, it was not "offered" at all. In mid-November 1620, the Pilgrims on the *Mayflower* were cold, weary and low on food. They dropped anchor at the first land they saw, the farthest tip of Cape Cod, near what is now Provincetown. In a longboat, a scouting party set out to explore the Cape and find "a place fit for situation." The Nauset Indians, seeing them coming and having previously lost some of their people to English slave traders, withdrew to the woods and observed the newcomers. Mourt's journal, published in 1622, gives eyewitness accounts of what happened:[46]

> There was a heap of sand ... it was newly done, we might see how they had paddled it with their hands—which we digged up, and in it we found a little old basket full of fair Indian corn, and digged further and found a fine great new basket full of very fair corn of this year, some thirty-six goodly ears of corn, some yellow, and some red, and others mixed with blue, which was a goodly sight. ... It held three or four bushels, which was as much as two of us could lift up from the ground, and was very handsomely and cunningly made ... we concluded to take as much of the corn as we could carry away with us. If we could find any of the people ... we would satisfy them for their corn.

Later they came back for the rest of the corn, "about ten bushels, which will serve us sufficiently for seed. And sure it was God's good providence that we found this corn ... sundry of us desired to make further discovery and to find out the Indians' habitations."

The scouting party poked through the Nausets' wigwams and into several graves, "taking away the prettiest things." Then they rowed away toward another part of the Cape.

The Nauset were part of the Wampanoag confederacy, and the moccasin telegraph spread the word. When the Pilgrims arrived at the next beach, they encountered "hostile" Indians. They named this place the "First Encounter." Prudently, the Pilgrims moved on. The *Mayflower* arrived at Plymouth in mid-December. The site was cleared for cornfields but apparently deserted. A plague (probably smallpox) brought by earlier voyagers had recently reduced the Wampanoag by half. Before the cruel winter was over, half of the Pilgrims had also died. Only fifty-two were left in the spring when Samoset, "a man of seemly carriage," walked out of the forest and said in English, "Welcome." This is where the Told Story takes up.

Samoset introduced the Pilgrims to Massasoit, whom they described as a "lusty man, in his best years, able in body, grave of countenance and spare of speech." He was chief of the Wampanoag confederacy, which included much of eastern Massachusetts, Cape Cod and Rhode Island. Massasoit became a staunch friend of the Plymouth Colony, which he saw as a valuable ally against the powerful neighboring tribe, the Narragansett. They had not been touched by the plague.

Massasoit gave the colonists a large tract of land and entered into a treaty of friendship with a mutual protection clause. As a further gesture of friendship, the Wampanoag offered the Pilgrims corn—the grain and its sacred meaning. The Pilgrims took the grain—and ate it. But perhaps because they were "folks" and used to the cycles of sowing and harvest, they had a more amiable attitude toward the grain and the people who offered it than did the Virginia colonists. The Wampanoag taught the Pilgrims how to plant, hunt and fish. And in the fall, Indians and Pilgrims together celebrated a thanksgiving for the harvest, a tradition long-practiced by both peoples. This was the "Thanksgiving of the Companions."

This peaceful relationship held for almost a generation. As the Pilgrims grew stronger, however, they expanded their territory, and attitudes began to change, especially after 1830, with the coming of the Puritans, who were more rapacious and less tolerant. To justify taking Indian land, the governor of the Massachusetts Bay Colony, John Winthrop, invoked secular English laws of property, which were contrary to the Indians' sacred law of communal use. He said the Indians had not "subdued" the land and therefore had only a "natural right" to it, but not a "civil right." "Natural right" had no legal standing. The Puritans claimed biblical justification: Psalms 2:8. "Ask of me, and I shall give thee the heathen for thine inheritance, and the uttermost parts of the earth for thy possession." And to justify use of force, they cited Romans 13:2: "Whosoever, therefore, resisteth, resisteth the ordinance of God: and they that resist shall receive to themselves damnation."[47]

In 1636, the Puritans broke their uneasy peace with the Pequot, who occupied what is now southern Connecticut and Rhode Island. They attacked the Narragansett on Block Island, then raided Pequot villages along the mainland coast. An officer on the expedition wrote, "The Indians spying on us came running in multitudes along the waterside, crying, 'What cheer, Englishmen, what cheer, what do you come for?' They not thinking we intended war, went on cheerfully. ... "[48]

War soon strangled all cheer. On both sides, the fighting was fierce. The English used deliberate attacks on noncombatants to terrorize the enemy. One of these was the mass murder of seven hundred Indian men, women and children, who were celebrating their Green Corn Ceremony— their own Thanksgiving—in a place called Mystic Fort in what is now known as Groton, Connecticut. Finding the Indians gathered in their own meeting house, the soldiers ordered them from the building and shot them as they came out. Those who remained inside were burned alive. To commemorate this "victory over the enemy," the governor of the Massachusetts Bay Colony in 1637 proclaimed the first official "Thanksgiving Day," which was celebrated for the next one hundred years.

Proof that he did so remained buried in archives for over three centuries, and history rarely mentioned this massacre. But the memory of the People is long. They did not forget the seven hundred. In the 1970s, a contemporary Penobscot professor, William Newell, who has degrees from the University of Pennsylvania and Syracuse, went in search of the missing proof. He found it in documents stored in Holland libraries, as well as in letters, log reports, journals and other documents written during the mid-1600s.[49] (United Press International newswire released a story about his findings November 24, 1977.) This was the "Thanksgiving of the Corn Borers"—a celebration of the burgeoning concept of manifest destiny.

Among the most outspoken colonists of the Companion attitude was the Calvinist nonconformist, Roger Williams, pioneer of religious freedom. From 1631, when he arrived in the Bay area, Williams preached on two major themes: the separation of church and state, and the invalidity of the king's patent (to seize land). He insisted that only direct purchase from the Indians gave a just title to the land. Plymouth rejected the latter theme. The civil authorities of Massachusetts Bay rejected both—and banished Williams. In 1636, Williams founded the Rhode Island colony, purchasing the land directly from Narragansett. He earned their trust and often in the following decades helped make peace between them and the surrounding colonies. As early as 1640, he used the Indian example to support his case for religious tolerance of minorities.

Meanwhile, the Puritans continued the war with the Pequot and the Block Island Indians, often pitting tribes against each other. Forty years later, the Puritans turned on the Wampanoag, who occupied the south shore of Massachusetts Bay. By this time many of the Plymouth colonists were also land-hungry. Massasoit was dead. His son Wamsutte had been killed by the English, and his other son, Metacom (whom the English called King Philip), led the confederacy. Attitudes had changed greatly since his father's time, when the colonists were dependent upon the Wampanoag for survival. Enforcing their views of property rights by force of arms, the English also made the Indians subject to their own harsh laws of justice.

As friction mounted, Metacom became the first Indian leader to realize that only a united Indian front could withstand the English. Some tribes were eager to join against the colonists; others were against unifying because they were economically dependent on the English. Some tribes were jealous of Metacom's leadership. The Christian Indians remained loyal to the British. After nine years of planning but well before he was completely prepared, Metacom was betrayed by his personal secretary, a Christian Indian named John Sassamon, who warned the Plymouth Colony of the conspiracy and his chief's strategy. When Sassamon was later found dead, the colonists captured three Indians and hanged them. Metacom's people considered this an intrusion into Indian affairs and were infuriated. Confrontations escalated.

The war began in late June 1675, when the cornfields were in bloom. Colonists of the Companion attitude were not silent. Roger Williams charged the English with camouflaging their aggression. Although many of the small farmers refused to fight, the colonial forces outnumbered and outgunned the Indians. A year later, during the season of green corn, the most savage war in the history of New England was over, and with it, effective resistance to English domination. Statistics tell little of the tragic loss of life on both sides. Although they had sustained a loss of six hundred soldiers and twelve of their fifty-two towns, the English had won. They killed three thousand warriors, destroyed crops, and sold into slavery captured Indian women and children, including Metacom's wife, Nanuskooke, and their son. Metacom himself was killed, his body quartered and his head displayed for over a year in the Plymouth public square—as a warning.[50]

Most of the colonists had come to see the land and the Indians as "its" to use and consume. To them the ruin in the fields was mere silage to be ploughed under. But the Indian survivors knew that beneath the burned and trampled stalks, milk from mangled ears had soaked, like blood, into the ground. The survivors kept the watch. Within four generations, the Corn-Mother would return, this time in the form that would ultimately bring Native people back from the brink of extinction.

A New Strain of Democracy

Through the Iroquois and America's Founding Fathers, Corn, Mother of Us All, became a central part of the Constitution of the United States.

It came about in the same way it would if you planted the seed I gave you at the beginning of our path to Selu. First the soil is prepared. Then the seed is planted. During the process of germination, the seed is out of sight, imbibing energies from earth and rain and sun. Then it sprouts—the first hair-fine taproot takes hold and others branch out. When the root system is established, it pushes up a green shoot—"first the blade and then the ear ... then the full corn does appear. ... "

Those who conceptualized the Constitution were men of great common sense. To found a new country, they would need a new form of government and a plan for creating it. The plan had to come first. It was the stump the Founding Fathers set on for more than forty years, thinking it through. Should the colonies be put under one rule? Or should they be put under individual stateship? Or could a plan in between be found?

The Thinkers considered the depth and breadth of the roots of democracy, beginning with the Greek and Roman ideals and the works of philosophers such as Locke and Rousseau. The theories were sound, but how to make them work? The Thinkers had the "hardware" of democracy from the Old World, but they needed "software" programmed for the New World. Through long association with the Iroquois, many of the Thinkers, led by Benjamin Franklin, had been intrigued by the Great Law of Peace, and not only on a philosophical level. They had observed the workings of the Great Law on practical terms.

For almost a century and a half, the British in America had prospered from alliances with the League of the Iroquois, which was the most powerful confederacy, politically and militarily, east of the Mississippi River. Although it was based in New York, with the central fire, or capital of government, near present-day Syracuse, the League's influence reached west to the Mississippi River and south through Tennessee and Virginia. Its power to control the fur trade, land sales, a host of subordinate tribes and the making of peace or war made it prudent for other tribes, as well as the colonists, to stay on the good side of the League, or Six Nations, as it was also called.

Trying to come up with a government in a new place, it is common sense to study a government that has worked in that place for a long time. The Thinkers had long been interested in the Great Law's strength, based on unity in diversity and representative self-rule. It was a working federalism that gave maximum internal freedom while providing for a strong defense. When colonial representatives met with the Six Nations at Lancaster, Pennsylvania, in 1744, they were receptive to what the Iroquois chief, Canassatego, seeded into their minds. He spoke of the Law's origins.

> Our wise forefathers established union and amity between the Five Nations. This has made us formidable. This has given us great weight and authority with our neighboring nations. We are a powerful confederacy, and by your observing the same methods our wise forefathers have taken, you will acquire much strength and power; therefore, whatever befalls you, do not fall out with one another.[51]

The Thinkers continued to talk and ponder until, like atoms, their thoughts fused into something visible. In his historic drafting of the Albany Plan of Union in 1754, Benjamin Franklin modeled federal, representative self-rule on the Iroquois example, and he used many terms from the Iroquois language to do it. Historians agree that in its federal aspects, the Albany Plan foreshadowed the Articles of Confederation and the Constitution itself. In its final form, the Iroquois rhetoric is replaced by the simplicity of Madison's language, "We, the People. ... "

There are similarities and differences between the Constitution and the Great Law of Peace. The fundamental structure of the United States—its system of checks and balances, the separation of powers—clearly was modeled on the Iroquois Grand Council. But the differences are also fundamental. Within the Iroquois system it was (and is) the women who had the right to elect the chiefs, oversee their work and recall those who did not work for the good of the people. Also, one of the qualifications of leadership within the Iroquois government has always been that the leader must be honest in all things. The U.S. Constitution *as a document* is a combination of European democracy of the Great Stag and indigenous democracy of the Corn-Mother.

At the Constitutional Convention in 1787, John Rutledge of South Carolina, who chaired the Committee of Detail that wrote the first draft of the U.S. Constitution, had long been familiar with the Great Law. He opened the convention with passages from it that related to the sovereignty of the people, peace and unity. Rutledge had asserted earlier that a great empire was being created, so it must be firmly rooted in American soil. On a federal level, as the Constitution was born, the Companion attitude toward Native people prevailed. In 1776, the new United States government had reaffirmed a treaty with the Indians always to protect their rights of land and justice, "for as long as the grass grows green, as long as the water runs downhill, and as long as the sun rises in the east and sets in the west."

With the rise of political pressure for western expansion—and the acquisition of more land—the season changed and shadows deepened as the Corn Borer attitude ascended. Once more, Indians were characterized as "savage and heathen"—it was not convenient to remember that those deemed expendable were civilized. And so the story of the Iroquois and the Great Law was forgotten. Thomas Jefferson, who during the Revolution had called himself "the savage from the mountains" and had held up Indian ideas of democracy against the "civilized" monarchies of Europe, shifted U.S. policy from economic alliance to assimilation and removal.

The result of this policy created more than a century of suffering for Indian peoples. They were wrenched from their land and denied citizenship, dignity and the right to educate their children in their own heritage and religion. Depending on who gives the statistics, the Native population at white contact varies between fifteen and twenty million. What is certain is that by 1923, there were scarcely 220,000 Indians left in the United States. The number now is about two million.

In spite of all despair, the People kept their eyes fixed on the Constitution, on the hope that one day their rights would be restored. In the early twentieth century, the season slowly began to change again, a change that continues in our own time. In 1924, citizenship was restored. Under the 1934 Indian Reorganization Act, tribal governments could be re-established. In 1978 came the Religious Freedom Act. But the federal government can still seize Indian lands without due process or compensation—and does seize them. The Constitution protects other American citizens from this act. Litigation to restore the Indian right to protection is now in process through the courts. Perhaps the Companion attitude will one day prevail and remain.

Researching this chapter, I gradually began to understand the answer to the question I had asked at Tellico: Why have Native people continued to place their trust in a Constitution that has failed so often in its promise? The answer clicked into place when I read this passage by the Seneca scholar

John Mohawk, words that evoked what my parents had told me over a decade ago: "Give the Constitution time to work—it's like the land.":

> The Constitution of the United States, you know everyone's saying, "Wow! This is a great document!" And it really is just a document. *But the idea of the Constitution of the United States is much bigger than a document, is it not?* [italics mine.] What we think the Constitution of the United States is, especially if we don't read it carefully, is our compact with the government of the United States. We think it's our compact that guarantees our rights and liberties. But what it really is, is part of a tradition that found its way into the American people of the 20th century that says that the rule of law is sacred. The arbitrary thoughts of a dictator or somebody else are not sacred, and a people have said they will die unless they can be ruled by a rule of law based on a principle of fairness. They have insisted, from the time of the first signing of the United States Constitution until today that they increase and hone and develop and make grow that idea of fairness.[52]

"This is called Democracy, it is in the land, it is in the seed. The Law is in the Corn ... "

The Constitution Is Alive

> Ginitsi Selu is in The Law,
> part of its power to nourish and sustain.
> The Great Stag is in The Law,
> part of its power to provide and protect.
> Continuance in the midst of change *is* The Law.
> We-the-People are part of its power,
> Women and Men and Children
>   doing our part
> to make the idea of fairness grow.
>
> The Constitution is alive!

SELU SINGS FOR SURVIVAL

'I will be the Corn-Mother ... don't ever forget.' From that beginning there became so much corn that everyone in the world had some.

In the course of seeking the Corn-Mother's wisdoms, we have delved into three of the four metaphorical senses in which Native Americans have traditionally perceived corn: enabler, mother, transformer. Evidence that she is also a healer has been clear, but the secrets of the healing traditions and of the sacred significance of pollen are kept in the rituals and ceremonies of the Native people who know them, preeminently the Navajo. Following the Corn-Mother's teaching, we've kept a respectful distance from her private work. However, it's comforting to know that this healing tradition continues and that we can become part of it in respectful, commonsense ways. In both weavings, the scent of corn—from pollen and from the sweet heart—has been used to evoke the healing power of Ginitsi Selu.

Wounds and shadows are still deep in America. The use and consume attitude is still strong, and many Americans feel that they are considered expendable by the society, the marketplace, the government. The things that divide us are many—race, religion, gender, sexual preference, education, on and on. But unity in diversity is the Corn-Mother's cardinal survival

320

wisdom. In the grain, genetic diversity is the key to an immune system that enables adaptation and survival. Unity in diversity is also the basic principle of the Constitution, one that we should consider carefully as America becomes ever more culturally diverse. This issue is even more complex than it appears on the surface, because people "sow seeds" (sperms and eggs) wherever they go. From this perspective, the diversity in Americans may equal that of maize itself. If only Ginitsi Selu would speak directly to us on this issue. Maybe she already has. The story of a twentieth-century woman leads me to believe it. Through the work of her biographer, Evelyn Fox Keller, we are able to hear the story from the lips of the one who lived it.

We find her as a young woman, working hard in a cornfield in Ithaca, New York. The century is twenty-five years old, and she is two years younger. Petite, perky, sun-browned, she might be called pleasant looking—until we see the intense gleam in her eyes, the gleam of a "See-er," one who thinks purposefully, with unity of mind/heart/soul. What she is thinking about—and will continue to think about until the end of her days—is *Zea mays*. People say she sees things in corn that no one else can. Remarkable in one so young.

I sense a story, don't you? Maybe she will tell it. Her Celtic father comes from a storytelling tradition. The ancestors of both of her maternal grandparents were on the *Mayflower*. Intriguing to think that their descendant is working in a field of the same kind of corn they took from the beach near Provincetown three hundred years ago. There is a mystic quality in this connection—and in the See-er herself. But she is straightforward, too, and immediately answers our question, "Why can you see in corn what others can't?"

> You must have time to look, to hear what the material says ... the patience to hear what the material has to say to you, the openness to let it come to you. You need to have a feeling for every individual plant. ...
>
> No two plants are exactly alike. They're all different, and as a consequence, you have to know that difference. I start with the seedling and I don't want to leave it. I don't feel I really know the story if I don't watch the plant all the way along. So I know every plant in the field. I know them intimately. And I find it a great pleasure to know them.[53]

> Animals can walk around, but plants have to stay still to do the same things, with ingenious mechanisms. ... Plants are extraordinary.

For instance ... if you pinch a leaf of a plant you set off an electric pulse. You can't touch a plant without setting off an electric pulse. There is no question that plants have all kinds of sensitivities. They do a lot of responding to their environment. They can do almost anything you can think of. But just because they sit there, anybody walking down the road considers them just a plastic area to look at as if they're not really alive.[54]

Obviously, the corn is not an "it" to the See-er. She feels the persona, the life within the grain. As she continues, we realize that she is studying maize as subject, not object. She touches the leaves and ears with great respect, explaining that "every component of the organism is as much of an organism as every other part"—including the gene. All of it is alive, active, responsive. Her eyes twinkle with merriment. All around us the corn "talks in the wind, in the language of movement," in harmony with what the See-er is telling us. Her credo is that nature is lawful. But to get to the laws, reason and experiment will not suffice. She agrees with Einstein that "only intuition, resting on sympathetic understanding, can lead to these laws ... the daily effort comes not from deliberate intention or program, but straight from the heart."[55]

You and I smile at each other. It seems we've heard this story before. ... It comes as no surprise when she says, "I have learned so much about the corn plant that when I see things, I can interpret them right away."

"In the beginning the Creator made our Mother Earth, then came Selu, Grandmother Corn. ... " The Medicine Man and the See-er are singing the same song—in counterpoint.

In her early twenties at the time we encounter her, Barbara McClintock has already made her first major discovery in genetic research with maize, the initial step of a journey that will lead to the Nobel Prize in 1983. Perhaps it will also lead one day to a change of thinking in all of us about who we are.

In her first year as a graduate student at Cornell, McClintock was a paid assistant to another cytologist who had been working a long time at the problem of identifying maize chromosomes—of distinguishing the individual members of the sets of chromosomes within each cell. "Well, I discovered a way in which he could do it, and I had it done within two or three days—the whole thing done, clear, sharp, and nice," McClintock says. Her employer was not overjoyed with her success. "I never thought I was taking anything away from him; it didn't even occur to me. It was just exciting. Here we could do it—we could tell one chromosome from another, and so easily! He had just looked at the wrong place, and I looked at another place." Having found the right place to look, McClintock spent the following years doing just that.[56]

Readers of this book will understand that corn genetics is hard work, physically and mentally. The methods of growing the crop are the same ones Selu gave her grandsons. You have to clear a bright sunny place, plant, water, weed and "hoe and hoe and hoe." Mental hoeing is necessary, too, because compared to other plants and insects used in genetic research, corn is slow, slow, slow to grow. But it is sure, for the colors of kernels on a cob of maize are "a beautifully legible, almost diagrammatic expression of genetic traits."[57]

The central dogma of genetics had been—and would remain for many years—that once information gets into the cell it can't get out. When I was taking botany in the 1950s, genetics still was very boxed. If you crossed a purple bean with a white bean, for example, the subsequent colors could be precisely figured out through the principle of dominant and recessive genes. (Presumably, human genetics functioned the same way.) Life could be boxed, labeled, stacked in a very orderly manner. And scientists also anticipated discovering the atom's ultimate "bead." Just as we humans believed everything could be perfectly ordered and controlled, Mother Nature said, "Surprise!" The atom eased off into a thought. And the Corn-Mother gave the first intimation of what is now popularly called jumping genes.

In 1931, when she was twenty-nine years old, Barbara McClintock and her student, Harriet Creighton, published a paper in the *Proceedings of the National Academy of Science*. The paper was called "A Correlation of Cytological and Genetical Crossing-over in *Zea mays*." It demonstrated that the exchange of genetic information that occurs during the production of sex cells is accompanied by an exchange of chromosomal material. This work, which has been referred to as "one of the truly great experiments of modern biology," finally and incontrovertibly secured the chromosomal basis of genetics. In his *Classic Papers in Genetics*, James A. Peters introduces McClintock's work, "This paper has been called a landmark in experimental genetics. It is more than that—it is a cornerstone." Maize could now be used for detailed cytogenetic analysis of a kind that had never previously been possible with any organism.[58]

Continuing her researches, letting her material "guide and tell" her what to do, McClintock developed and conclusively proved that what she called "transposition" takes place in genetic material. That genes, in short, "jump." And genetic changes are *under the control of the organism itself.*

McClintock used a new kind of integrated language to present her theories. It was not the almost mathematical vocabulary scientists were used to hearing. Many stonewalled her. There were years when she couldn't communicate with the scientific community as a whole, years of lonely, solitary—and brilliant—work.

It is another of the mysterious circles that just as *Rising Fawn* was published in October 1983, and I was setting out with my deerskin pouches of corn seed, my mother sent a clipping that Barbara McClintock had won the Nobel Prize in Medicine. I had never heard of her. Mother wrote a note on the clipping, "Thought you'd be interested. Might come in handy one day."

Blessings on Mother!

McClintock said that Evelyn Witkin, a young geneticist who came to assist her at Cold Spring Harbor, New York, in 1944, was the "only one who had any understanding of what I was doing." Witkin said that what McClintock was finding was "completely unrelated to anything we knew. It was like looking into the twenty-first century."[59]

McClintock's discovery may well make as big a change in the Western mind as Einstein's theory of relativity has done. Through the atom we have learned that everything in the universe is connected, not just philosophically but concretely through energy. Now, through blood and markers in the chromosomes, we may come to see that we humans are truly sisters and brothers—one family in fact, as well as philosophy. All the boxes and labels society forces people into explode in a vision of a great, shining web of peace and creativity. The Corn-Mother engenders dreams.

Barbara McClintock says that science often misses understanding the whole picture because it focuses on an isolated part. She emphasizes over and over that one must have "a feeling for the organism." In fact, that is the title of Evelyn Fox Keller's biography of her. *Organism* is the name

McClintock gives to the living, responsive sum and parts of *Zea mays*, the organism that in her own words "guided and directed her work, that spoke to her." It is interesting to think what name she would have given *Zea mays* if her ancestors at Plymouth had accepted the Indian's gift of whole corn: the grain and its story, its spiritual meaning. The important thing is that this great See-er communed with the mystery that is Ginitsi Selu. She made her first discovery on the ancestral lands of the Iroquois and continued her inquiry in the vicinity of where the Flemish missionaries centuries ago encountered a smell so sweet "that we stood still, because we did not know what we were meeting." What their hearts did tell them is that they were encountering a Presence. And if they had looked closely at the cornfield's edge, they might have seen a stag standing regal and staunch—maybe gleaming white—Awi Usdi himself.

As so many Americans do who have not been educated in Native American thought, Barbara McClintock connected her unified way of thinking only with the East (Tibet and China). In this aspect, her example underscores the importance of including indigenous history and culture in our national educational system. But McClintock's great work—her interpretation of what her "material told" her—and her integrated language have created a path for understanding among Americans of all races and have provided ways for us to make connections as human beings.

The Corn-Mother has been talking to us for a long time.

THE CIPHERS

I promised that in the end I would take you to Washington, D.C., to see and decode the secret ciphers, the guiding messages for the twenty-first century. Just as seven thousand years ago, Native farmers looked at a certain wild grass and saw a sacred gift, so Barbara McClintock looked through her microscope and instantly read the small dots on the corn, which she called ciphers. Other people couldn't decode them, but she could.

It is the same with the ciphers in Washington. They are in plain view. But most people probably pass them every day without recognizing what they really are. You will know instantly and decode them for yourself, because the stories have given you a synapse in the mind, a lens in the eye, a drum in the ear and a rhythm in the heart.

At sunrise we stand quietly in the middle of the Washington Mall. The sky is clear, the air fresh and sweet. Looking toward one end of the mall from the corners of our eyes, we see the Washington Monument—tall and sharp—the great white prong of a deer antler. And looking toward the other end, to the top of the Capitol dome, we see the figure of a woman whom many have called an Indian because of her flowing robe and the headdress that resembles feathers. From where we stand her robe is green and the feathers are a plume of brown silks, stirring in the wind.

Awi Usdi, Little Deer
Ginitsi Selu
Corn, Mother of Us All
in perfect balance
in perfect union.

The Creator offers us a gift ...

Future Unfolding

This painting represents the beginning
of life on earth:
the sacred circle, sacred fire, the forming.
Purification by smoke and eagle feathers.
The important Four Directions.
The corn provided to sustain life.
The deer and other animals that interact
to maintain all life and provide direction.
The important number seven—
in the seven eagle feathers
and seven ears of corn.
The four circles
represent the four stages of earth,
with the last one vague,
as yet to be determined
by our care and spiritual growth.

—Mary Adair

NOTES

Weaving I

1. Jack F. Kilpatrick and Anna G. Kilpatrick, *Friends of Thunder* (Dallas: Southern Methodist University Press, 1964), pp. 129–34.

2. Jack F. Kilpatrick and Anna G. Kilpatrick, *Walk in Your Soul* (Dallas: Southern Methodist University Press, 1982), p. 22.

3. Alfonso Ortiz, "Cultural Meanings of Corn in Aboriginal North America," in *Northeast Indian Quarterly* (now *Akwe:kon*): "Cultural Encounter II: Indian Corn of the Americas—A Gift to the World" (Ithaca, NY: American Indian Studies at Cornell University, 1989), p. 64.

4. Kilpatrick, *Friends of Thunder*, pp. 141–44.

5. Michael J. Caduto and Joseph Bruchac, "Awi Usdi, the Little Deer," in *Keepers of the Earth* (Golden, CO: Fulcrum Publishing, 1988), pp.173–74.

6. Consultation with Sue Thompson, Cherokee basketweaver and teacher, Talequah, Oklahoma, September 1991. Thompson teaches annual basket-making workshops at the National Indian Education Association Conference and the Johnson O'Malley Joint Tribal Conference.

7. Kilpatrick, *Walk in Your Soul*, p. 19.

8. American Heritage Publishing Company, *The American Heritage Book of Indians* (New York: Simon and Schuster, 1961), p. 417.

9. Jefferson Chapman, *Tellico Archeology: 12,000 Years of Native American History* (Knoxville: University of Tennessee Press, 1987), p. iv.

10. *The New York Times*, November 11, 1979.

11. William Bruce Wheeler and Michael J. McDonald, *TVA and the Tellico Dam* (Knoxville: University of Tennessee Press, 1986), p. 215.

12. Marilou Awiakta, revised from a version in the *Tennessee Conservationist*, May/June 1981, p. x.

13. *The Commercial Appeal*, November 11, 1981.

14. *The Commercial Appeal*, December 4, 1979.

15. *The Chatanooga Times*, April 16, 1980.

16. Wheeler and McDonald, *TVA and the Tellico Dam*, p. 218.

17. *The New York Times*, May 8, 1988.

18. Pat Alderman, *Nancy Ward* (Johnson City, TN: Overmountain Press, 1978), p. 80.

19. Ilene J. Cornwell, "Nancy Ward," in *Heroes of Tennessee* (Memphis: Memphis State University Press, 1979), p. 41.

20. Alderman, *Nancy Ward*, p. 69.

21. Kilpatrick, *Walk in Your Soul*, pp. 72–73.

22. Susan Peterson, *The Living Tradition of Maria Martinez* (San Francisco: Kondansha International, 1981). All quotes from Maria and Barbara are taken from this book.

23. Sylvia Wynter, "Challenging Canonical Knowledge," from her presentation at the conference, "Using Black, Ethnic and Feminist Perspectives to Integrate the Sciences and Humanities," Tufts University, 1988.

24. Leslie Marmon Silko, *Ceremony* (New York: Penguin-Viking, 1977), p. 2.

25. T. E. Mails, *Pueblo Children of the Earth Mother* (New York: Doubleday, 1983), Vol. I, p. 115. Mails is quoting from C. A. Amsden, *Prehistoric Southwesterners from Basketmakers to Pueblo* (Los Angeles: Southwest Museum, 1949).

26. Anne Fausto-Sterling, "Gender, Race and Nation: The Anatomy of 'Hottentot' Women in Europe 1815–1817," in *Deviant Bodies,* Jennifer Terry and Jacqueline Urla, eds. (Indiana University Press, 1993).

27. Parks Lanier, Jr., ed., *The Poetics of Appalachian Space* (Knoxville: University of Tennessee Press, 1991), pp. 193–210.

28. Gaston Bachelard, *The Poetics of Space,* Maria Jolas, trans. (Boston: Beacon, 1969).

29. Ibid., p. 5.

30. Ibid., p. xxxii.

31. Ibid., pp. 46–47.

32. Ibid., p. 18–20.

33. Ibid., p.101.

34. Ibid., pp. 51–54.

35. Ibid., p. 101.

36. Ibid., pp. 144–45.

37. Ibid., p. 197.

38. *Ms.* magazine, September 1989.

Weaving II

1. Jeanette Armstrong, "Entering the Canons: Our Place in World Literature," presented at "Returning the Gift: A Festival of North American Native Writers," University of Oklahoma at Norman, OK, July 9, 1992. Armstrong, an Okanagan, quoted the medicine man in the discussion following her presentation.

2. Caduto and Bruchac, "The Coming of Corn," in *Keepers of the Earth*, pp. 137–39.

3. Merle Severy, ed., *America's Historylands* (Washington, DC: National Geographic Society, 1962), p. 29.

4. Ibid., p. 29.

5. William Benton, "Corn," *Encyclopedia Britannica*, Vol. 6, p. 503.

6. Howard Zinn, *A People's History of the United States* (New York: Harper and Row, 1980), p. 3.

7. Ibid.

8. *Encyclopedia Britannica,* p. 503.

9. Ivan Von Sertima, *They Came Before Columbus* (New York: Random House, 1976), pp. 240–51.

10. Jack Weatherford, *Indian Givers* (New York: Fawcett Columbine, 1988), p. 71.

11. *Encyclopedia Britannica*, p. 503.

12. Mississippi Band of Choctaws, *Chata Hapia Hoke: We Are Choctaw* (Philadelphia, MS: 1981), p. 7.

13. Kilpatrick, *Friends of Thunder*, p. 5.

14. Bill Brescia, ed., *Our Mother Corn* (Seattle: United Indians of All Tribes Foundation, 1981), p. 18.

15. Ibid., p. 21.

16. Ibid., pp. 21–22.

17. Ibid., p. 18.

18. Ibid., p. 14.

19. Frank Waters, *The Book of the Hopi* (New York: Penguin Books, 1982), p. 134.

20. Arturo Warman, "Maize as Organizing Principle," in *Northeast Indian Quarterly* (now *Akwe:kon*): "Cultural Encounter II: Indian Corn of the Americas—A Gift to the World" (Ithaca, NY: American Indian Studies at Cornell University, 1989), p. 21.

21. Alex Jacobs/Karoniaktatie, "The Law Is in the Seed," *Indian Roots of American Democracy,* José Barreiro, ed. (Ithaca, NY: Akwe:kon Press, 1992), p. vi.

22. Brian Swann, *Song of the Sky: Versions of Native American Songs & Poems* (Ashuelot, NH: Four Zoas House, Ltd., 1985), p. 16.

23. Kirke Kickingbird and Lynne Shelby Kickingbird, *Indians and the U.S. Constitution: A Forgotten Legacy* (Washington, DC: Institute for the Development of Indian Law, Inc., 1987), p. 12.

24. Sally Roesch Wagner, "The Iroquois Influence on Women's Rights," in *Indian Roots of American Democracy,* pp. 115–34.

25. Jacobs, *Indian Roots of American Democracy*, p. 11.

26. Ibid., pp. 30–33.

27. Brescia, *Our Mother Corn,* p. 57.

28. John Mohawk, "Economic Motivations: An Iroquoian Perspective," in *Northeast Indian Quarterly*, "Indian Corn of the Americas," pp. 56–63.

29. José Barreiro, ed., "Mother of Nations: The Peace Queen," in *Northeast Indian Quarterly*, "Cultural Encounter I" (Ithaca, NY: American Indian Stuides at Cornell University, 1988), pp. 68–70.

30. Jacobs, *Indian Roots of American Democracy,* pp. 36–42.

31. Kilpatrick, *Friends of Thunder,* p. 61.

32. Rennard Strickland, *Fire and the Spirits* (Norman: University of Oklahoma Press, 1982).

33. "Marriage," in *Ancient Village Manual* (Talequah, OK: Cherokee National Historical Society, 1989).

34. Robert J. Conley, *Mountain Windsong* (Norman: University of Oklahoma, 1993), p. 96.

35. Warman, "Maize as Organizing Principle," p. 21.

36. Mary Regina Ulmer Galloway, comp. and ed., *Aunt Mary, Tell Us a Story, A Collection of Cherokee Legends and Tales as Told by Mary Ulmer Chiltoskey* (Cherokee, NC: Cherokee Communications, 1990), pp. 40–41.

37. "Lincoln," *Life,* Vol. 14, No. 2, February 1991, excerpt from a speech given by Abraham Lincoln at Edwardsville, Illinois, September 11, 1858.

38. José Barreiro, *Indian Chronicles* (Houston: Arte Público, 1993).

39. Kickingbird, *Indians and the U.S. Constitution*, p. 2.

40. Ibid., p. 3.

41. E. Raymond Evans, "Notable Persons in Cherokee History: Ostenaco (Outacite)," in *Journal of Cherokee Studies* (Cherokee, NC: Museum of the Cherokee Indian), Summer 1976, pp. 43–53.

42. James C. Kelly, "Notable Persons in Cherokee History: Attakullakulla," in *Journal of Cherokee Studies* (Cherokee, NC: Museum of the Cherokee Indian), Winter 1978, pp. 3–29.

43. Kickingbird, *Indians and the U.S. Constitution*, p. 18.

44. Thomas A. Strohfeldt, "Warriors in Williamsburg: The Cherokee Presence in Virginia's Eighteenth Century Capital," in *Journal of Cherokee Studies* (Cherokee, NC: Museum of the Cherokee Indian), Spring 1986, pp. 5–8.

45. Kickingbird, *Indians and U.S. Constitution,* p. 5.

46. Mourt's Relation, *A Journal of the Pilgrims at Plymouth,* edited from the original printing of 1622 by Dwight B. Heath (New York: Corinth Books, 1973), pp. 15, 59. *Note*: The full subtitle of the above is "A RELATION OR JOURNAL (sic) of the English Plantation settled at Plymouth in New England, by certain English adventurers, both merchants and others."

47. Zinn, *People's History*, p. 14.

48. Ibid.

49. *Commercial Appeal*, November 24, 1977.

50. Frederick J. Dockstader, "Metacom" and "Massasoit," in *Great North American Indians* (Atlanta: Van Nostrand Reinhold and Company, 1977), pp. 172–74.

51. Bruce Johansen and Donald A. Grinde, Jr., *Exemplar of Liberty* (Los Angeles: American Indian Studies Center at University of California, 1991), p. 93.

52. Jacobs, *Indian Roots of American Democracy,* p. 26.

53. Evelyn Fox Keller, *A Feeling for the Organism: The Life and Work of Barbara McClintock* (New York: W. H. Freeman, 1983), p. 198.

54. Ibid., p. 199.

55. Ibid., p. 201.

56. Ibid., p. 40.

57. Ibid., p. 3.

58. Ibid., p. 3, 4.

59. Ibid., p. 137.

INDEX OF POEMS BY AWIAKTA

PERMISSIONS AND CREDITS

The author would like to thank the following for permission to reprint:

Excerpts from *Friends of Thunder* by Jack F. Kilpatrick and Anna G. Kilpatrick, © 1964 by Jack F. Kilpatrick and Anna G. Kilpatrick. Reprinted by permission of Jack F. Kilpatrick, Jr.

Interview with Wilma Mankiller, "Rebirth of a Nation," by Marilou Awiakta in *Southern Style* magazine, September/October issue, © 1988 by Whittle Communications, L.P. Reprinted by permission of Whittle Communications.

Poem "Ceremony" from *Ceremony* by Leslie Marmon Silko, © Leslie Marmon Silko. Reprinted by permission of Wylie, Aitken & Stone.

The last message to his people of John Kruger, Okanagan medicine man and Elder, is quoted by permission of his son, Jack Kruger, who speaks for the family in British Columbia, Canada.

Excerpts from *Our Mother Corn,* edited by Bill Brescia, © Daybreak Star Press. Reprinted by permission of United Indians of All Tribes Foundation.

Excerpt from "Introduction" to Brian Swann's *Song of the Sky* by Paula Gunn Allen, © by Paula Gunn Allen. Reprinted by permission of the author.

Excerpts from *Indian Roots of American Democracy,* edited by José Barreiro, © 1992 by Akwe:kon Press. Reprinted by permission of Akwe:kon.

Excerpt from *Aunt Mary, Tell Us a Story: A Collection of Cherokee Legends and Tales as Told by Mary Ulmer Chiltoskey*, compiled and edited by Mary Regina Ulmer Galloway, © 1990 by Mary Ulmer Chiltoskey and Mary Regina Ulmer Galloway. Reprinted by their permission.

Excerpts from *A Feeling for the Organism: The Life and Work of Barbara McClintock* by Evelyn Fox Keller, © 1983 by W. H. Freeman and Company. Reprinted with permission.

Poems from *Abiding Appalachia: Where Mountain and Atom Meet* by Marilou Awiakta, © 1978 by Marilou Awiakta. Reprinted by permission of the author and Iris Press.

Excerpt from *Rising Fawn and the Fire Mystery* by Marilou Awiakta, © 1983 by Marilou Awiakta. Reprinted by permission of the author and Iris Press.

The following essays by the author were previously published. "Baring the Atom's Mother Heart" appeared in *Homewords: A Book of Tennessee Writers*, edited by Douglas Paschall and Alice Swanson, © 1986 by the University of Tennessee Press. Reprinted by permission of the author and the University of Tennessee Press. "Amazons in Appalachia" appeared in *A Gathering of Spirit: Writing and Art by North American Indian Women*, edited by Beth Brant, Sinister Wisdom Books, 1984. "Out! Children at Play on the Atomic Frontier" and "Honor to the Founding Elders of Oak Ridge" appeared in *These Are Our Voices: The Story of Oak Ridge 1952–1970*, edited by James Overholt, © 1987 by the Children's Museum of Oak Ridge. Reprinted by permission of the Children's Museum. "Daydreaming Primal Space" appeared in *The Poetics of Appalachian Space*, edited by Parks Lanier, © 1991 by the University of Tennessee Press. Reprinted by permission of the author and University of Tennessee Press.

Excerpts from "The Press: Watchdog with a Blind Eye" are reprinted from the *Houston Chronicle*. "Red Clay: When Awi Usdi Walked Among Us" first appeared in *Southern Exposure*. "Cherokee Eden" first appeared in *Milkweed Chronicle*. "Living in the Round: What Maria's Bowl Teaches Me" first appeared in *Sonoma Mandala*.

For poems reprinted in this volume, acknowledgment is made to the following periodicals: *The Greenfield Review, Appalachian Heritage, Appalachian Journal, Now & Then, The Tennessee Conservationist* and *Ms*.